A
QUILTER'S
Companion

A QUILTER'S Companion

Dolores A. Hinson

ARCO

New York

TO THE READER

The pattern for the quilt shown on the cover—Mariner's
Compass #36—can be ordered by mail. Send $1.50 in check
or money order, postage included, with your order to:

The Stearn & Foster Company
Quilt Center
P.O. Box 15380
Cincinnati, Ohio 45215

Ninth Printing, 1980

Published by Arco Publishing, Inc.
219 Park Avenue South, New York, N.Y. 10003

Library of Congress Catalog Card Number 72-3333
ISBN 0-668-02666-9 (Library Edition)
ISBN 0-668-04605-8 (Paper Edition)

Printed in the United States of America

CONTENTS

Foreword

THE CRAFT OF QUILTING

There are many of the crafts which are popular at present, such as ceramics, oil or watercolor painting, crewel work or needlepoint embroidery and others. They all have one thing in common: they need a capital outlay for original equipment and are usually expensive to maintain. Some are messy and take up much space. None of these drawbacks need apply to quilting; but all of the benefits, such as being soothing to the nerves, creative and ego satisfying, are included in the work of making a quilt.

To make a quilt, you need about six yards of cloth in several colors. These can be large and small sewing scraps or about a half yard or a yard and a half from the bargain counter. You also need a batt of cotton or dacron which retails for less than five dollars, a sheet of backing for less than three dollars, a spool of thread, and needle. The quilting frame can be four one by two boards, two 9 feet and two 10 feet long plus four 'C' clamps. If you do not have enough room, you may buy a table-sized quilting frame from any catalog service for less than fifteen dollars. You may also do as many of my friends do—lay out the three layers of top, filler and backing on the floor and baste it firmly all over. Quilt the result on your lap without a frame. The four edges of the finished quilt must be bound with about two packages of bias tape. All of the value in a quilt comes from the work your hands put into these simple materials and the hours of work you choose to give.

There are only two sewing stitches which are used in making a quilt—the running stitch and the blind or hem stitch. If you are hand-making a dress, the running stitch is used to make the side seams and the blind or hem stitch is used to sew up a hem. To make a quilt, you piece and quilt with the running stitch and appliqué with the blind or hem stitch. To piece a pattern put two pieces of cloth together and sew a seam along one edge. To appliqué lay one piece of cloth on a larger one, and sew the smaller piece to the larger without any of the stitches showing. (See the two diagrams.)

Anyone can piece or appliqué a beautiful quilt. If you have never sewn before, get some cloth and practice the two stitches before cutting the cloth for the first quilt. These stitches should be as small as you can possibly make them. They must also be as even in length and space as you can make them.

All of the patterns in this book are for Amer-

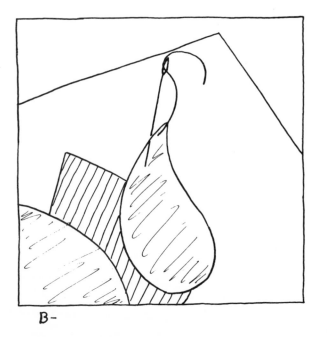

B-

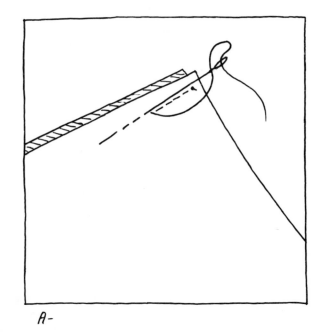

Aican Type quilts. An American Type quilt is first made in blocks. These blocks are sewn into rows which are sewn into a top. The basic block can also be called a patch. Quilting is a folk art which grew without special rules, hence many of the names are interchangeable. The filler is the cotton or dacron batting put in the middle of the quilt. The backing is just that, the back of the quilt.

When cutting any of these patterns, trace the outline of the pattern on a piece of tissue paper first. Cut out this traced outline and retrace it on cardboard, sandpaper or hard plastic. For a pieced pattern, trace the outline of the pattern on the WRONG side of the cloth. For an appliqué pattern, trace the pattern on the RIGHT side of the cloth. You will use these pencil lines as a guide for your stitches. Draw the patterns on the cloth and leave one-quarter inch all around each traced pattern for a seam allowance. I have added this seam allowance on the Clamshell quilt pattern to show how large it must be. Do not trace the pattern and sew inside the traced line or leave too small a seam allowance when cutting out the material, for if you do the quilt will not come out right.

Use the directions with each pattern to put it together. To piece two pieces of cloth, place them face to face and put the seam side up. Sew across, open the seam, and smooth the center with your fingers. Press the two sides firmly.

To appliqué a square, cut out all of the appliqué pieces and place them on the background square. When they are in the correct places, baste or pin them firmly. Clip the seam allowances for all curved edges as near as possible to the penciled line. For tight curves clip these edges close together and for shallow curves further apart. Fold the seam allowance under and sew each piece in place starting with any which are under other pieces.

There are three ways to put the blocks together: first, set the blocks into a top with an all-over pattern. This means the blocks are set next to one another each one pieced or appliquéd alike. Next, make every other block plain white, plain color, or printed. The third way is to place lattice strips between the pieced or appliquéd blocks. These lattice strips can be as narrow as two inches or as wide as one half the width of the other blocks used in the top. I have illustrated all three of these methods in some of the complete tops shown in this book.

All of the above information belongs to the craft of quilting. The art of quilting is to choose a pattern for the blocks, a color combination, a method of setting the blocks together, and a border and quilting patterns which will all blend together to make a lovely and decorative quilt when finished. There are 150 pieced and appliquéd patterns and 50 border and quilting patterns in this book. All are traditional and all have been used for many years to make lovely quilts. You should have no trouble in choosing a combination of patterns which will make one, two, or two hundred different beautiful quilts from the patterns in this book. All of them are taken from my large collection of quilt patterns. Some of them are as old as two hundred years while others are as new as two years; all are my favorites. I have been careful to tell you if the pattern is easy or hard to work on, so choose carefully to suit your own skill. I hope you have as much fun in using this book as I have had in compiling it.

A
QUILTER'S
Companion

One Patch Patterns

Mary Schaffer's Clamshell

MARY SCHAFFER'S CLAMSHELL

Mary Schaffer is one of the best quilters I know. She wins prizes consistently with her quilts, which are either exact copies of antique quilts or her own variations of old patterns. This is a variation of the old colonial New England pattern, Clamshell, which heretofore has usually been done in dull, dark, scrap-pattern materials of wool. When I saw this variation with its bright pastels and white, I fell in love with it. The quilt was made in 1968 and won the Sweepstakes Ribbon at the Saginaw County Fair which entitled Mary to enter it in the Michigan State Fair that year. It was entered in the National Quilter's Association Exhibition in 1970; it won a Blue Ribbon for pieced quilts and the Popular Prize Ribbon for best-liked quilt.

It is said that this top may be pieced together patch by patch. To keep them in straight lines, baste the pieces on a sheet. To start with, put a shell on the backing and baste it in place. Put a second shell next to the first with the lower edges touching it. Start the next row by placing a shell between the lower points of the two shells in the first row. When placing a shell, turn the seam allowance of the upper curve under and baste it. The seam allowance of the two lower curves should not be turned under but should be left flat to be sewn under the shells of the next row.

There are two rows of white shells all the way around the quilt as a border. Count the shells in the remainder of the pattern and piece them as shown in the drawing of the full quilt top. Be neat and careful and this will not be a hard quilt. Quilt the top ¼ inch inside the outline of each shell.

A. CONVEX

B. CONCAVE

5

Mrs. Schaffer has generously shared with us her method for piecing this quilt as well as the pattern for it. Her directions are: cut the patches on the vertical grain of the material (see large arrow on pattern); allow the ¼ inch seam allowance shown on the pattern on each cut piece; clip all concave sides.

Sew one quarter of the shell at a time. Always sew with the concave side up (towards you). Mark the center of the convex side with a penciled dot (small arrow on the pattern). Place a straight pin vertically through the two pieces of cloth at each end of the side of the seam you are about to sew. This allows you to move the two shells enough to keep the two penciled seam lines together as you sew around the curve. With every two or three stitches taken, check on the underside and see that the stitches are following both lines. If the shell on the underside has moved, gently move it back into line with the shell above. Do not try to work quickly, and take out any seam which goes wrong. If you do not work slowly and carefully, the lines of the shells will go astray and give you a crooked quilt top.

Mrs. Schaffer has added interest to her pattern by carefully centering a printed motif in some of the shells. These, spaced among the shells with all-over printed designs, give something for your eyes to follow.

ZIGZAG BLOCK

This pattern depends as much on the colors used as on the shape of the pattern elements. In the original, these colors were medium brown for the background, orange and yellow and green and yellow for the designs. These design elements were so placed that the two color combinations form diagonal lines across the quilt top.

To form the design, place a No. 1 square over the center of a No. 2 strip and sew. The longer center strip is made by piecing a No. 3 strip on each side of a No. 2 strip. Sew this center strip under the No. 2 strip already in place. Again, center another No. 2 strip under the center strip and sew it in place. Finish the pattern by sewing a second No. 1 square at the center and bottom of the design element.

Sew these design elements together with No. 4 blocks as shown in the drawing. To start the quilt, make a partial block like the ones shown in the drawing and edge the quilt with partial blocks to complete the design at the sides. This is a one-patch quilt and except for piecing the design elements, the remainder of the top must be pieced into the pattern as it is pieced into a top.

There could be several other color combinations including one which would use a print background with pastel design elements. I would not think that this top would look well as a scrap pattern. A twin-bed size quilt will take three full design elements across and seven elements in a row down. This would mean that you must piece eighteen design elements and place them in four rows of three designs and three rows of two designs. Add one more design element to the side of each row across to make a double bed quilt.

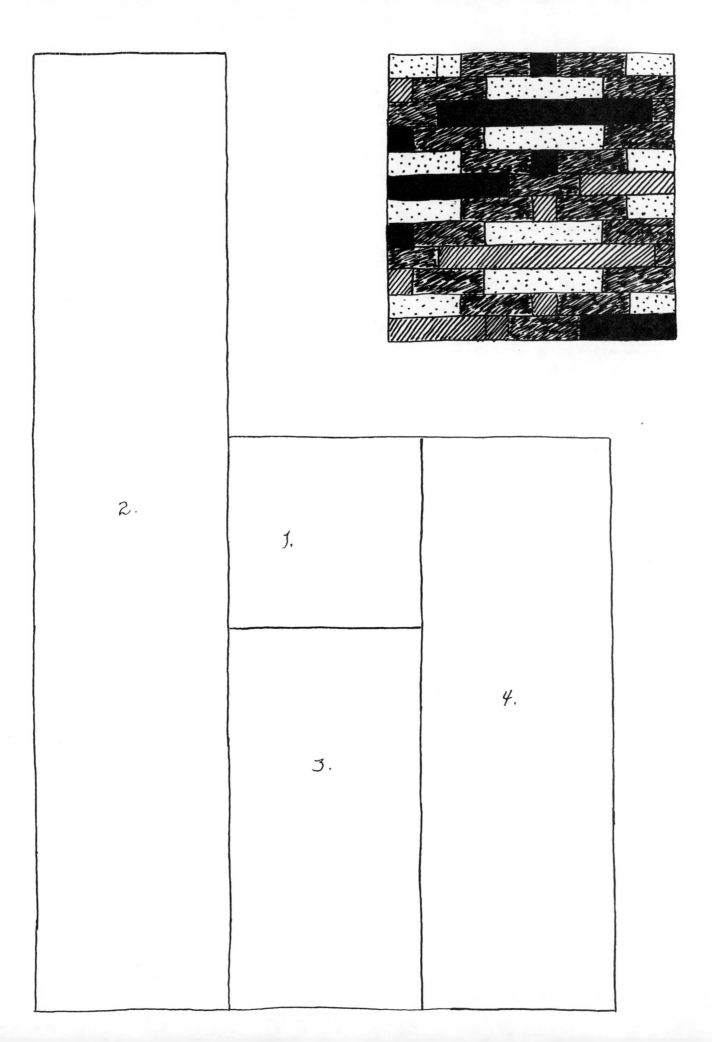

SPOOLS

This pattern was popular during the latter part of the eighteenth century and perhaps in the very early nineteenth century. This is a true scrap quilt as it has no pattern or color indications at all. Just use dark and light colors, similar or contrasting, prints or plain materials in any way that pleases you. This is a one-patch quilt. You must start in the upper left hand corner of the quilt. Make the first row of patches which are arranged first upright and then sideways alternately. A twin bed quilt should be about five feet wide, and a double bed quilt about seven feet wide. Make a second row in the same manner as the first row and then sew them together. Continue making these rows and sewing them together until your quilt is eight feet long.

To sew the motifs together, clip the seam allowance all the way around the two cut-out pattern pieces. Remember to add one-quarter inch wide seam allowances to the material you cut out because all of these patterns are given in the finished sizes. Place the rounded end of one block face down to fit one side of the cut-out side of the other block placed face up. Sew along the pencil line, a few stitches at a time. Move the edges of the two pieces together as you sew. When you sew the curve, the pieces behind the stitches will tend to curl; disregard this. After two pieces have been sewn together, turn the patches right side up and iron the seam flat. This will save you from having much trouble with a design that will be crooked if the pieces are left unironed.

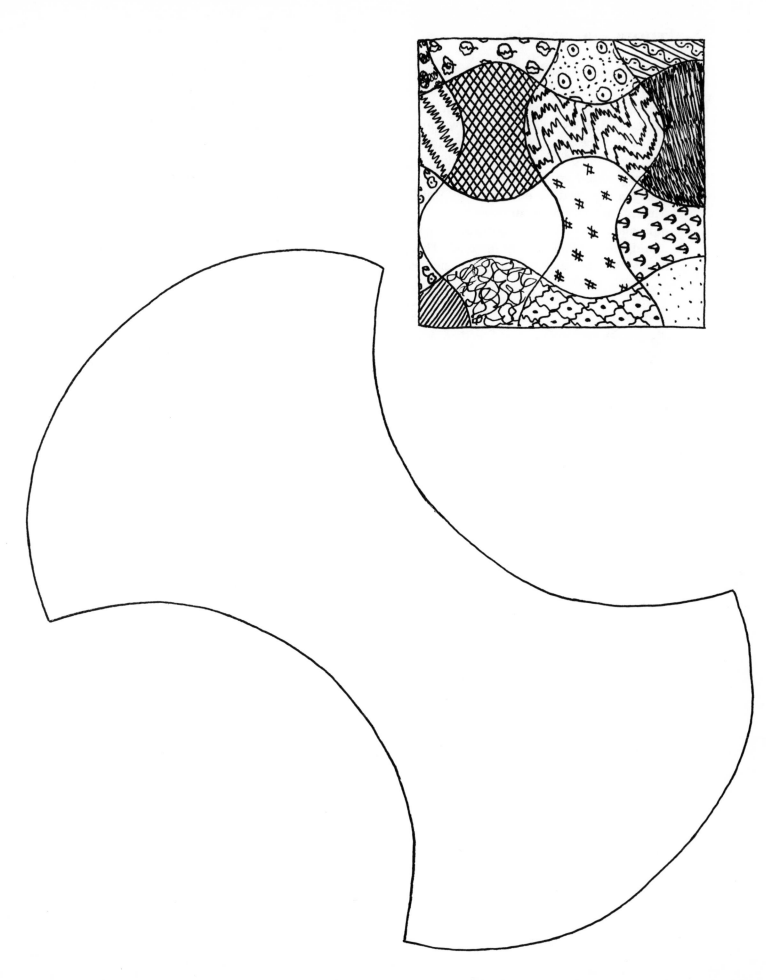

THOUSAND PYRAMIDS

This is also known as STREAK O'LIGHT-NING, ZIG ZAG, RAIL FENCE and SNAKE FENCE. I have three patterns to put this quilt together: the two variations shown and the one where the point of one triangle meets the bottom points of the two others on top.

The pattern in B and the one described above are pieced in one color or print and white. The pattern in drawing A is a scrap quilt and each of the two dark rows shown are of a different plain or print material. This pattern is for one patch quilts; hence the designs are the same all over the quilt tops. Piece one line of the triangles reversed alternately. For a twin bed quilt, this line should be five feet long; for a double bed quilt, it should be seven feet long. Piece a second line exactly like the first with every other triangle reversed, then sew the two lines together. Repeat with other lines of triangles until the quilt top is eight feet long.

This pattern is so easy that even a beginner should be able to make an attractive quilt. Take care to make the seams straight and the points even.

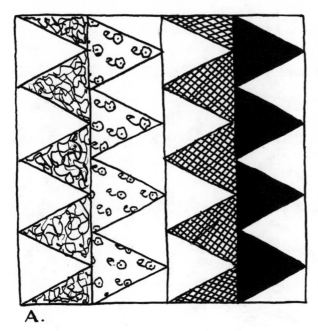

A.

B.

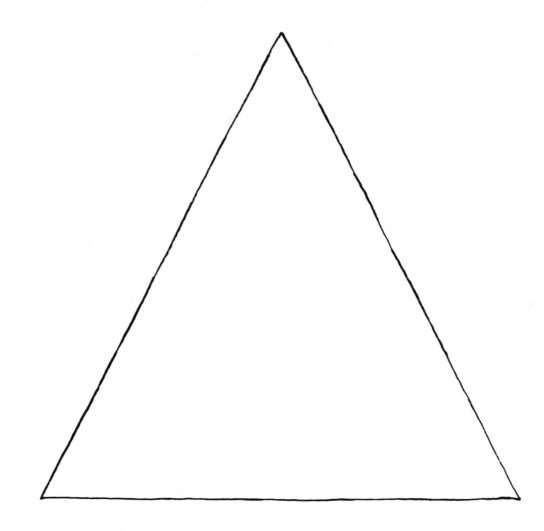

Two Patch Patterns

MARYLAND BEAUTY

There were two kinds of quilts made in Maryland because there were two cultures before the automobile came along and gave people more mobility. The first culture was along the waterways of the Chesapeake Bay area. The people who lived along these waterways had access to the cloth and civilization of the cosmopolitan city of Baltimore. Their quilts were quite elaborate and mostly appliquéd. The inland dwellers were more restricted in the amount of cloth and the new ideas that could be brought to them over the bad roads. They

made pieced quilts which were mostly of several Sawtooth variations. This Maryland Beauty pattern is one of those. It was found in a small town in Maryland in the 1930's and was published for the first time in a newspaper quilt column. To my knowledge, it has not been published since. It is not hard to piece and will make a beautiful red print and white or scrap quilt. If you make this into a scrap quilt, use the same print in all three sections of this pattern and change prints only when you start the next full block.

Cut out a large triangle (No. 1) by measuring with the triangle marked No. 2. The larger triangle should be two triangles No. 2 on each of its three sides or 12 x 12 x 17¼ inches. This triangle should be cut from white cloth. Cut one No. 2 triangle of white cloth. Cut three triangles No. 3 of your print cloth. Lastly, cut 33 white triangles and 27 print triangles No. 4. Divide these last No. 4 triangles into three equal piles of 11 white and 9 print triangles and place each pile with one print No. 3 triangle.

Begin to piece this pattern by making a square of one print and one white No. 4 triangle. There will be nine of these squares. Now piece two rows of these squares, placing a white triangle beside a print one until there are four squares in one row and five in the other. Place these two rows on the two short sides of the print triangle No. 3 (see the drawing). Add two white triangles No. 4 to the ends of the rows to make the finished piece triangularly shaped. Sew this pieced triangle along the longer side to the white triangle No. 2 to form a square. Repeat the above instructions with the two other piles of triangles to form two more pieced triangles. Sew the two triangles and the square into a large triangle with the white triangle No. 2 in the center. Sew this pieced triangle along the long side to the large white triangle No. 1 to form the finished square.

I have drawn the finished top for this section from the Maryland Beauty pattern. On the top the blocks are pieced together in the manner of a "Delectable Mountains" quilt top. It seems to me a more interesting treatment of this pattern than the traditional top design in which all of the patches are placed in the same direction forming diagonal lines across the quilt. The traditional colors for this quilt are brown on white which were the colors used from the

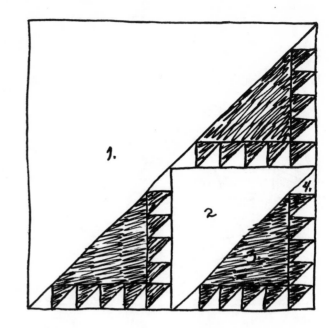

1830's to 1850's and from the 1870's to 1880's; and red print on white, used in the 1860's and the 1890's. Either color combination is pretty. This quilt could also be made as a scrap quilt with each block a different print on white.

The traditional manner of quilting this top is to use an outline on the pieced portion and a curved feather in the white triangle all over the quilt top.

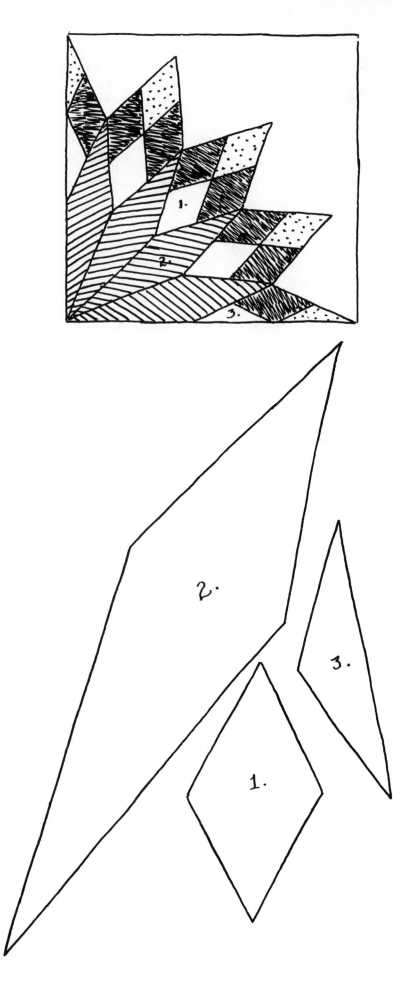

FRINGED ASTER

This is another pattern from the rich heritage which the 1930 quilt designers have left us. It is a variation of the old fan patterns with some four patch diamonds added. The colors given for this pattern are green diamonds for leaves, then white, two orange and a yellow diamond pieced together for the flowers against a white background. The pattern is given for a 12 inch block.

To piece this pattern, cut out 12-inch square blocks of white material with ¼ inch seam allowance on all sides, one for each block needed for the quilt top. Next, for each pieced block, cut four green leaves pattern No. 2, three white diamonds pattern No. 1, eight orange diamonds pattern No. 1, three yellow diamonds pattern No. 1, two white triangles pattern No. 3 and two yellow triangles pattern No. 3.

Piece together three diamonds of one white, two orange and one yellow diamond pattern No. 1. Then piece together two half diamonds or triangles of one white triangle and a yellow triangle on either side of an orange diamond No. 1. Sew one of these three pieced diamonds on the left side of one of the green diamonds. Then sew a second pieced diamond to the other side of the same green diamond. Sew the second green triangle and then the third to either side of this unit and then add the diamonds and half diamonds. Finish the Fan shape. Appliqué this fan to one corner of a white square.

For a twin bed quilt there should be seven rows of five blocks each. A double bed will take seven rows of seven or nine blocks each. This pattern would be prettiest put together with every other block plain. I think a soft pastel green square between the pieced blocks would be my preference. You might try to make this pattern as a starburst by placing the green leaf corners together in the center of four pieced blocks. In this case you could use other color combinations than the one given above. To quilt this block, use outline on the pieced fan section and a more elaborate design on the plain sections.

HILL AND VALLEY

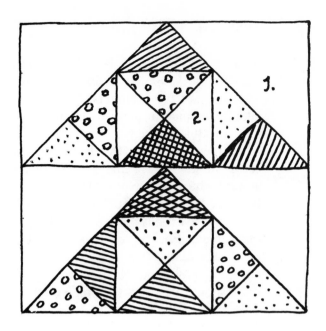

This pattern is a new version of the old Flying Geese. It does not seem to be a very old pattern; I cannot date it back further than the 1940's. This could be one of the first quilts tried by a beginning quilter. It has only two pattern sections and needs only to be pieced with straight seams to come out perfectly. It may be pieced with either a scrap pattern which uses different color combinations or you might try working out a color scheme of your own. In the original pattern there are four triangles each of three colors and two triangles of a fourth color plus four small white triangles and four large ones. Remember to add ¼ inch seam allowance always to all sides of the patches you cut out.

To piece this square, first make four triangles by sewing together two of the smaller triangles in each. Sew two of these larger triangles together into a square being sure that the small white triangles are in the places shown in the drawing. Add the other two triangles to the sides and the remaining single triangle for the point of the pieced triangle. Add two of the large white triangles to each side to form an oblong and repeat the above directions with the other triangles to form the other half of this block. Sew two oblongs together. This pattern is for a nine-inch finished size block.

There are several ways to piece this block into a quilt top. The prettiest, in my opinion, would be to make a strip of ten pieced squares. This strip will be 7½ feet long. On either side of this nine-inch strip, place a white or dark colored strip of cloth three inches wide by 7½ feet long. There should be five pieced strips and six of the three-inch strips in a twin-bed size quilt. For a double bed quilt add two more pieced and two plain strips to one side of the quilt. To quilt this top, use either outline quilting or a plain, all-over, background quilting pattern.

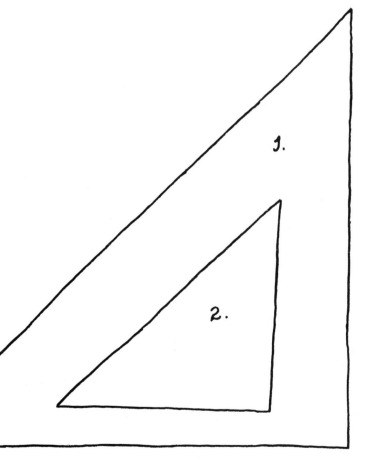

VASE OF FLOWERS

This is another of the beautiful patterns designed in the 1930's. It is also quite rare. This pattern is not for beginners, because it takes some experience to piece its complicated sections together correctly.

For the background of the square cut the pieces No. 1, 6, 9, 11 and 13 from white. For the vase, cut pattern No. 12 from blue cloth or choose a color or print which is pleasing to you. For leaves, cut patterns No. 4, 5 and 10 from green. For flower petals cut patterns No. 8 in a dark color. For the centers of the small side flowers cut No. 7 in yellow. Pattern No. 3 should be of dark color. For the petals and center of the large center flower use yellow for No. 2.

To piece this quilt block, first sew the curved side of No. 13 to the convex bottom of the vase piece No. 12. Carefully piece the two side pieces No. 11 to each side of the vase No. 12. Lay this section aside. Piece the flower from two pieces of No. 3 and one piece of No. 2 patterns and then piece the two side flowers from the two No. 8 and one No. 7 pieces each. Piece one of the side flowers to the green leaf No. 10 and add the white corner section No. 9. On the other side of the flower center, sew a white triangle No. 6 and add the green diamond No. 5. Lay this section aside and repeat the above directions to make the corner section for the other side. Take the large center flower and sew two green triangles to the bottom corners. Sew the side pieces to the bottom triangle containing the vase. Add the center section. Finish the square by sewing the two No. 1 white pieces to the top of the center flower.

Because this block is so elaborate, it should be pieced with plain blocks between the pieced blocks in five rows of seven blocks each for a twin bed quilt and seven rows of either seven or nine blocks each for a double bed quilt. Use outline quilting on the pieced blocks and a rather plain motif in quilting the plain blocks. A background pattern may also be used on the plain blocks and the white portions of the pieced blocks.

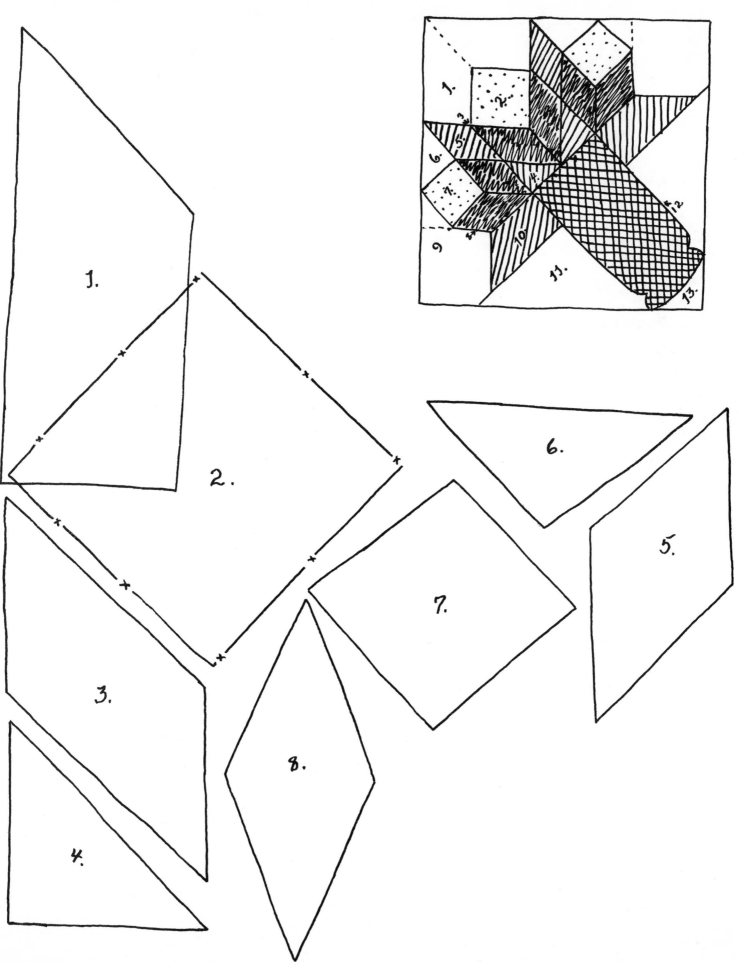

1.

2.

3.

4.

6.

5.

7.

8.

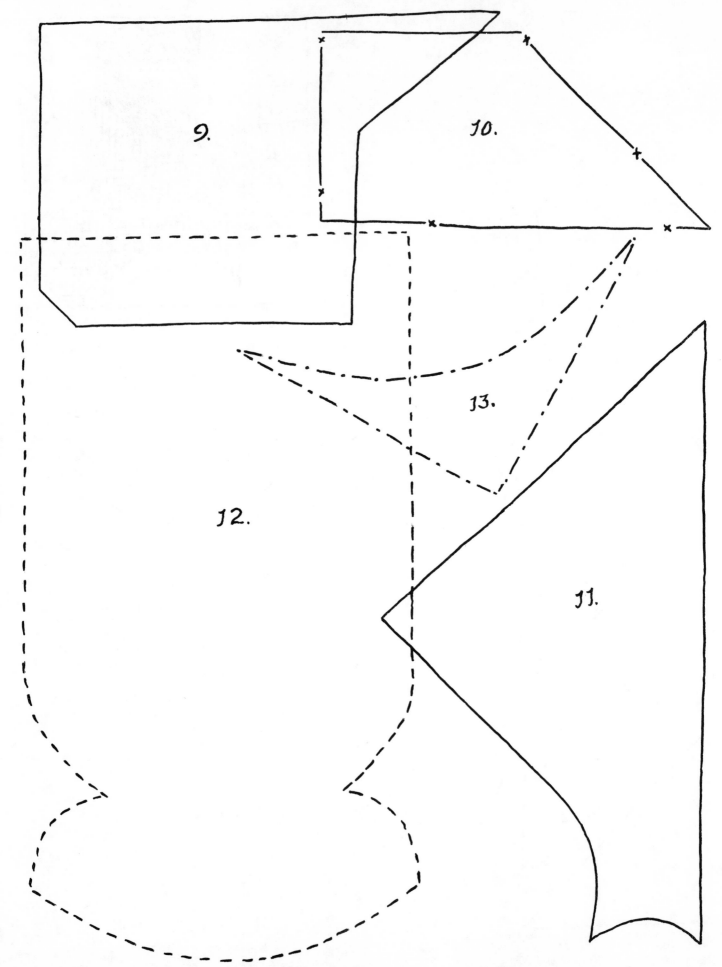

9.

10.

13.

12.

11.

18

FLOWER BASKET

This looks like all of the other old traditional Basket patterns but it has at least two differences. First, it is pieced in pink and scrap materials alternately, which is certainly not traditional. Second, it is quite large for a pieced square since it is 18 square inches. Third, the handle is pieced from two No. 2 patterns and six No. 3 patterns. The No. 2 patterns are the outside pieces of the handle. The basket is pieced from twenty-nine pink triangles and twenty-two assorted print triangles. This triangle is pattern No. 1. Piece the basket and the handle, then appliqué it to an 18-inch square block of white material.

There are only five rows of five blocks in a finished quilt top for a double bed quilt of this pattern. I believe the square is too large to make a pretty twin-bed size quilt. You may make the top with every other block plain and use only thirteen pieced blocks with twelve plain blocks to make your quilt. The quilting of the plain blocks should be a rather elaborate flower medallion with outline quilting and a plain background pattern for the remainder of the top.

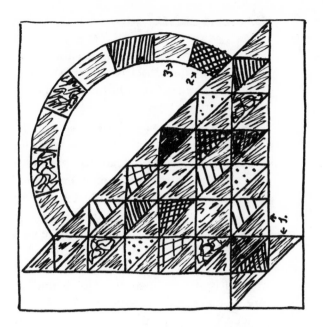

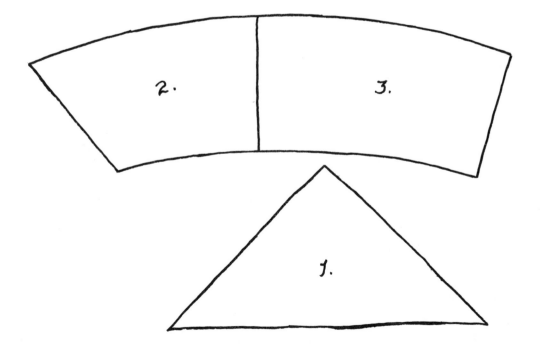

BASKET AND IRIS

This is a pattern I designed for my mother because her name is Iris. The basket is a very slight variation of the old favorite. The flowers are an entirely new design.

The basket is pieced from sixteen No. 10 brown triangles and nine yellow ones plus one No. 9 yellow square. You may piece this basket and then piece the remainder of the background square from No. 11, 12 and 13 patterns in white. Or you may piece the basket and appliqué it to a 12-inch square of white. When the basket and the background square are finished, appliqué the basket handle, No. 1, three iris flowers patterns No. 6 and 7; four green leaves from pattern No. 4 which is placed half under the handle, No. 8 and two No. 5; two pieces of stem which can be narrow bias tape and five flower buds patterns No. 2 and 3. Place the leaves, buds, stems and flowers either where they are shown in the drawing or make your own arrangement.

This block looks much more complicated than it really is. It should be pieced with plain squares or with lattice strips. The baskets should all be alike in color but you may use any color and shade of plain or print material for the flowers. Use a darker shade for the inner petal of the flower and the No. 2 piece of the buds. Each basket should contain one color of flower and each block should have a different color flower. Remember that the other name for iris is rainbow flower. Quilting should be an outline and a plain background pattern.

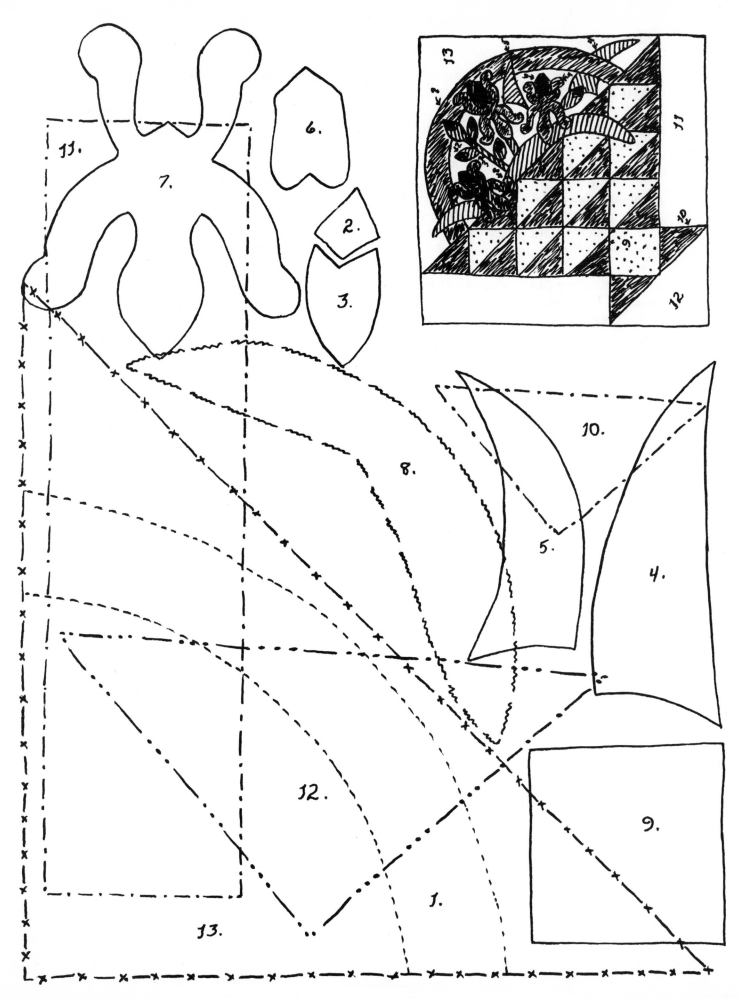

21

FLO'S FAN

Everyone loves the old fan patterns but I tried to find a little known one for you. I think with Flo's Fan I have succeeded. Piece this pattern in any combination of colors that you wish because this is a scrap pattern.

The patterns No. 1, 2 and 3 are half patterns. Draw them on a piece of tissue paper. Place one edge of the patterns on a fold of the paper and cut them out doubled. Pattern No. 6 is also a half pattern. Place the right side of the pattern on the tissue paper so the fold is in the corner of the pattern where it fits into the corner of the block. The pieced row contains five No. 4 pieces of one color and four No. 5 pieces plus two No. 7 pieces of a second color.

To put this block together, piece the No. 4, 5 and 7 strip first. Then piece the patterns No. 1, 2 and 3 together to form one corner of the block. Add the pieced strip and then the No. 6 white strip to finish the block.

This is a 10-inch block and will take six rows of eight blocks to make a twin-bed quilt and eight rows of nine blocks for a double-bed quilt top. It might be interesting to place four blocks together with the No. 1 points at a common center. This would make a sunburst pattern.

The pieced pattern in this block is quite plain, so use an elaborate background quilting pattern in an over-all design. Ignoring the pieced pattern would be the best for this top.

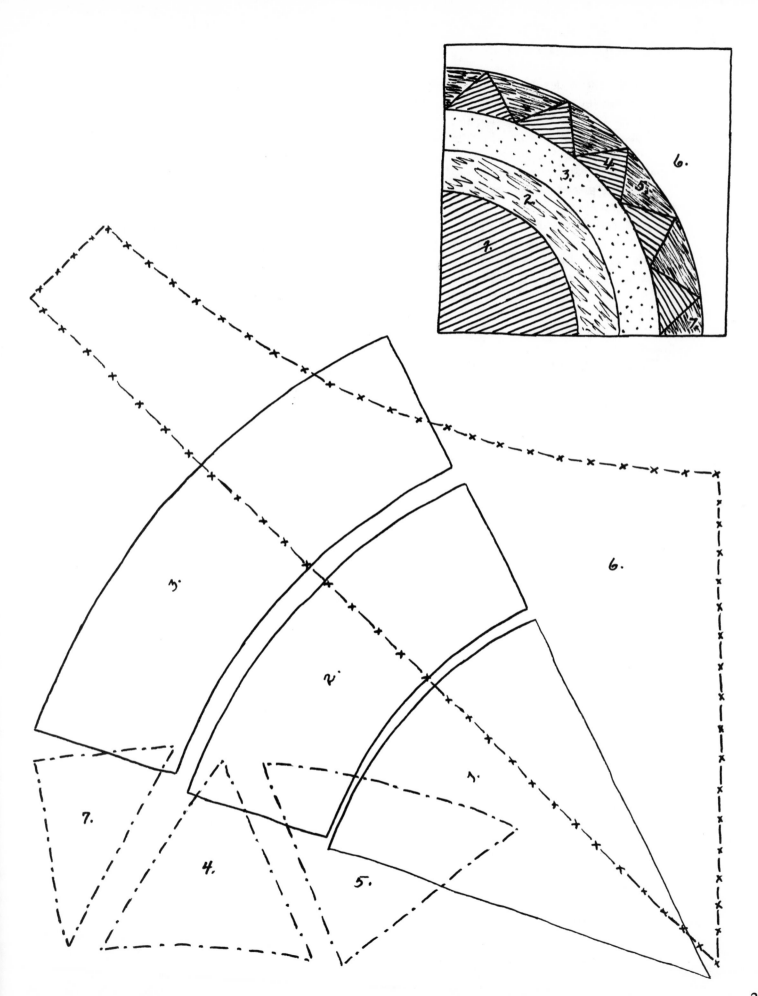

TREE OF TEMPTATION

Among the oldest patterns in American quilting are the pine tree patterns. The variation offered here is an apple tree and the name suggests that it is the tree which grew in the Garden of Eden. See how low its branches bend to offer its tempting fruit.

Make the pieced background by cutting out eight white No. 1 squares, five white No. 2 squares, two brown No. 2 squares, fourteen green No. 2 squares, twenty-two white No. 3 squares and twenty-two red No. 3 squares. Also cut out the brown trunk from pattern No. 4. Use white in No. 5 if you plan to piece the trunk into the patch; otherwise, just appliqué the trunk to the square after it has been pieced.

Piece the twenty-two apple squares with two red and two white No. 3 squares each. Piece these together in strips with the green No. 2 squares, adding the brown No. 2 squares where indicated in the drawing. Finish the center with the five white No. 2 squares and one white No. 1 square. Add the seven white No. 1 squares around the two sides. Appliqué the trunk in place.

You may piece the top together with alternate plain blocks but the white strips of pattern No. 1 will provide a lattice strip between the pieced sections. The plain blocks are not really needed.

Use outline and a plain background quilting pattern on this quilt top. The block is 14 inches square so you will need only four rows of five blocks each for a twin-bed quilt and five rows of six blocks each for a double-bed quilt top.

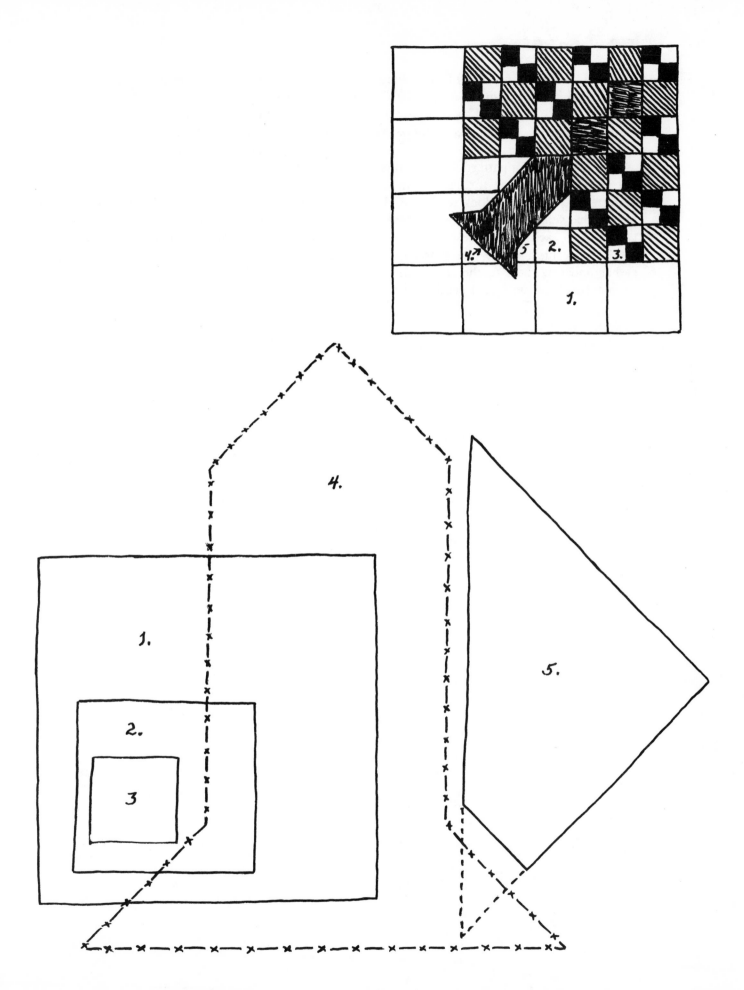

25

TULIP GARDEN

This is another of my 1930 favorite designs. It appeared in the Baltimore Sun in 1933 and in other papers, as well. This is not as easy a pattern as it looks. It is all pieced curves which always need special care.

Cut two pieces for patterns No. 2 and No. 3, but cut only one piece for each of the other patterns. To piece the block sew a No. 3 pattern to one side of the No. 2 petals. Sew these two units to each side of the No. 1 petal. Sew the No. 7 white and the No. 8 green leaf together and sew them to the right side of the flower. Sew a white No. 4 section to the top of the No. 5 green leaf and a white No. 6 section to the bottom. Sew this section to the other side of the flower and down the straight seam which makes the stem. This quilt top needs either lattice strips or a plain block between the pieced blocks.

This is a nine-inch block and will take 10 rows of seven blocks for a twin-bed quilt and 10 rows of nine blocks for a double-bed quilt. The quilting should be an outline on the pieced blocks and a fancy pattern on the plain sections of the top.

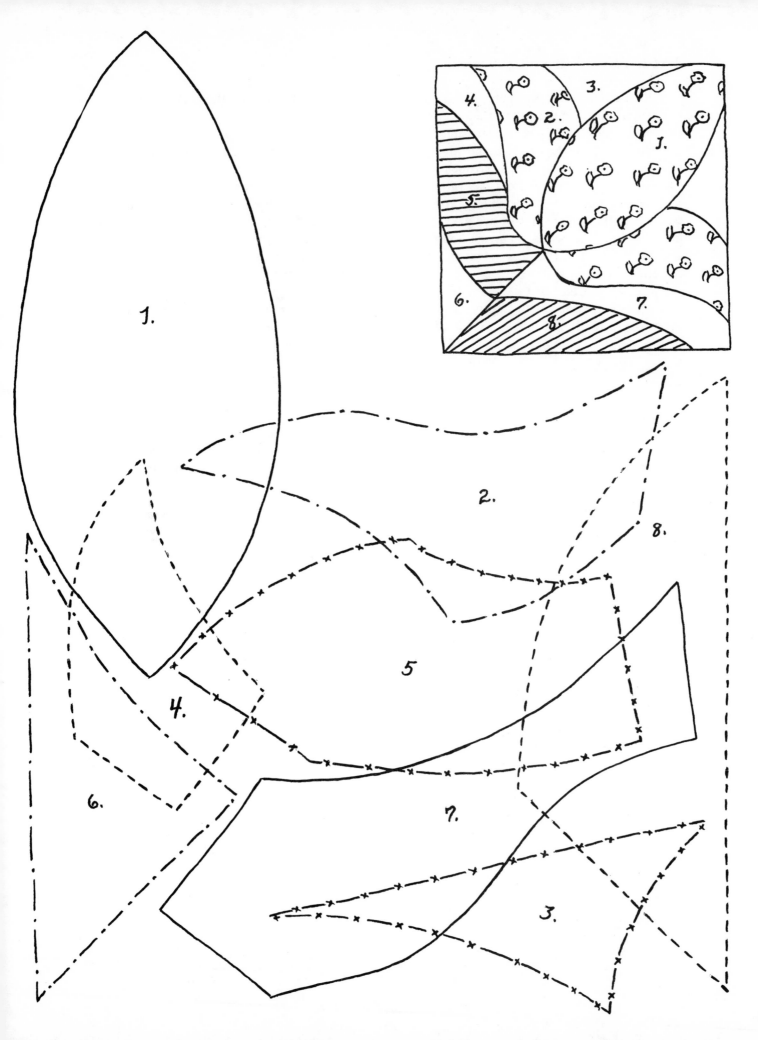

27

TALL PINE TREE

I don't know where this pattern came from or when it was designed, but it is another of my favorites. This is an all-over pattern and should be done only in shades of green and white. The finished size of the square is 12 inches. Cut two No. 1 green patterns from half of the No. 1–2 oblong and one whole oblong from the No. 1–2 pattern in green. Cut two green whole triangles from the No. 3–4 pattern, four green and six white half triangles from the No. 3 pattern.

Piece the top half of the square by sewing two white half triangles to the top of each of the two green whole triangles. Then add one of the half No. 1 oblongs to each side of the triangles after piecing the two sets of triangles together.

Piece the bottom half of the square by sewing one white half triangle and one green half triangle together until you have four units. Sew two of these together to make each side. Piece these sections to each side of the whole No. 1–2 oblong. Now sew the two halves of the square together.

Piece this top in five rows of eight blocks for a twin bed or seven rows of eight blocks for a double-bed quilt top. The quilting pattern should ignore the pieced pattern. A rather elaborate all-over design would be the best to quilt this top.

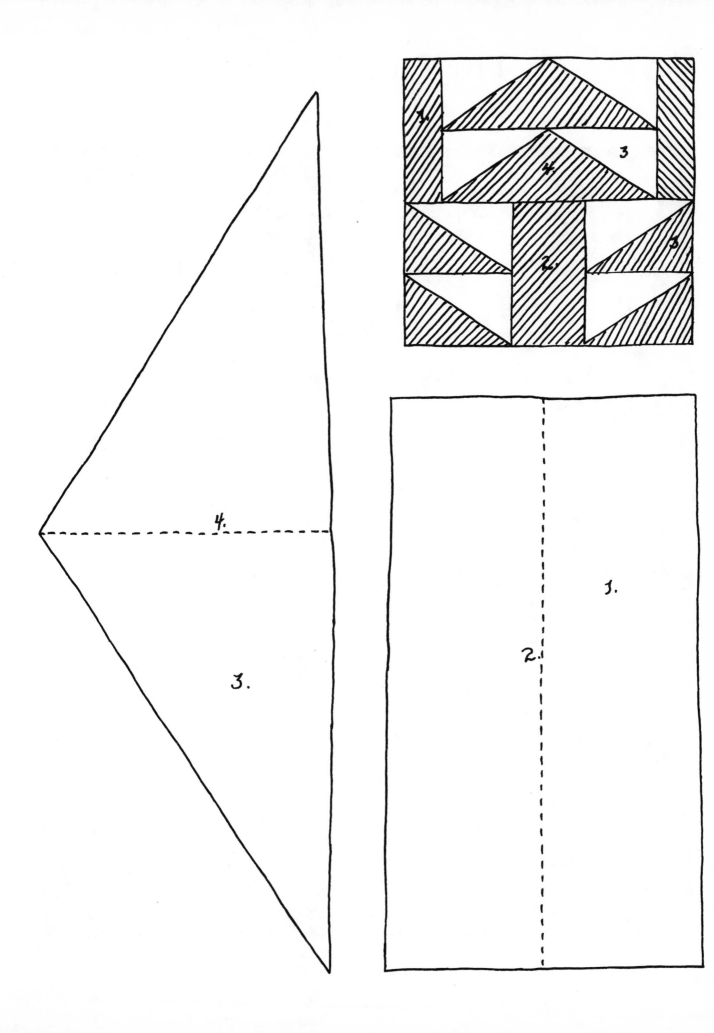

Five Patch Patterns

Doe and Darts

PLAID

This is an interesting design which I found as one of the blocks in a nineteenth-century album quilt. This block should be done in two shades of one color and a matching print plus white. It should be an all-over design without lattice strips or plain blocks between the pieced ones. There should not be any border on this quilt top. The design is easy enough to be pieced by even a beginning quilter.

Piece this design in five rows of the single and double blocks cut from the colors and put together by following the drawing. The dark stripes will then go lengthwise of the quilt top and the print stripes will run the width. Quilt this top in a fancy pattern without regard to the pieced pattern. This block makes a neat quilt with a woven look. This quilt will take seven rows of nine blocks each for a twin-bed size quilt.

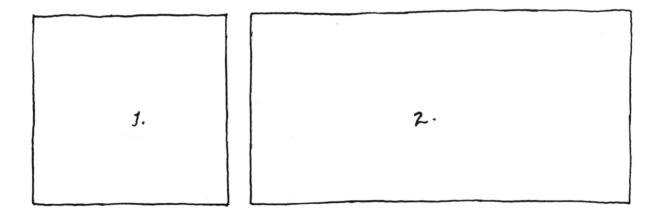

1.

2.

CHILDREN'S DELIGHT

I think the name of this pattern is cuter than the pattern. I wonder if the children found this pattern easy to do or if they were delighted that their mother had made them a quilt. There are so many of these unanswered questions in my study of old quilts. Anyway, the pattern is easy to do and may be done in an all-over pattern, with lattice strips or with plain blocks between the pieced ones. It may also be made with or without a border as you wish. I have shown it in green on white but it could be a scrap pattern. I would like to see it done with the large square in the center made from a bright flower print and the remainder of the dark sections in green. This would make it look like a geometric flower design. Why don't you try that with two-inch lattice strips between the blocks? This pattern can be made in four rows. The first row is No. 1 green, No. 1 white and No. 3 green. The second row is No. 1 green, No. 1 white, No. 2 either green or a bright flower print and No. 1 white. The third row is No. 1 green, No. 1 white and No. 3 green just like the first row. The last row is No. 3 white and No. 1 green strips. Sew these rows together until the finished block looks like the one in the drawing. To make a twin-bed quilt you will need six rows of eight blocks each and a small border.

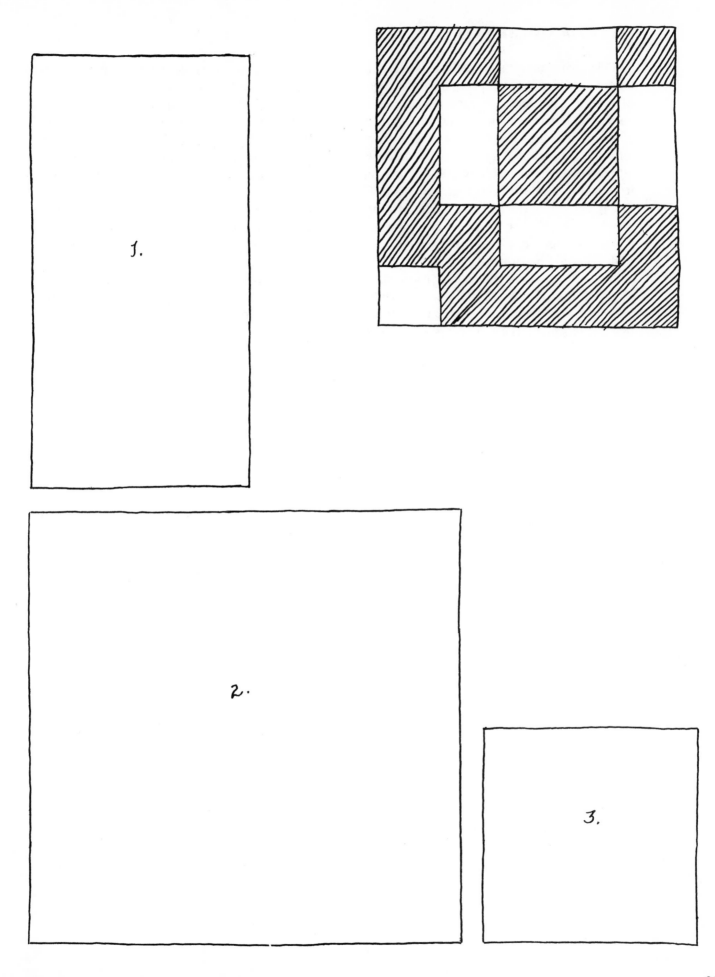

1.

2.

3.

DAVID AND GOLIATH

This pattern is also called MEXICAN STAR. This has to be a pattern from the early to middle nineteenth century because of the names and the style. It makes an interesting geometric design when done as an all-over pattern for a top but it may also be done with lattice strips or plain blocks. You may make it with or without a border as you wish. This design should be done in two colors or a plain color and a print on white. If not done in an all-over design, it makes an excellent scrap quilt. It is not hard to piece.

Begin by making all four corners. Use a light color for two No. 2 patterns and white in another two of the same pattern. Use white for one No. 4 square. These corners are triangles.

Now make the center by piecing three rows. The first and last rows are made up of two light-colored No. 3 triangles on each side of a dark No. 4 square. The center row is two dark No. 4 squares on each side of a light one. Piece these three rows together. Now add a dark square No. 4 to each of the dark squares in the center and add a No. 1 shape in dark cloth between these squares. Add the corners to the tops of the No. 1 shapes. This should give you your block. You may also make the design using the No. 5 oblong in dark cloth rather than using two dark squares. This design will make a twin-bed quilt by using seven rows of nine blocks each.

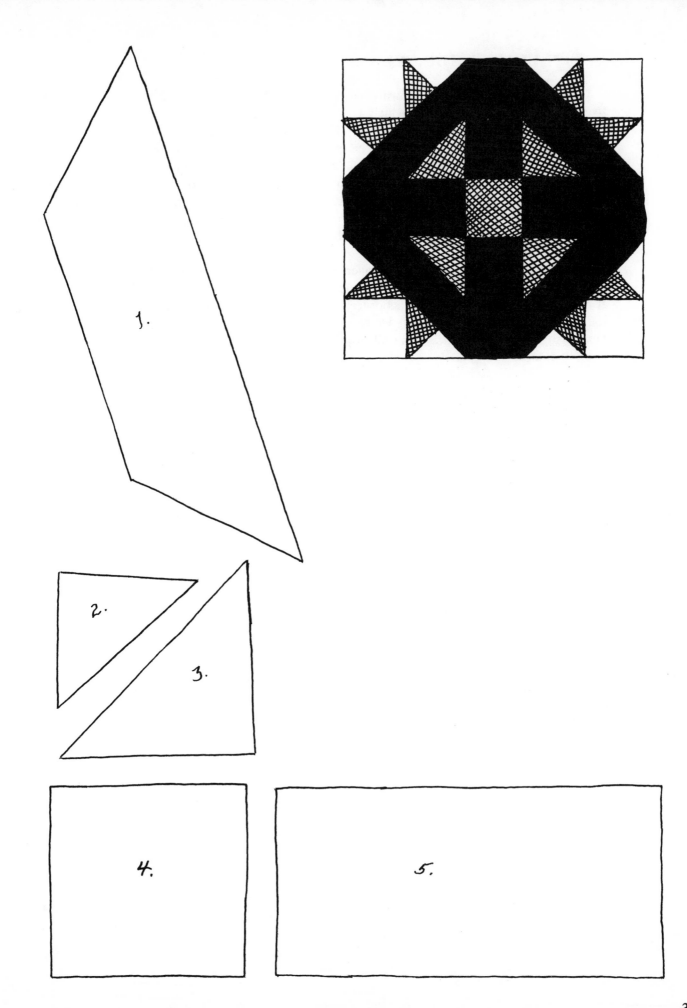

1.

2.

3.

4.

5.

QUEEN CHARLOTTE'S CROWN

One of the oldest and best known of all the five patch patterns is this one which is also known as INDIAN MEADOWS and MOUN– TAIN MEADOWS. It was named for the wife of George the Third of England, Queen Charlotte. During the Revolutionary War the good patriotic American ladies wanted to make this pattern but did not want to honor British royalty any longer, so it was then that the other names were thought up.

This pattern can be made in an all-over design, with lattice strips or with plain blocks. It can be made with or without a border like the other patterns in this section. However, I have a suggestion for putting this quilt top to-gether. A scrap quilt with the diamond shapes in one light plain color (like yellow) and the other colored pieces in dark prints, differing in each block, can be put together in an all-over pattern with a simple border.

Make two corner squares of the No. 3 tri-angles. To make the tulip-like corner, use four No. 1 diamonds, two No. 4 triangles and the No. 5 corner square. Add pattern No. 2 at the bottom. Put these four corners together with No. 2 in the center. This is not a hard pattern, but perhaps it should not be your very first quilt top. It will take six rows of eight blocks to make a twin-bed size quilt.

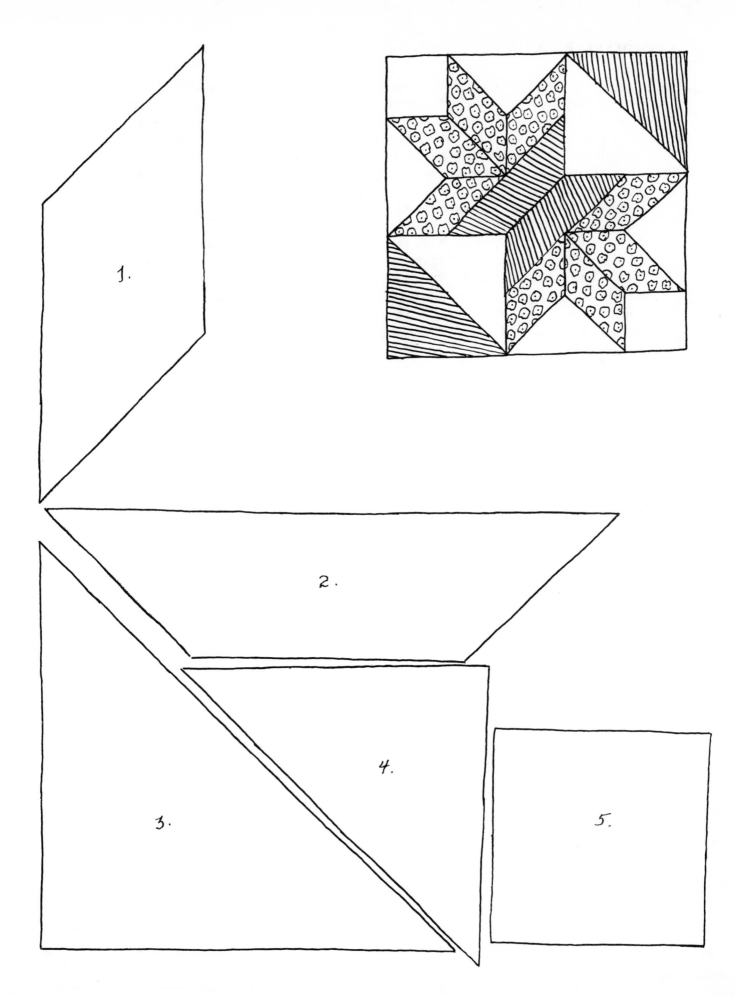

1.

2.

3.

4.

5.

GRAPE BASKET

Oddly enough this Grape Basket is a variation of the old Queen Charlotte's Crown pattern. Look at the base of the basket and compare it with the center of the other patch. This pattern will look well with plain blocks and lattice strips or it can be set together in an all-over design. It may be used with or without borders. It is a rather easy pattern, but it should not be your very first quilt top.

To make this block, break it up into sections. There are actually three squares in the block: one is composed of one square and triangles, while the other is made up of triangles only. To make the first square, use white for pattern No. 1 and make three white and three purple No. 2 triangles. For the other two squares, use two purple, two brown, and four white No. 2 triangles. Now make the other corner with two brown No. 5 patterns and two white No. 4 triangles. Put the three squares above the top white No. 4 triangle to form the second corner. Follow the drawing very carefully. Add two strips of three No. 1 white squares to fill out the last two corners.

You may wish to use grapes and handles in the No. 3 white triangles rather than the two squares. This 12-inch square will need six rows of eight blocks each to make a twin-bed size quilt.

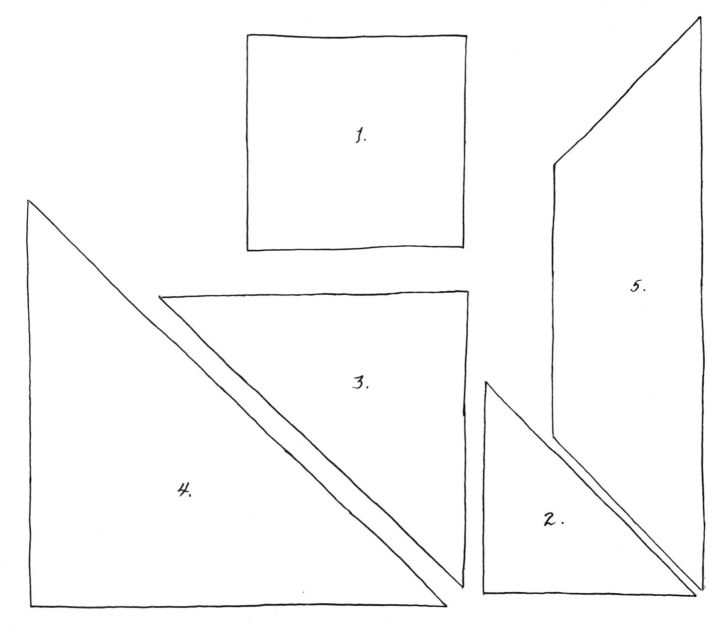

1.

3.

4.

2.

5.

DOMINO AND SQUARE

This is a simple pattern which makes a pretty, neat quilt. I do not know how old it is; it could have been designed any time from the middle of the nineteenth century to the 1930's. I believe that it could also make a pretty scrap quilt with white and another color or with a combination of two colors. Make this an all-over design rather than a quilt with plain blocks or with lattice strips. You may make the top with or without a border as you wish.

Piece this block in five strips. For the first strip, take a dark No. 5 square. On two sides, place two dark No. 2 triangles and one white No. 1 square. Finish it with a white No. 3 triangle for the corner.

For the second strip, use a dark No. 2 triangle, a white No. 1 square, a dark No. 1 square, a white No. 4 oblong, and two (dark and light) No. 1 squares. Finish with a dark No. 2 triangle.

For the center row, use a No. 3 white triangle for the first corner on this strip. Continue with a dark No. 5 square, a white No. 4 oblong, a dark No. 5 square, a white No. 4 oblong, 'a dark No. 5 square again (the third) and finish with a white No. 3 triangle for the other corner.

For the fourth strip, repeat the second strip, and for the fifth strip, repeat the first.

Sew all of the strips together in the order they have been made (from the first to the fifth). You should have a block exactly like the one in the drawing.

This is not too hard a pattern, but it should not be the first top you piece. A twin-bed quilt will take five rows of seven blocks each.

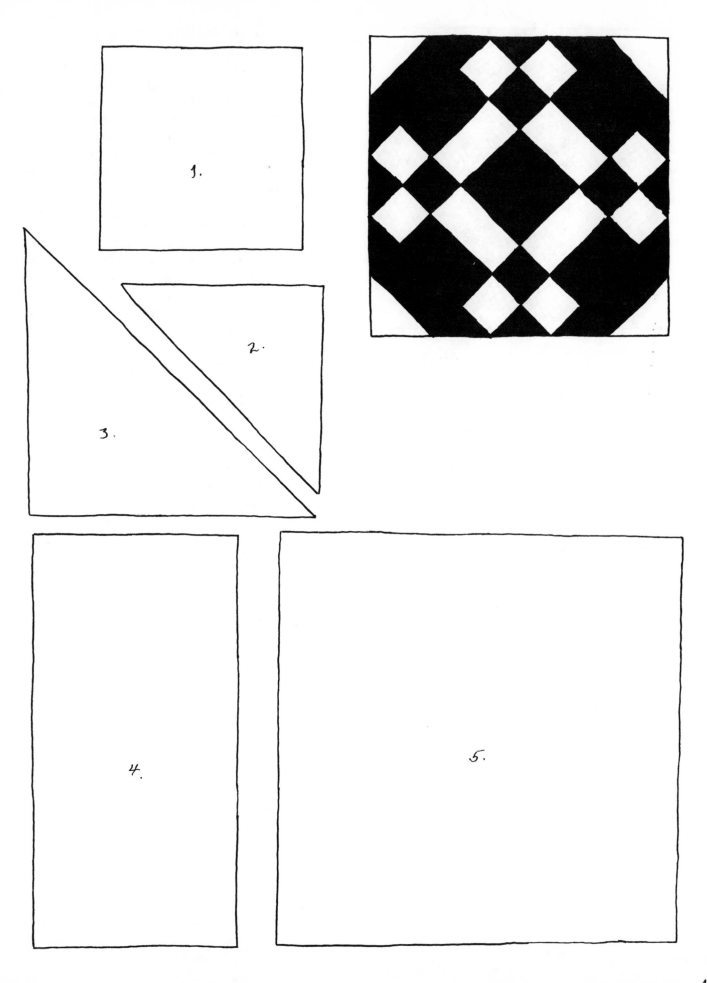

1.

2.

3.

4.

5.

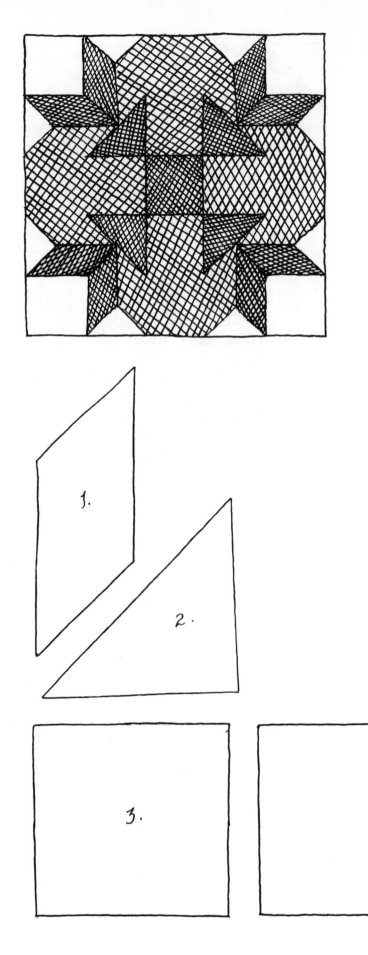

DOE AND DARTS

This pattern is also called DAVID AND GOLIATH, FOUR DARTS, BULL'S EYE and FLYING DARTS. It is a popular old favorite and dates from the early or middle nineteenth century. It is a variation of the David and Goliath pattern also found in this section. This pattern likewise makes a fine geometric if done in an all-over design; or it may be used as a scrap quilt if done with lattice strips or with plain blocks. You may use a border or not as you wish. This is an easy pattern for anyone to piece. It may be done in two shades of the same color, two colors or a plain color and a print.

To make this block, make the four corner squares by piecing a dark and a light No. 1 diamond and a white No. 2 triangle. Make two of these for each corner square. Sew these on each side of a white No. 3 square and add a dark No. 2 triangle to the other corner to fill out the square. Sew one of these large squares on each side of a light No. 4 oblong; this makes one strip. Make a second strip using the other two corner squares. The center strip consists of two light No. 4 oblongs on each side of a dark No. 3 square. Piece the other three strips together to look like the drawing of the finished block. This pattern will need seven rows of nine blocks each to make a twin-bed size quilt top.

Seven Patch Patterns

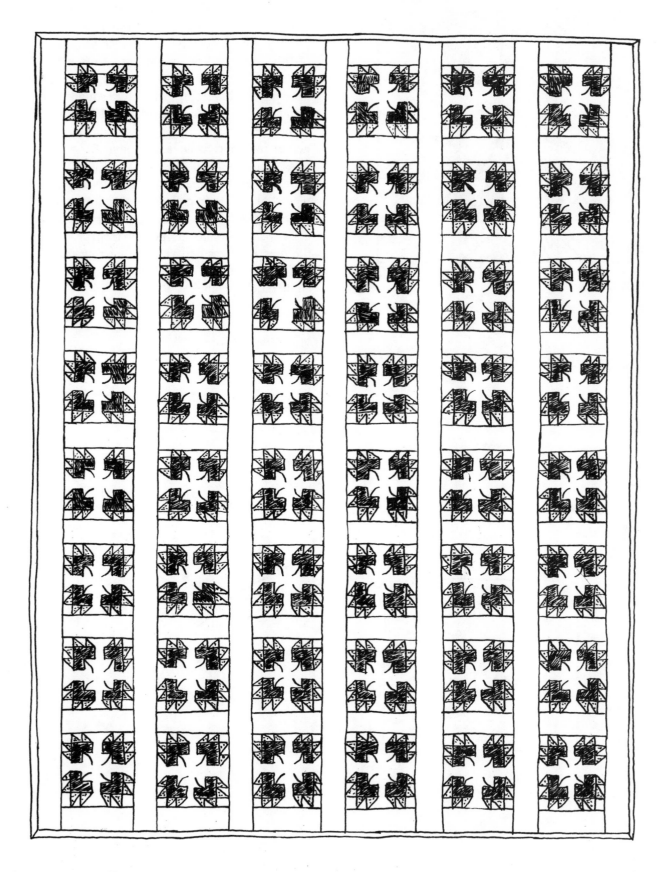

Autumn Tints

AUTUMN LEAF

When made in fall colors this is a striking quilt pattern. I do not think this is a very old pattern, but it goes back, at least, to the turn of this century. You cannot go wrong in making this quilt if you are careful in following the drawing and piecing the half squares into squares. Piece those and the solid squares together in seven strips, and sew the strips together in order. It is easy enough for a beginner. Appliqué the four stems to the correct square after the remainder of the block has been pieced. This block calls for either lattice strips or solid blocks between the pieced blocks. You may wish to make the border from a strip of the pieced leaves between two narrow strips of cloth. A twin-bed quilt will take six rows of eight blocks each.

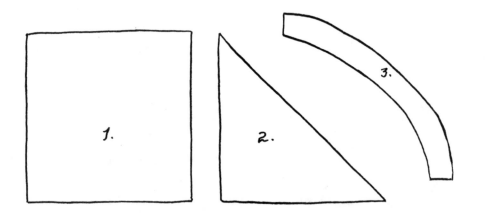

ORCHID HEMSTITCH

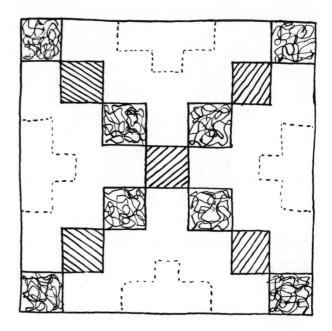

This pattern is from a rare 1930 pattern book. It is made in orchid and green on white. Piece the simple squares together with the alternating colored squares forming a cross in each block. Put these squares together in rows following the order of colors in the drawing. Then sew the strips together to form the same block as is seen in the drawing. The dotted line pattern should be drawn on the finished blocks as shown and then embroidered. This pattern must be an all-over design without lattice strips or plain blocks. It may have a border if you wish. It is certainly easy enough for any beginner to use as a first quilt top. It will take six rows of eight blocks each for a twin-bed size quilt top.

PRICKLY PEAR

This is a little harder pattern than should be pieced by a beginning quilter. It is a pretty old pattern dating from the late eighteenth century or early nineteenth century. I have seen it done in yellow and brown. Any two colors and white may be used. It may be pieced in an all-over design, with lattice strips or with plain blocks as desired. A border may or may not be added.

Piece four squares from a light and a white No. 3 triangle each. Sew two of these squares on either side of a strip made from a dark and a white No. 1 square. This is the first strip for the center. Repeat it with the colors reversed for the other side of the center. The center strip of this center portion is made of five No. 1 squares alternating in white and dark colors. Piece these strips together. Make four strips of one dark No. 1 square and five squares made from two No. 2 triangles each, in light and white colors. With the dark square in the corner each time, sew these four strips around the outside of the center portion already completed. This should give you a block which looks like the one in the drawing. A twin-bed quilt top will need five rows of seven blocks each.

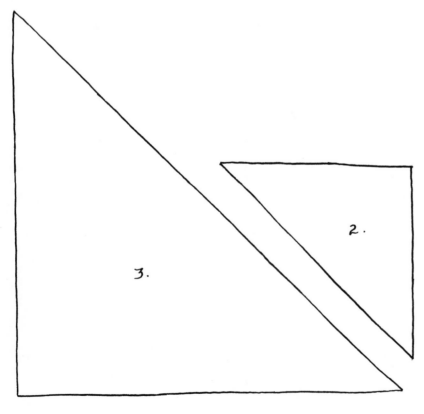

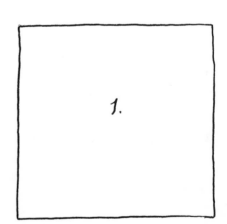

Four Patch Patterns

Harlequin Star

HARLEQUIN STAR

This star takes its name from the fact that the Harlequin Clowns of Italy wore costumes of diamonds sewn together in patterns of two colors. Choose any color and white for this pattern although gold and white would make a pretty quilt. The blocks are 12 inches square. It would be better to cut the white No. 1 triangle from cloth folded two times so the resulting piece of cloth is a diamond between the pieced stars. At the edges of the quilt, pattern No. 1 would be a long triangle rather than a diamond.

Cut four white and four gold No. 6 patterns, and four white and four gold No. 7 patterns. These will make the center of the star (see drawing). For each of the four rays of the star, cut one No. 2, two No. 3, three No. 4 and four No. 5 patterns. Sew the following patterns together in lines: Nos. 5, 4, 3 and No. 2. Then Nos. 5, 4 and 3. Thirdly, Nos. 5 and 4, and finish with a No. 5 triangle. This design is as easy to piece as it looks.

The drawing of the finished quilt in this chapter shows the border and quilting patterns to use with this design. There are five rows of six blocks for the top. The border is two strips of two-inch wide material and one strip of the white eight-inch wide.

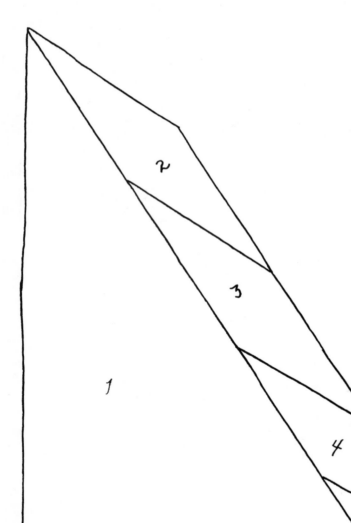

ETERNAL TRIANGLE

This pattern is also known as MERRY–GO–ROUND. It is a combination of small white squares and small white, colored, or printed triangles. The design was introduced during the latter part of the nineteenth century. In order to make the design appear clearly, put it together with alternate plain blocks in either white, plain-colored or printed triangles.

In each of the four sections of this block there are seven white squares, nine white and nine colored triangles. Piece the triangles into nine squares and then, following the drawing very carefully, piece all of the plain and triangular squares into the one-quarter design section. After making four of these pieced sections, sew them together into the finished block. There should be forty-two blocks in this quilt made in rows of seven blocks in six rows. Half of the blocks, twenty-one, should be plain and the other twenty-one should be pieced. This is not a hard quilt. A careful beginner should be able to piece it easily.

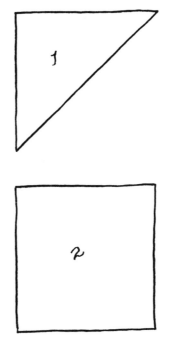

QUEEN OF THE MAY

This pattern is not difficult until you come to piecing the center ring into the dark frame. Choose a darker color for all of the frames in this quilt. The flowers may be of one print and a matching color lighter than the frames. The center and background of the flower circle should be white or cream. This may be made with flowers all the same or it would also be pretty as a scrap quilt. Cut half of the pieces of the No. 2 pattern reversed from the way the pattern is drawn here. Then sew two of these opposite-shaped patterns together on the longer side to make one of the six sides of the hexagon (see drawing).

Five rows of six blocks each will make a single bed quilt. This pattern is not for beginners, yet it is not one of the really hard quilts to piece either.

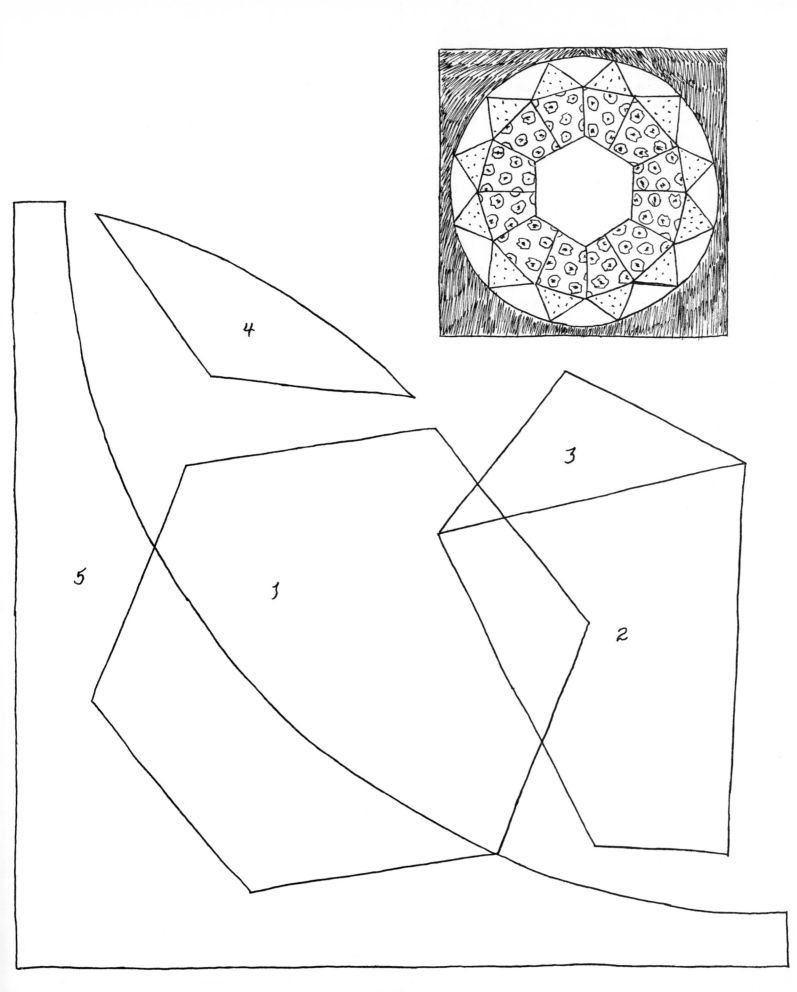

4

3

5

1

2

MY NOVA

The name means my new star for this is an original pattern printed here for the first time. It is based, however, on one of the old Dutch Rose patterns. I have shown it here in pale green and red on white. It is quite a difficult pattern that should not be attempted by a beginner.

Make the center triangles of red and white. On top of the white ones piece two smaller white triangles and a green diamond No. 2 and 3 patterns. On the red triangle piece two red No. 5 shapes and a green No. 3 diamond. Sew these triangles together. Fill in the outer points with white No. 6 pattern. Piece chevrons of pattern No. 7 and add No. 8 between them. When the rose-like center is finished appliqué it to the center of a 14-inch square of white material. It will take five rows of six blocks each to make a twin-bed size quilt.

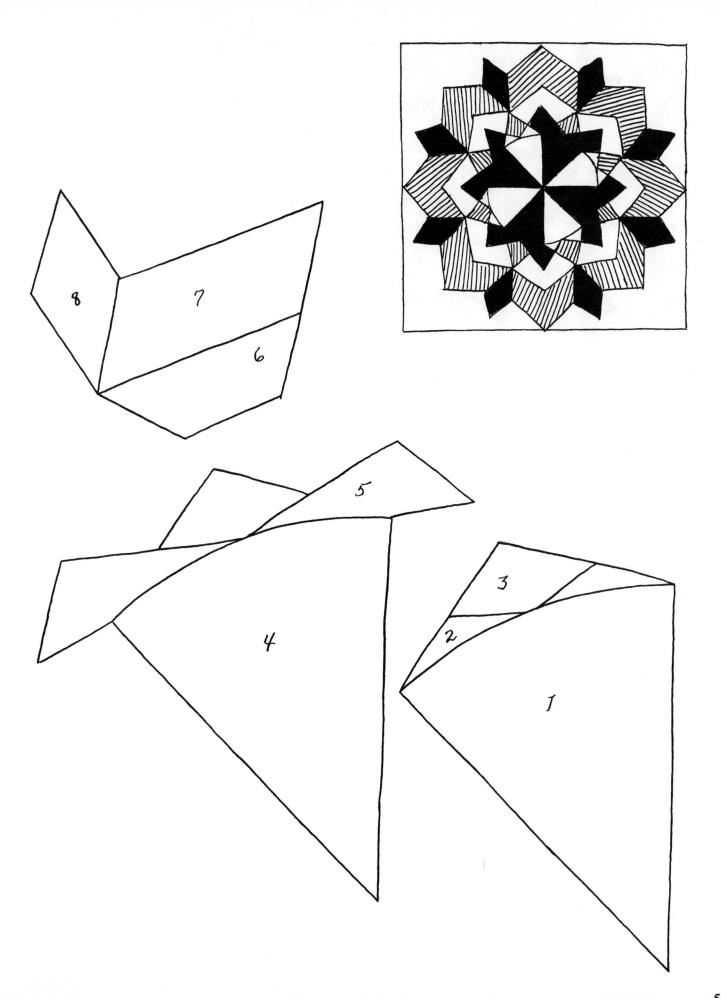

INDIAN TRAILS

This is a very old quilt pattern which was very popular for a long time. You can tell this because the pattern has many names. Here are the ones I have been able to find; FOREST PATH, RAMBLING ROADS, RAMBLING ROSE, CLIMBING ROSE, NORTH WIND, IRISH PUZZLE, WINDING WALK, OLD MAID'S RAMBLE, STORM AT SEA, WEATHER VANE, FLYING DUTCHMAN, PRICKLY PEAR, TANGLED TARES and BEAR'S PAW.

This pattern must be pieced in four sections. Each section will contain a large square made of two triangles cut from pattern No. 1. One should be of light and the other of dark color. On two sides of this square should be placed a strip of three small squares cut from the small triangle No. 2 pattern, in light and dark colors. Fill in the corner where the two strips come together with the light No. 3 square. Carefully place the four sections together so they look like those in the drawing. This is not a difficult pattern; it can be made by even a beginner of quilting. You will need six rows of eight blocks each for a twin-bed quilt.

1

2

3

UNKNOWN FOUR PATCH

This is one of the pretty patterns I found while walking along a sidewalk. It was on a navy blue and white quilt hanging on a clothesline and I have never been able to find out if this pattern has a name. The pattern makes a crisp, clean-looking quilt that is easy enough for the newest quilter and pretty enough for the most experienced.

There are only two shapes. Cut eight blue No. 2 triangles and eight white ones. These are sewn together into small squares to make the center square of this patch. Cut four blue No. 1 triangles and four white ones. Sew these into larger triangles for the four corners of the center square (see drawing). When the blocks are pieced together, they will form a series of alternating large and small triangular blocks. Seven rows of eight blocks each will make a twin-bed size quilt. You may wish to add a six-inch wide WILD GOOSE CHASE border all the way around this quilt top.

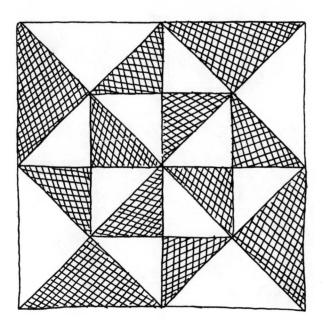

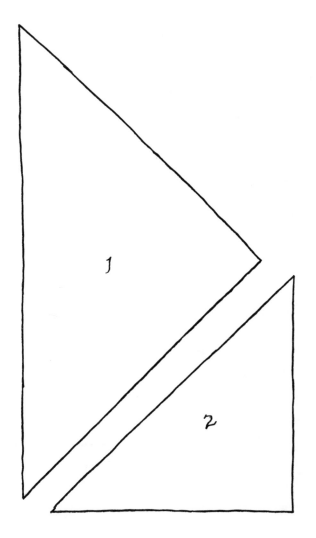

THE OLD WINDMILL

This old favorite is the scrap quilt par excellence. Mix or match your scraps as you choose; this old pattern will treat colors without favoritism and make a plain, good quilt. This pattern was used all through the nineteenth century as a utility quilt or one which could be made quickly, easily and economically. It can be made from cotton or wool; if you are lavish in your scraps, it can be made with the dark triangles in velvet and the light colors in silk.

This quilt can be made by the youngest child, the newest, beginning quilter, or by the most fussy who could make it quite grand. Make a number of squares from the small triangle of dark and light materials. Put them together to make the simple windmill pattern. The square shown here is 10 inches across; seven rows of nine blocks are needed to make a twin-bed quilt. This quilt may also be made with a plain dark border of any width to set off the pieced portion of the top.

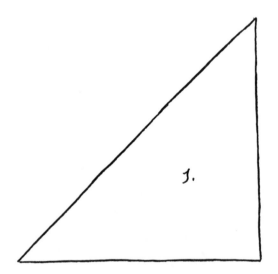

1.

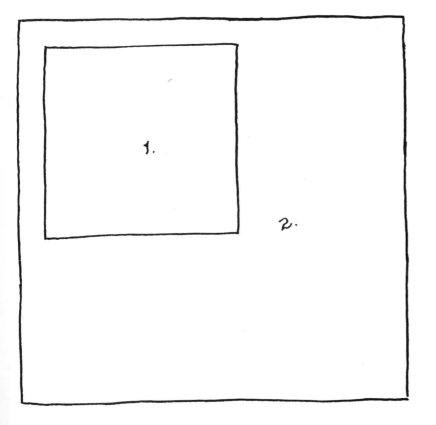

THE FOUR PATCH

All of the patterns in this section are variations of the basic four patch. The patterns in the drawings on this page are two of the most basic variations. The drawing on the left is done in orange, brown, yellow and green; it is called AUTUMN LEAVES. The pattern variation on the right is done in red, white and blue; it is merely called FOUR PATCH. These patches are all done with straight-line sewing and are easy enough for a child to make and pretty enough for the most discriminating adult. Each patch needs eight of the small squares (in the colors indicated by the drawings) and two of the large squares (again in the colors indicated). Sew four of the small squares together twice and add the large squares to make each block. Use your imagination in mixing and matching the colors for your tops. Since the pattern is very simple, the beauty of this quilt will depend on the colors used. A twin-bed size quilt will need seven rows of nine blocks each.

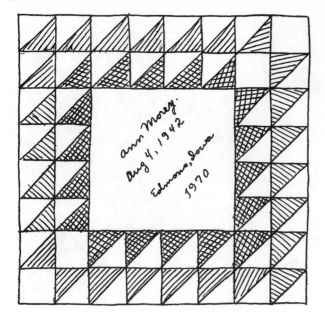

INDIAN PLUMES

This is a Friendship block but it may also be used as a pieced frame for a pretty quilted, embroidered or painted pattern. The style of this block is late 19th or early 20th century, so this is one of the patterns your grandmother could have done. I have shown the colors as light blue and green, but I think it would be effective in yellow and red or some other striking modern color combination as long as you match your two colors well. You might try this pattern in four colors, having two colors in each alternating block and the other two colors in the remaining blocks. This really should not be a scrap quilt.

Place 26 squares of one color of the triangles and 18 of the other color and white. Place the 18 squares together with two of the small white squares around the large white square. Then piece the remaining squares into a frame for the first set. A twin-bed quilt will take five rows of seven blocks each; this quilt does not need a border.

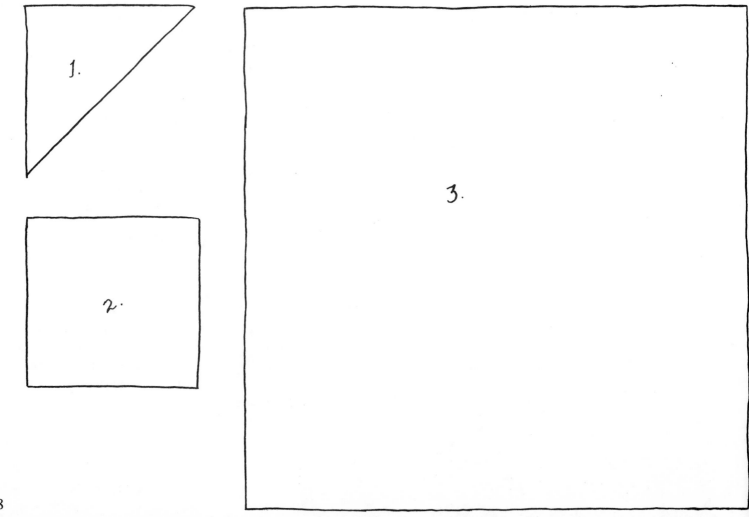

MODERN STAR

You will never make a more striking quilt than one from this pattern. It is based on the old red-and-green tulip quilts of the middle of the nineteenth century, but this one is from the 1930's. Piece the center star from four green and four white No. 3 diamonds. The peony or tulip-like corners are each pieced from six of the No. 1 diamonds. Add them to the four corners of the center star where the points are white. Finally add the four green triangles and appliqué the entire center to a white 12-inch square. This is a design which must be separated by white, plain squares between each two pieced blocks. The white spaces should be filled with as elaborate a quilting design as you can fit into the space. A fancy wide border could also be used effectively on this top. Four rows of six blocks and a 12-inch border all around the top will make a twin-bed size quilt.

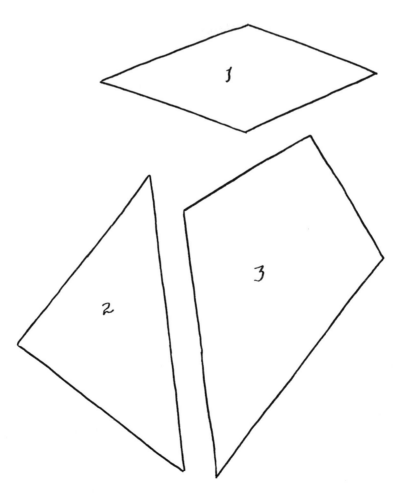

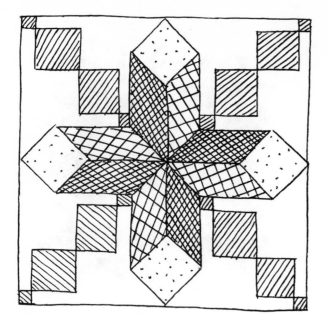

CENTURY OF PROGRESS

This is a pattern which is connected with one of the World Fairs so popular during the nineteenth and early twentieth centuries. The Chicago "Century of Progress" World's Fair was held in the years 1933 and 1934 and this pattern dates from those years.

Piece the center star from a dark solid color and a light matching print with the points of plain yellow. The paths to the corners, patterns No. 1 and 4 are made from a green print. The center star is appliquéd to the center of a 12-inch white square and then the pathway squares are appliquéd in place. This must be an all-over pattern and should not have the plain white squares between the pieced ones. You might set the squares together with a two-inch white lattice strip and a green No. 2 corner square between the pieced squares. Without the lattice strips, you will need six rows of eight blocks for a twin-bed size quilt. With the lattice strips, you will need five rows of seven blocks each and edge the quilt on all four sides with the lattice strips.

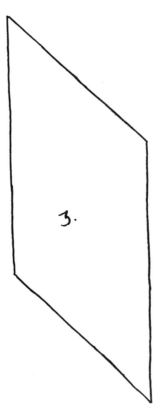

KANSAS DUGOUT

This pattern is one of those named for and designed during the troubles in Kansas just before and during the Civil War period. It is a simple pattern designed for a print and a white material. It should not be a scrap quilt; neither should plain blocks or lattice strips be used between the blocks. The square may be made (as shown) with the triangles in the outer corners, but it would be easiest to make the entire top with the squares between the larger patterns. Use only the triangles on the edges of the quilt top itself. In an all-over design, there should be 216 of the single designs with four of the No. 3 pattern and one No. 1 square in the center. There should be 28 rows of 32 blocks each with a square between them in each corner.

Do try this pattern; it makes a neat, pretty quilt and is not too hard for a beginner.

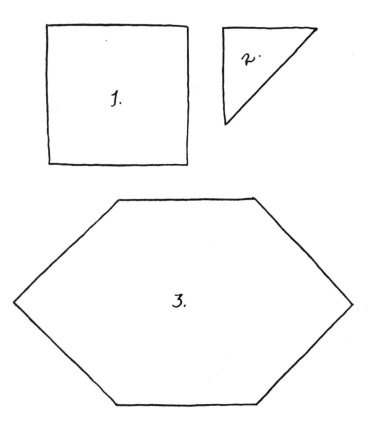

DELECTABLE MOUNTAINS

This is one of the few patterns that can be traced back to the colonial period of the eighteenth century. The drawing shows only the center row of mountains encircling a star. There will be three more rows of mountains around the outer edge of this quilt center. These outer blocks should be 12 inches square with half of the patch a pieced mountain made of patterns No. 3, 4, 5, 6, 7, and 8. The other half of the patch should be a plain triangle 12½ by 12½ by 18¾ inches. Make the center first and then arrange the blocks with mountains around the center. This will form four rows of mountains around the center star. The drawing shows only the first row of mountains.

Piece the center Star of Le Moine from patterns No. 1, 2, and 3. Make two of the pieced triangles which represent mountains with the No. 8 end triangles attached to each end and two more mountains without the No. 8 end triangles. Attach these four sections to each side of the center star and then attach four of the plain triangles to the outside of this pieced center. Make a row of eight pieced mountains and the plain triangles next. Make a further row of 12 pieced mountains and plain blocks for the third row. The fourth or outer row will need 16 of the pieced mountains. This will mean that you must piece 60 of the mountain squares for a double-bed size quilt. There should not be any border around this quilt as the pieced mountains will make four rows of borders around the center star. The quilt will be eight feet square which is large enough for a double bed. One more row will make it a queen-size bed quilt and two more rows will make it large enough for a king-size bed. Any color combination of dark and light colors may be used to make a beautiful quilt, i.e., blue and white, green print and tan, or orange and ecru.

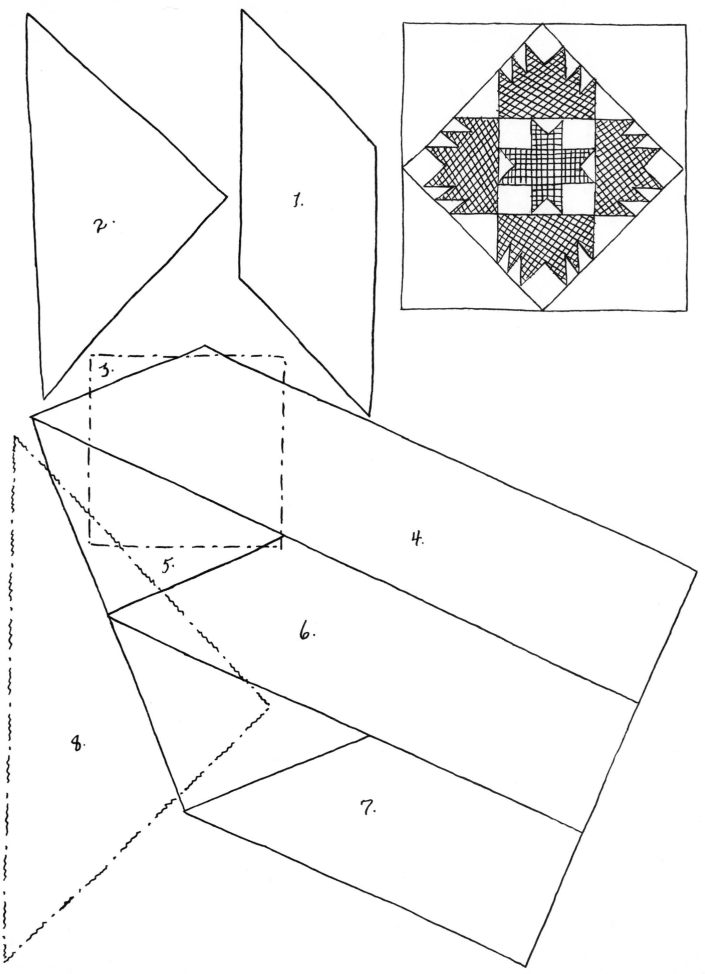

2.

1.

3.

4.

5.

6.

8.

7.

63

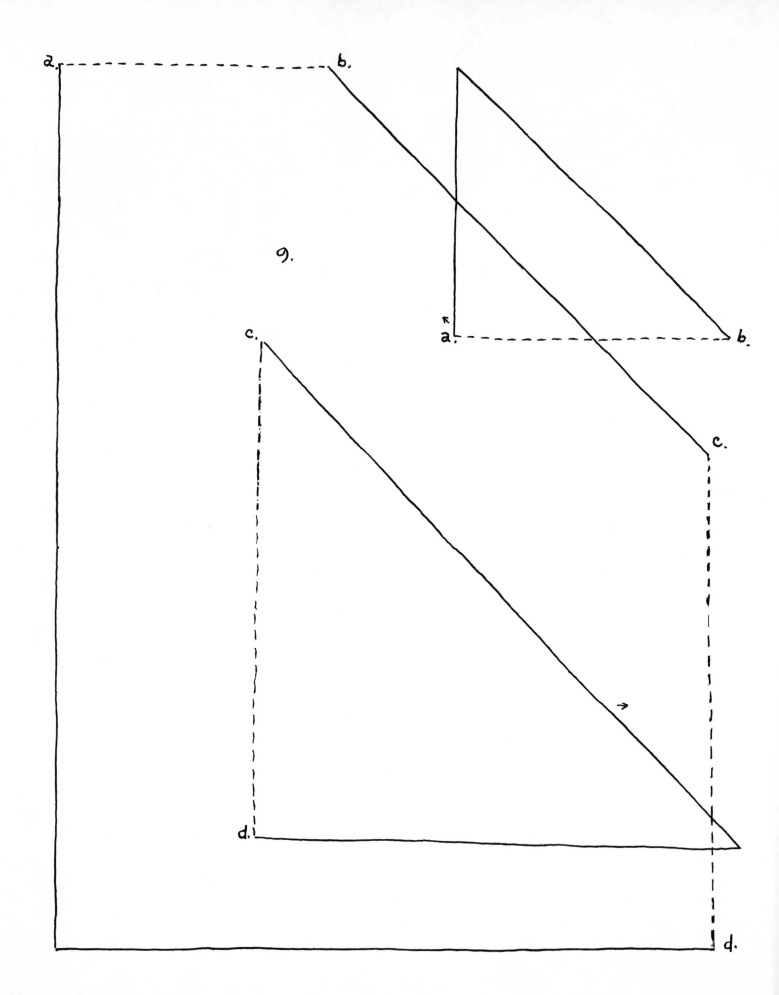

9.

a.

b.

b.

a.

b.

c.

c.

c.

d.

d.

d.

64

BLACKFORD'S BEAUTY

This pattern makes a neat quilt in green and white. Unfortunately, I do not know anything about the origins of this pattern except that it dates from, at least, the middle of the nineteenth century. It is easy enough for beginners and should be made as an all-over design without plain blocks or lattice strips. You might try a simple border such as two or three strips on this quilt. Piece four of the diamond sections, two No. 1 diamonds and two No. 4 triangles at each end to make this a strip. Make four corner sections, two green and three white No. 3 squares plus two green No. 2 oblongs to form a square. Place one of the corner squares on each side of a diamond strip. Make two of these strips. Place the remaining two diamond strips sideways on one large white No. 5 square. This makes the center strip of the block. Place the two strips with the corner squares on each side of the center strip. The blocks will be only eight inches square so it will take sixteen rows of fifteen blocks each for a twin-bed size quilt. This should not be made as a scrap quilt.

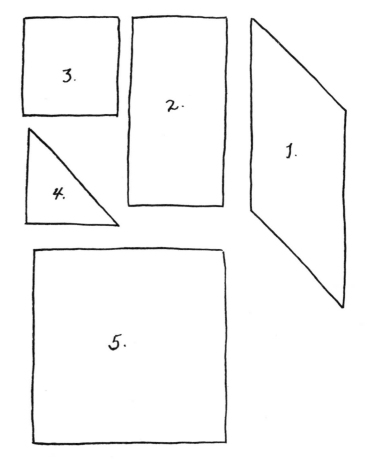

THE PHILIPPINES

This is a red and white quilt which, from the name and type, seems to date from 1898 or 1899. It is one of the Feathered Stars which was so popular toward the end of the nineteenth century. This pattern is one of the harder ones and should not be attempted until you have made several others of the easier patterns.

Frame the white No. 5 square with the No. 6 strips. This makes the center of the Star. Make four star points by making red and white strips of each of the following: four red of No. 3, and five white of No. 2. Join these with the No. 1 diamond in red. Place these strips on each side of a No. 4 triangle in white. Place one of these four points on each side of the center square. Pattern No. 7 is one half of the triangle needed between the star points. Place the bottom line on a fold of the cloth when cutting it from white fabric. Add one of these larger triangles to each of the four sides of the square. This pattern should be pieced together into a top without plain white squares or lattice strips between the blocks. It might have a small Wild Goose Chase border if you wish. This might also be pretty worked out as a scrap quilt. It will need five rows of seven blocks each to make a twin-bed size quilt.

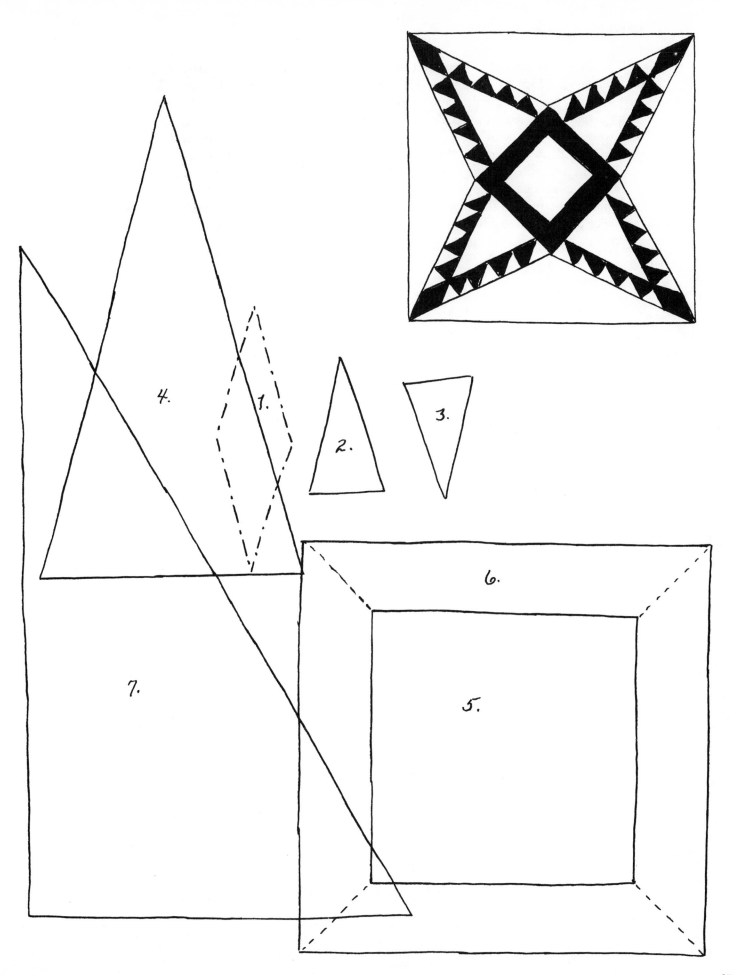

4.

1.

2.

3.

6.

5.

7.

67

NORTH STAR

This pattern is one of the prettiest stars in my collection. It also is known as STAR TULIP. It is not for the beginning quilter as it has many small curved seams in it. The colors are red, white and blue with the small petal-like shapes around the center in yellow.

Piece the center by adding one of the No. 2 sections to each side of the No. 1 piece. Add the eight semi-circles to the outside of this center. Piece the No. 5 and add two No. 4 sections together; add one No. 6 piece to one side of this. Make four of these. Carefully sew the corner sections to the petal-shaped pieces of the center and finish the four seams between these sections. This is not an easy pattern but it is effective when done carefully. You might wish to place a plain block between each of the pieced blocks. This quilt will take seven rows of nine blocks each for a twin-bed size quilt. You might also like this quilt with an elaborate wide border of a flower meander in the manner of an early nineteenth century quilt.

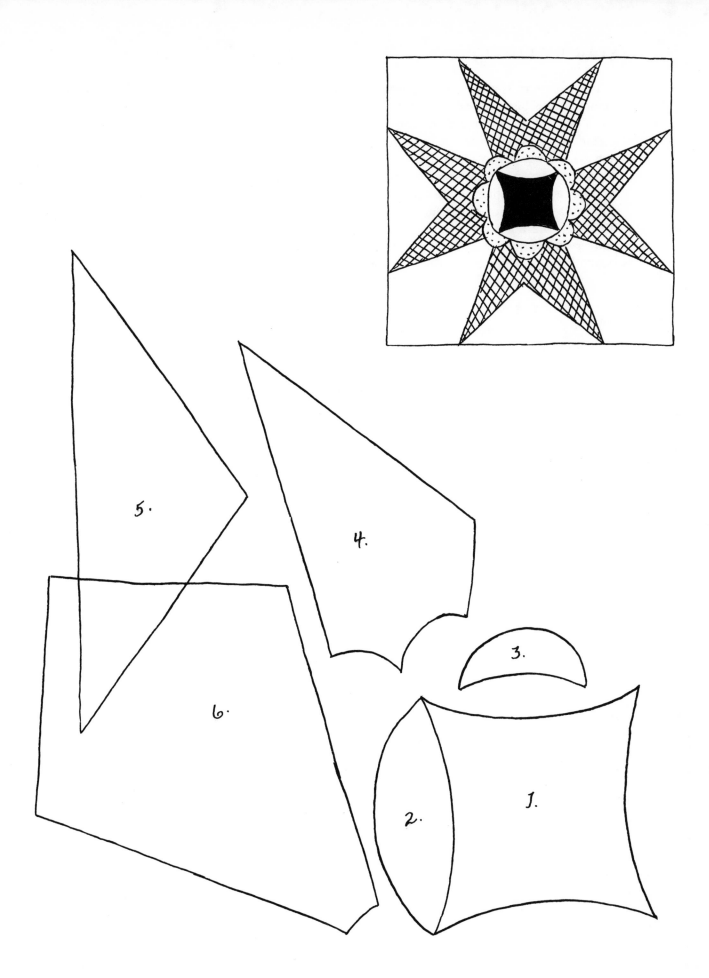

STAR OF LE MOINE

If this pattern is made with a printed rather than a white background, it is called STAR OF THE EAST. It is one of the very old basic variations of the plain Star of Le Moine. It is not a hard pattern to piece, but it does take special care to piece the points to make them come exactly together in the center. If you allow the corners of the seams to wander a little, you will not produce a pretty quilt. This pattern can be done in an all-over pattern, with plain blocks or with lattice strips as you please.

First sew the diamonds together from the two triangles. Then sew two diamonds to either side of a No. 2 triangle, making four of these sections. Finish the blocks by adding the No. 3 corner squares and sewing the four sections together down the remaining seam. Four rows of six blocks each will make a twin-bed size quilt. You may wish to add a simple border to this top. It might be pretty as a scrap quilt if you are careful in matching your colors.

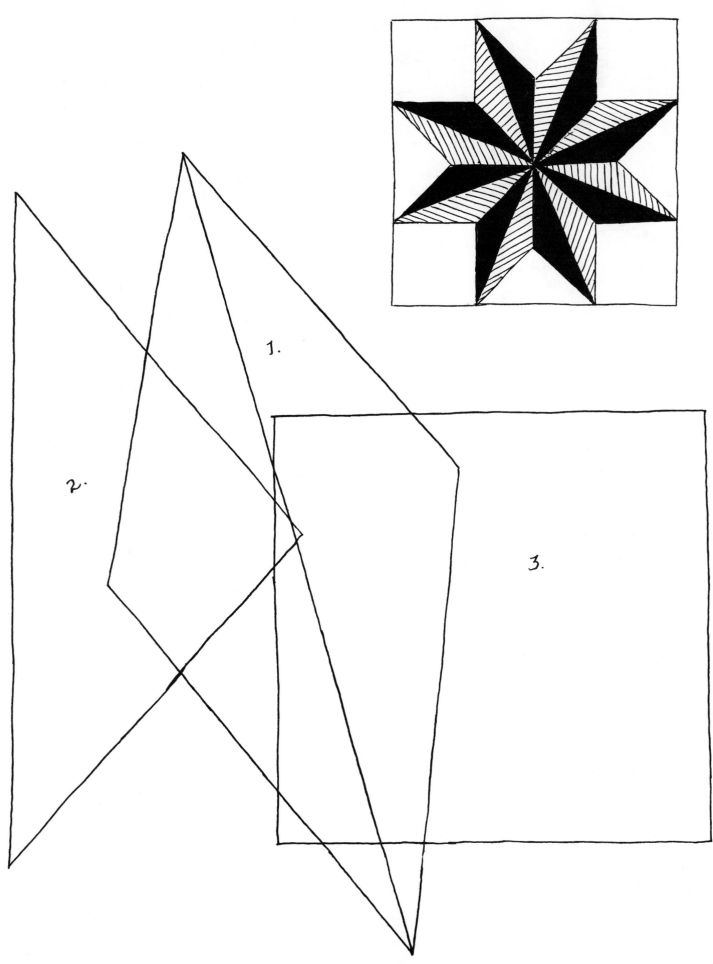

1.

2.

3.

ODD FELLOWS CHAIN

This is another of the anonymous patterns that seem to just pop up in a collection. I do not know the age nor the history of this block. It is another block that must be done in two colors and in an all-over design. Do not use plain blocks or lattice strips. You may add a simple border pattern to this top if you wish.

To piece the block, divide the pattern into smaller blocks. The four corners with the bow tie-like pattern are one set. These are pieced from two print and two white No. 3 triangles and two white No. 2 squares. The next set of eight squares are pieced from one No. 4 triangle, one printed No. 3 triangle plus three white No. 3 triangles. Piece the star in the center of the block from one white No. 1 square, four white No. 2 squares, eight green No. 3 triangles and eight white No. 3 triangles. Piece two of the corner squares on either side of two of the next squares for the first strip. Piece two each of the next squares on either side of the center square for the second strip and make another strip just like the first one. Sew the three strips together. You will be amazed at the pattern which emerges when these blocks are put together into a top. Do not make this a scrap quilt as that would spoil the design. It will take six rows of eight blocks each to make a twin-bed size quilt. This pattern is easy enough for a beginner.

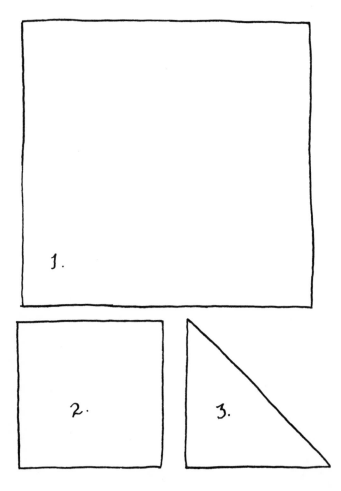

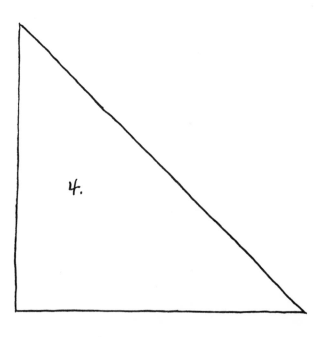

72

UNKNOWN STAR

This attractive pattern is copied from a square in an old nineteenth century Friendship quilt. It was red on white and is quite a simple pattern to make. Piece one large eight pointed Star of Le Moine from the large diamond pattern No. 1 and four small stars from the tiny diamond pattern No. 2. Appliqué these stars in position on a large 18-inch white square and add the three large, red diamonds in a row across each corner. Piece the squares together in an all-over design. This is a very easy pattern and will make an attractive quilt even for a beginner. You might even try this as a scrap quilt. A twin-bed size quilt will need four rows of five blocks and you may add a simple border, if you wish.

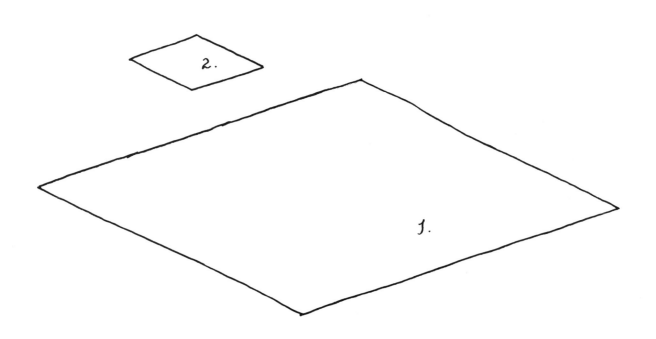

2.

1.

LOG CABIN STAR

This beauty is a variation of the old fashioned String Quilt. You will use up scraps from your sewing that you never dreamed of being able to use. To make this type of quilt you must first make a sheet of cloth on your sewing machine from all of the odd, long, narrow scraps you can find in your scrap bag. Anything from ¾ of an inch wide to five or six inches wide will do. Mix and match the colors and prints as you make your sheet of cloth so the colors look well together. When finished, lay the pattern No. 1 lengthwise on the sheet of cloth so the strips go from side to side (see drawing). Make eight of these diamond shapes. Piece them together into an eight-pointed star. Fill in the points with a solid color from pattern No. 2. Add the four semi-circular corner pieces to make the blocks a square. This block takes a little experience to make but it is not as hard as it looks.

This quilt should be an all-over pieced top without plain blocks or lattice strips. It will take five rows of seven blocks each to make a twin-bed size quilt. It needs only a very simple border if one is used with this top.

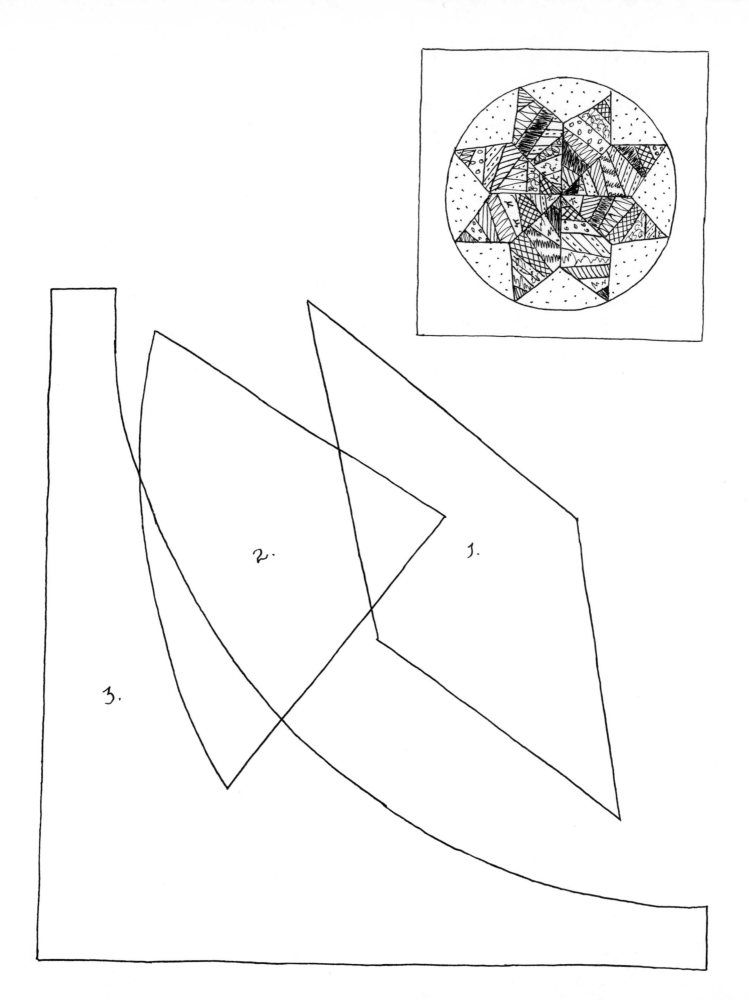

2.

1.

3.

LAFAYETTE ORANGE PEEL

This is also called ORANGE PEEL and MELON PATCH. The story behind this patch is that it was made up when the good Marquis de Lafayette visited our country for his triumphal journey in 1824–1825. During this visit he was especially honored with a feast in the city of Philadelphia. At a banquet, oranges were served as part of the dessert and M. Lafayette took his knife and divided the skin of the fruit into exactly four equal parts before peeling it away. A young lady in her teens sitting nearby begged the skin of the fruit as a souvenir of the occasion and M. Lafayette gave the peels to her. She took the peels home and used them as a pattern to make the very quilt block of this design. It is a pretty tale and is supposed to be quite true. The pattern was spread all over the new United States where it took its popularity both from its own beauty and the love of every American lady for the Marquis de Lafayette, the Hero of our Revolution.

The quilt may be done in any color and white or in two colors. Prints are also quite pretty but this is not a scrap quilt. It is also not for a beginner because of the curved seams. The top should be done in an all-over pattern without lattice strips or plain blocks. Piece two of the sections, using patterns No. 1 and No. 2. Sixteen of these squares put together, as shown in the drawing, will make one block. Seven rows of nine blocks each will make a twin-bed size quilt top. This quilt may have a very simple border, but it does not really need one.

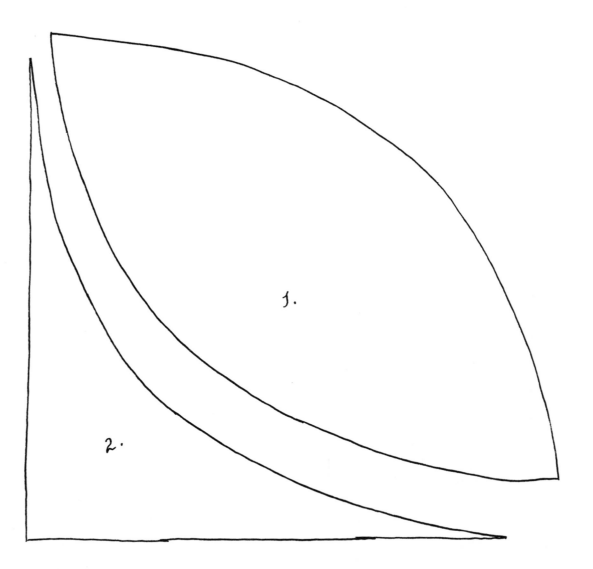

1.

2.

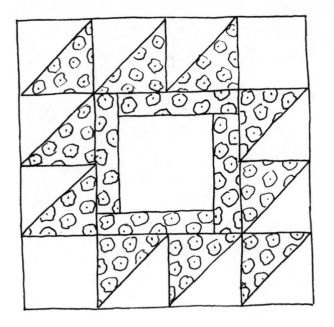

ROCKY MOUNTAIN PUZZLE

This is definitely a scrap pattern that is easy enough for any beginner. You may make it with lattice strips or plain blocks between the pieced blocks. Add a large or small border or any other way of making this quilt top and this pattern will still look neat and pretty.

To piece the block, make twelve squares from triangle No. 1 using plain and printed materials. Make one center square from the white No. 3 square and four printed No. 2 strips. Sew the small squares made from triangles around the center square after sewing them first into strips of four blocks for the top and bottom and two blocks each for the two sides of the quilt. This top will need seven rows of nine blocks each for a twin-bed size quilt top.

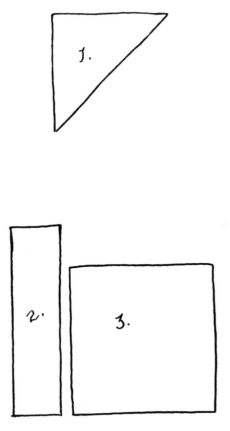

WANDERING FOOT

This pattern when used as a quilt on a boy's bed will cause that boy to leave home and begin a life of eternal wandering. Of course, you can call this same pattern TURKEY TRACKS and then it has no effect on boys or anyone else. At least that is how the old superstition runs. I'll bet it would have no effect either way. This is a pretty, old nineteenth century pattern. It calls for a print and a matching plain color on white in each block. It would make a very pretty scrap quilt.

The blocks are nine inches square. Piece a No. 2 oval on each side of the No. 1 center. Appliqué this motif to the exact center of a white nine-inch square. At each of the four points of the No. 1 pattern, place a tulip made from two of the No. 2 ovals on either side of a No. 3 piece. This quilt top takes eight rows of twelve blocks each for a twin-bed size quilt. This pattern would look very nice with a large, elaborate border. This quilt is not for beginners because of the curved seams.

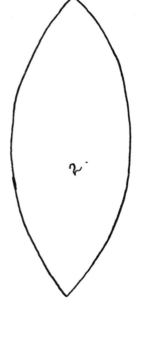

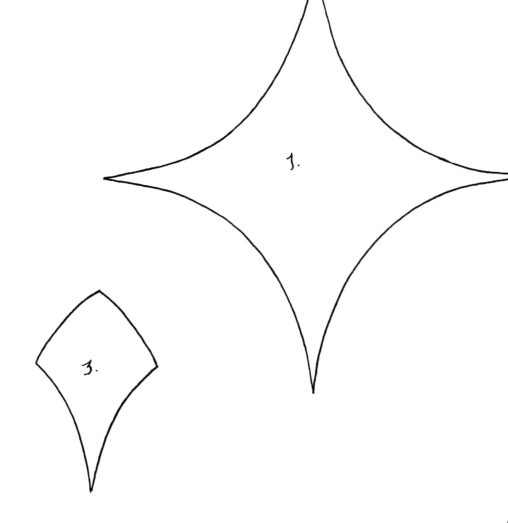

WORLD WITHOUT END

This is also called GOLDEN WEDDING RING. It is an early nineteenth century religious pattern and one of the really wonderful geometric designs that have been used in quilting. This pattern uses no curved lines at all and thus may be made easily by any beginning quilter. The wonder of this design is that when the blocks are put together the designs form large and small circles all over the quilt top. Piece each of the four sections separately and then sew them together to look like the drawing. A twin-bed size quilt will take six rows of eight blocks each. Do not put plain blocks or lattice strips in this quilt. It also does not need a border. The colors should be one plain color or print and white.

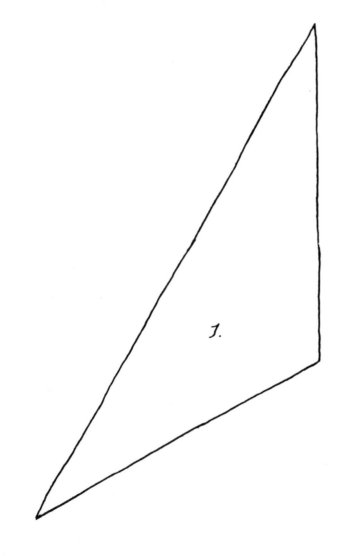

1.

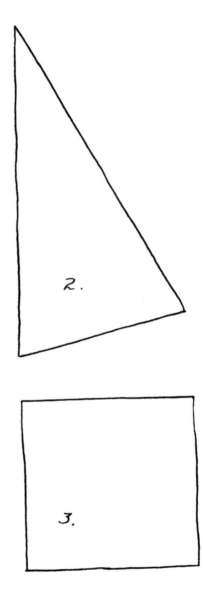

2.

3.

CROSSES AND LOSSES

This nineteenth century utility pattern is called "X," DOUBLE X and OLD MAID'S PUZZLE. It may be made from plain color or print on white, or with a color, matching print and white. This is a true scrap pattern. It is easy enough for a child or a beginner to make a pretty quilt from this pattern. It can be used with or without a border, and with or without lattice strips or plain as desired. Make the four sections one at a time and put them together to look like the drawing. This is such a tiny pattern that it may be used as a pot holder or an apron pocket as well as a quilt. The finished quilt top in twin size will take twelve rows of sixteen blocks each.

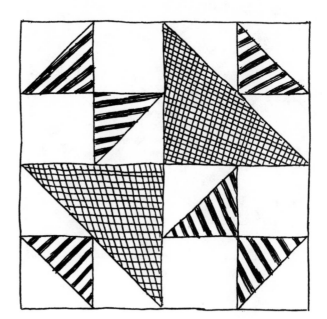

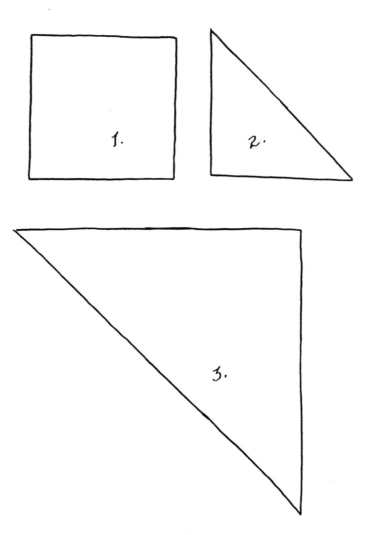

SHADED TRAIL

This is an "eye fooler" design. It should be done in an all-over design without lattice strips or plain blocks. The nice thing about this pattern is that it is easy to piece. Piece the four sets of No. 4 pattern in dark and light materials. Sew two of these sets together and add a set of dark and light No. 2 and No. 3 squares on each side. Work this all the way around until the center of the block is finished. Add the No. 1 corner triangles.

It will take sixteen rows of fifteen blocks each to make a twin-bed size quilt top. You may or may not add a border to this quilt.

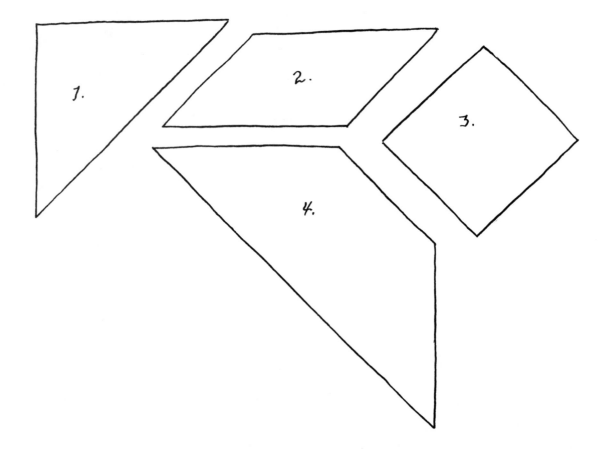

NIGHT AND DAY

This is another "eye fooler" design which should be made in an all-over design without lattice strips or plain blocks. This design, too, is easy enough for beginners. To make the block, sew together to make a large triangle: a light No. 1 triangle, a dark No. 3 pattern and a light No. 2 triangle. Sew a second triangle with the same shapes but the colors and the way the shapes face each other should be reversed. Sew these two large triangles into a square and repeat the previous steps three more times. Sew the four triangles into a block which looks like the drawing. This pattern needs six rows of eight blocks each, but it does not need a border for a twin-bed size quilt.

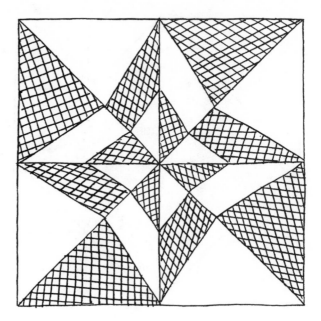

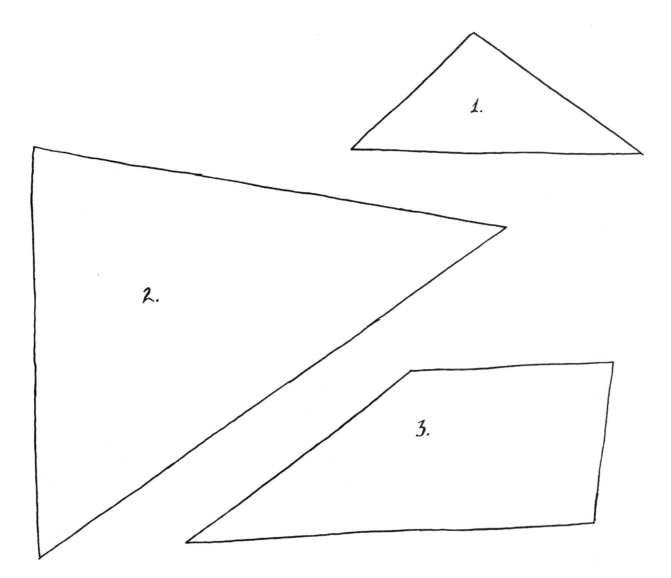

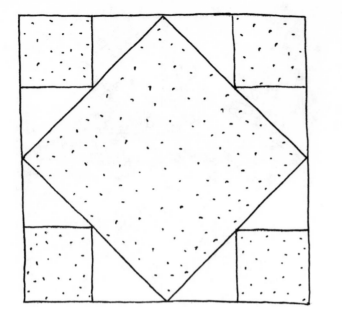

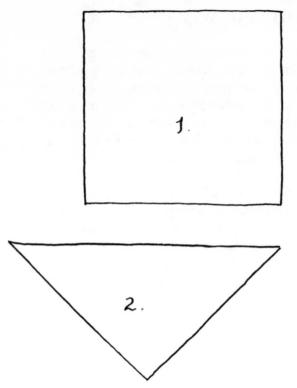

1.

2.

3.

FOUR SQUARE

This is one of the simplest and neatest quilt patterns in this book. It may be put together in any way you wish with plain squares in an all-over design or with lattice strips. It may or may not have a border or it may or may not be a scrap quilt. To piece the block, make a triangle of two white No. 2 triangles on each side of the darker No. 1 square. When you have pieced four of these, sew them to the sides of the large No. 3 square. This would be an excellent pattern for any beginner to make as her first attempt at quilting.

WINDBLOWN SQUARE

This block is also known as the BALKAN PUZZLE and ZIG ZAG TILE QUILT. It is one of the older patterns but there is no telling just how old this pattern is. It was very popular in the 1930's. This is another pattern which is easy enough for a beginning quilter. It may be made with plain blocks, in an all-over pattern or with lattice strips. It would also look well either with or without a border. If it is not used in an all-over pattern it may be made as a scrap quilt.

To piece this pattern, make a square by piecing two triangles together. One of these triangles must be made of two of the large No. 1 triangles. The other may be made by placing the small side of a No. 2 triangle against the short side of the No. 3 diamond. The long side of triangle No. 2 should be placed against the long side of diamond No. 3. Make four of these squares and piece them together to make the block as shown in the drawing. A twin-bed size quilt will need eight rows of ten blocks each.

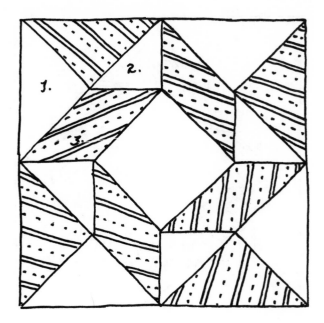

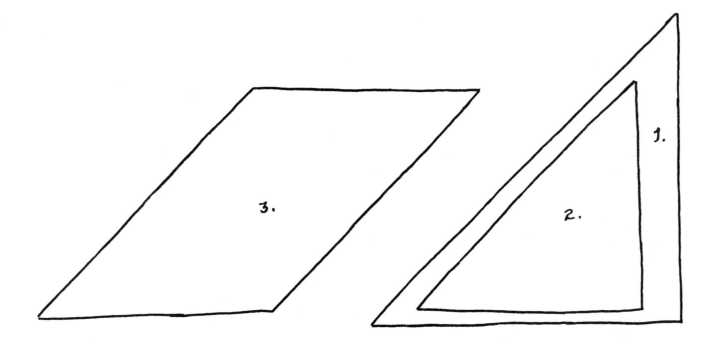

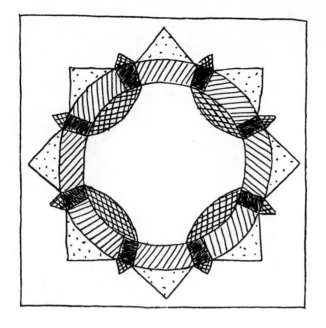

STRAWBERRY

This pattern is also called FULL BLOWN TULIP and ORIENTAL STAR. It is one of those patterns that should not be attempted by a beginning quilter. Piece the patterns together in four sections by sewing together and alternately No. 3 and No. 2 patterns (the arrow on the No. 3 pattern points to the top of the pattern). Sew the No. 1 pattern on each of the No. 2's and the No. 4 pattern on each of the No. 3's. Then add the No. 5 pattern on the bottom of the first two No. 3 and No. 2 patterns. Repeat this four times and sew all four sections to make a ring. Appliqué this ring on an 18-inch white square. This should be an all-over pattern or you may use a three-inch wide lattice strip between the blocks. The top will need four rows of six blocks each for a twin-bed size quilt. You may use a narrow, fancy border for this quilt if you wish.

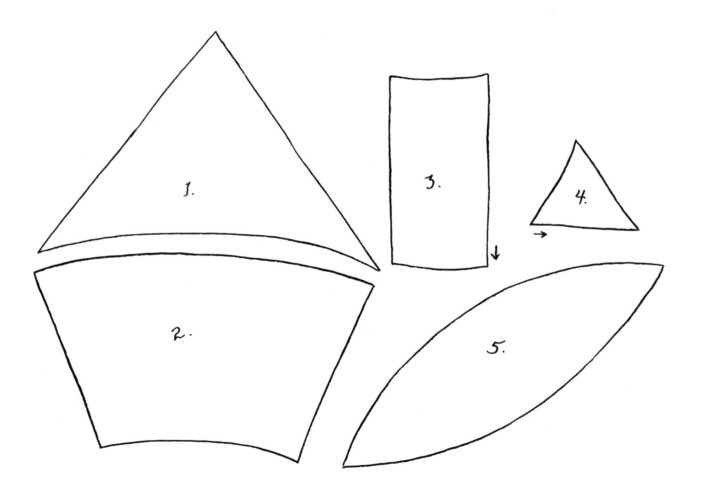

THE COMPASS QUILT

This pattern was first printed in a 1930 newspaper column. It is an all-over design in a dark color or print and white. This top does not need a border. You will be happily surprised at the beauty of this geometric pattern but it is not for a beginner. Make a square of one light No. 2, two dark No. 1 and one dark No. 3 patterns. Repeat this color combination in seven more squares and reverse the color combination in eight squares. Look at the drawing very carefully and sew the squares together so they look exactly like the square in the drawing. A twin-bed top will need eight rows of twelve blocks each.

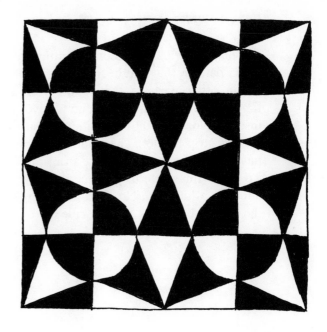

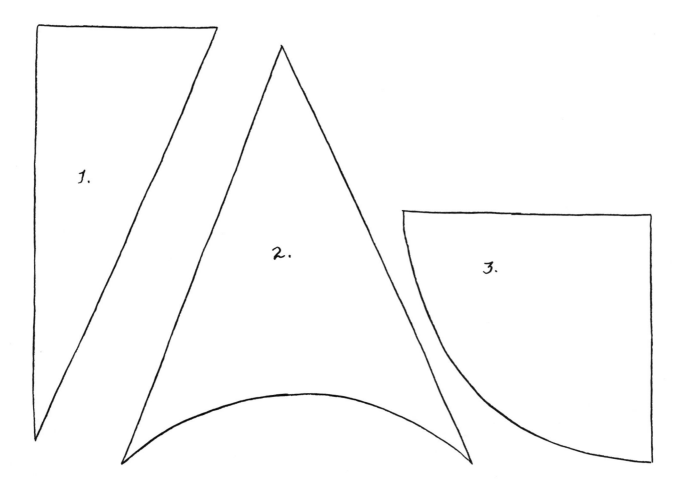

STAR AND CRESCENT

This is an early nineteenth century Pennsylvania pattern that had been a favorite of quilters in other parts of the country for a long time. It looks best if done in an all-over design in one color of print on white and with just a narrow strip border. The traditional colors are navy blue with a small white print and white. To piece this pattern, join the patterns No. 2 and 4 in white with No. 3 in blue. Sew one of the large diamonds to one side of this unit.

Add the background corner in white. This is pattern No. 5 made double by placing the lower straight seam beside the curve on a fold of the material (the dash line is the fold line). Make four of these sections and then sew them together to make the fifteen-inch square. Four rows of six blocks plus a border will make a twin-bed size quilt. If you use a border, it should be a simple one.

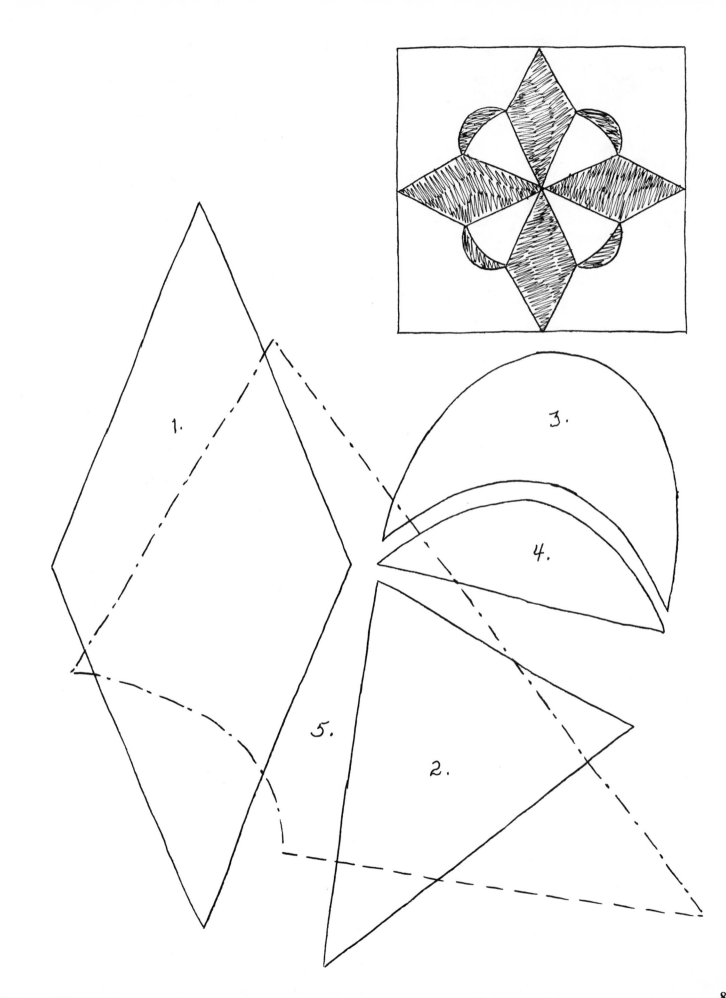

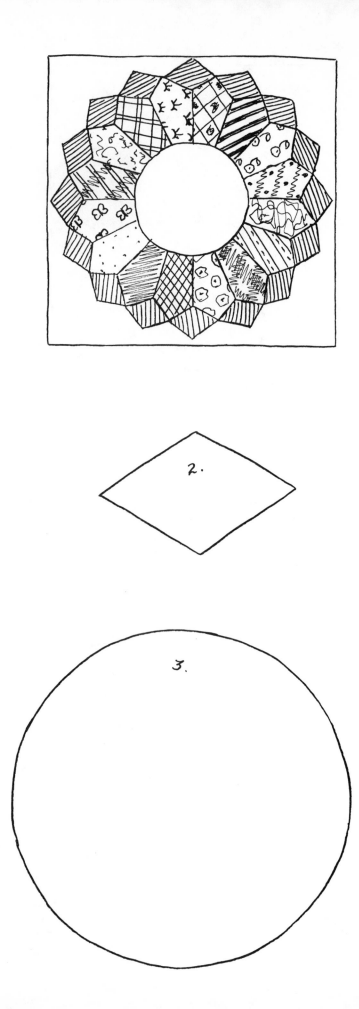

DRESDEN PLATE

This is one of the prettier of the old favorite Dresden Plate designs. Using the patterns given here, you may make at least three of the forms this pattern comes in.

First, make the pattern as shown in the drawing. Set two of the No. 1 petals together and place a green No. 2 diamond for a leaf between them. Repeat this eight times and set the pairs of petals together into a circle. Appliqué this to a twelve-inch square block.

Second, make the simpler traditional Dresden Plate pattern without the green diamond leaves, and set this on the twelve-inch block.

Third, make this pattern into a sunflower or another flower. Add a No. 3 circle to the center of the circle of petals when you appliqué it to the background square. The center circle can be in yellow or any other color.

The old Dresden Plate is a twentieth century design which cannot be traced back much further than the early 1900's. It proves that inspiration has not died out of American quilting. This should be put together in an all-over design without plain blocks or lattice strips as desired. The pattern does not call for a border, although an interesting one could be worked out using half circles of the petals joined with every other circle reversed to form a meandering line. This can be appliquéd to an eight-inch wide border strip with a one-inch colored strip on each side. This border could be used on quilt tops of other patterns. This block may be made by even a beginning quilter if the appliquéd circles are carefully set in the exact center of the background blocks. This quilt top calls for six rows of eight blocks each for a twin-bed size quilt top.

INDIAN WEDDING RING

Someone pointed out to me that Indians did not use a wedding ring but this is probably the kind they would have thought of using, if they had. It is a variation of a favorite among the favorite patterns of the twentieth century quilter—the Double Wedding Ring.

Make each of the four corner squares separately; cut No. 5 by using folds of the cloth on the two straight sides to make it a square. Make a semi-circle of a red No. 1 pattern, seven dark blue No. 3 patterns, six red No. 2 patterns and another light red No. 1 pattern. Make a second strip of seven dark blue No. 3 patterns and six red No. 2 patterns. Make these two strips into a pointed oval by sewing them to either side of a white No. 4 oval. You may make four of these and then place them in a circle around a squared form of white No. 5 pattern. Place a white semi-circular No. 5 on each side of the pieced oval and sew the four blocks together. If you use the squared No. 5 patterns, make all of the circles you will need and then join them with more of the white squares between four blocks each. In this method, leave the edges of the outer rings as the edge of the quilt top to make a scalloped quilt edge. This is, by necessity, an all-over pattern without a border. It takes a little more skill and effort than a beginning quilter should attempt in her first few quilt tops. The top will need six rows of eight blocks each to make a twin-bed size quilt.

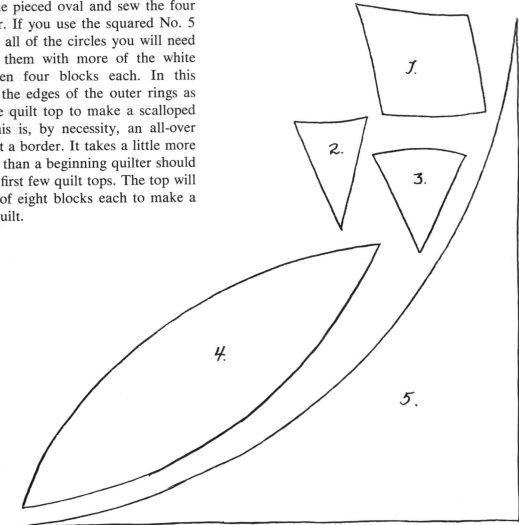

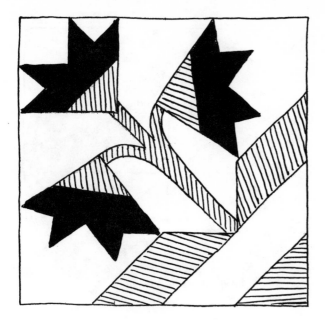

ANTIQUE SHOP TULIP

This pattern may also be called a DOUBLE TULIP. I found the pattern on a lovely old quilt in an antique shop. Ten years ago the quilt was at least 100 years old. This is a red print and green on white quilt and is one of the large family of the favorite nineteenth century Double Tulip patterns. Do not use a solid red for the petals of the flowers if you wish to make an antique reproduction quilt. The original patterns were worked in red chintz prints and either a blue-green or a faded yellow-green for the leaves. Use plain blocks between the pieced blocks in this top and have a simple border; the quilting should be quite elaborate. I do not think a beginner should try this design.

Piece three tulips from four red No. 1 diamonds and a green No. 2 triangle. Appliqué a No. 2 green triangle in the lower corner of a white twelve-inch square block and one of the tulips in the opposite corner. Lay the stem between these two motifs and pin it first. Then pin the two large No. 3 green diamonds on each side of the lower end of the stem and add the other two tulips. Each of these motifs should be correctly placed and pinned before you start to appliqué them permanently in place. This quilt will need six rows of eight blocks each for a twin-bed size quilt.

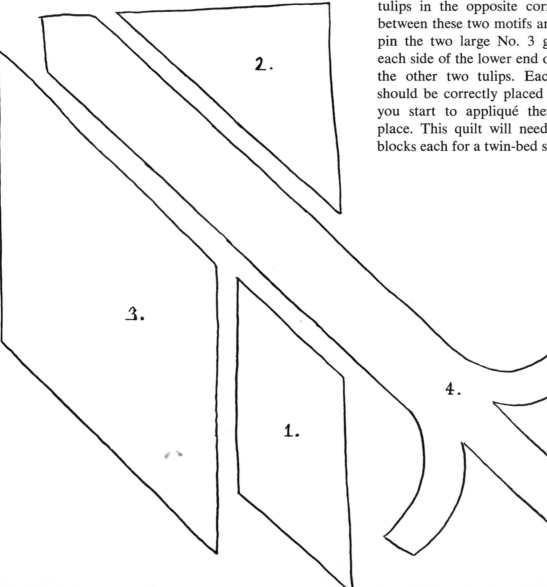

VICTORIA'S CROWN

I cannot trace this pattern back beyond the 1930's. However, from the name and its resemblance to other crown patterns of the nineteenth century, I am inclined to think it belongs to the middle decades of that century. I have the original pattern in rose and green. It must be pieced in an all-over pattern without plain blocks or lattice strips. Choose a color scheme which blends with the bedroom colors for the dark sections. The lighter areas can contrast or blend with that color scheme. Or use these lighter areas to use up print scrap materials. A narrow border should be used for this top.

Make the center by piecing four of the No. 4 patterns together. Add four white No. 2 patterns to make this center a circle. Make a ring of No. 1 and No. 3 alternating patterns and piece this around the center. Appliqué this to a twelve-inch white block. To finish the design, appliqué four No. 2 ovals in each corner. These will form a chain between the motifs when the blocks are set together.

I do not think a beginner should try to make this quilt as a first attempt; but it is not too hard a pattern to make if you are careful in placing motifs on the square. This quilt will need six rows of eight blocks each for a twin-bed size quilt.

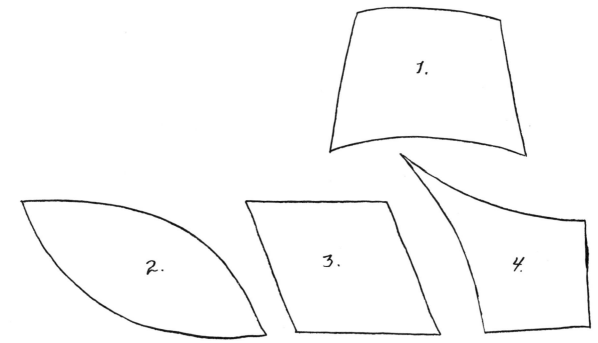

QUEEN'S PRIDE

How old this pattern is or who the queen was is not known. It is, however, an interesting scrap quilt, but it is not for beginners. This pattern will be prettiest as an all-over design. A border may or may not be used.

Make each of the four corner blocks from one No. 4, two No. 5, and one No. 3 patterns. The four side sections are made from two No. 2 and one No. 6 pieces. Make two strips of the two corner squares and one side section each. Place a side section on each side of the No. 1 center square. Finish the block with the two strips placed at the top and bottom of the center section. It will take six rows of eight blocks each for a twin-size bed quilt.

2.

1.

3.

4.

5.

6.

95

NEW YORK BEAUTY

This is the hardest pattern in this section; do not try it until you have been making quilts for some time and are sure of your sewing. The pattern is in red, white and blue and makes a beautiful and striking quilt when made carefully. It is an all-over design without a border.

Piece together four strips twelve inches long, making two-color strips from patterns Nos. 5, 6 and 7. The No. 5 pattern goes at each end of these strips. Sew pattern Nos. 6 and 7 alternately. Sew these two-color strips to each side of the No. 4 white strips. The central Star of LaMoine which joins these strips is made from patterns No. 1 and 3 in white and No. 2 in red and blue. The twelve inch blocks between the strips are appliquéd in each corner with a pieced strip of pattern Nos. 8, 9 and 10 and two semicircles No. 11 and 12. Lay out your blocks as you finish them until you have a twin-bed quilt approximately six feet by eleven. This should take about 35 of the star squares and 48 each of the other strips and squares.

97

STAR FLOWER

This is a late nineteenth century or early twentieth century pattern and is quite easy to make. Each block needs one dark plain color and three print materials; hence, it is an excellent scrap quilt. Put this top together in an all-over design, with lattice strips or plain blocks and with or without a border, as desired. Make a ring of No. 1 petals and No. 2 tiny triangles. Place the No. 3 circle in the exact center of a ten-inch white block and appliqué the petal circle on the white block background. Seven rows of nine blocks each will make a twin-bed size quilt in this pattern.

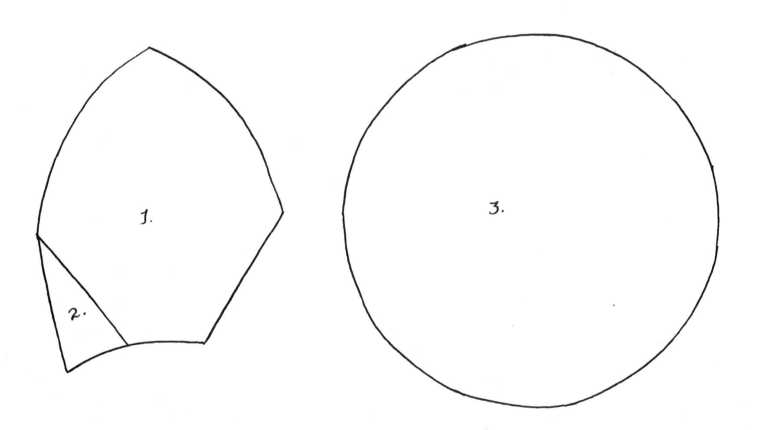

Nine Patch Patterns

Mexican Star (pattern on page 140)

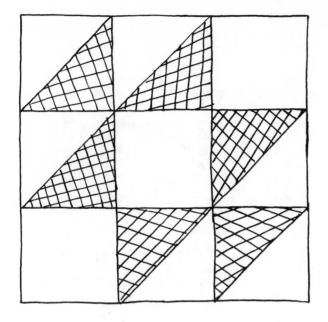

DOUBLE X

This seems to be a rather old pattern because of its simplicity. It is just a basic nine-patch with the squares cut in half to form triangles. Any color or print and white would make a pleasing quilt; however, this pattern will also be pretty as a scrap quilt. Cut three of the No. 1 squares in the background color and piece six squares from two of the No. 2 triangles. Put these together to look like the drawing of the finished block. It will take eight rows of ten blocks each to make a twin-bed size quilt. Make this an all-over pattern, or with plain blocks or lattice strips with or without a border, as you please. This pattern is easy enough for any beginning quilter, adult or child.

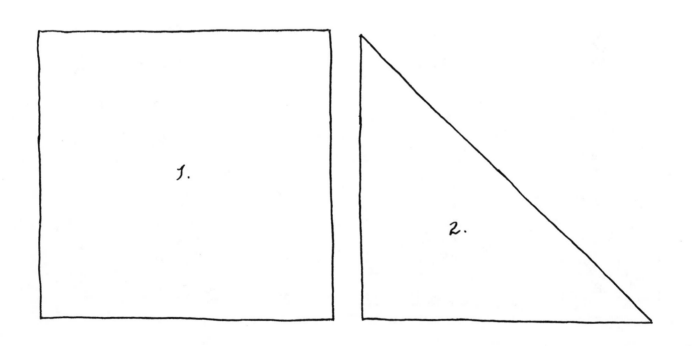

NORTH WIND

This is another pattern which may be old yet it is certainly easy enough for any beginner to piece. It may be made in plain color or print material and white or as a scrap quilt. This design would look well as an all-over pattern, with lattice strips or with plain blocks. Also, it would look well with or without a border. Piece together three squares of two of the small No. 2 triangles. Add one light-colored triangle to the side of the square with the dark triangle. Sew these three into a diagonal strip and add a dark and a light triangle to each side to fill in the corners and make the square look like the one in the drawing. A twin-bed size quilt will take six rows of eight blocks each.

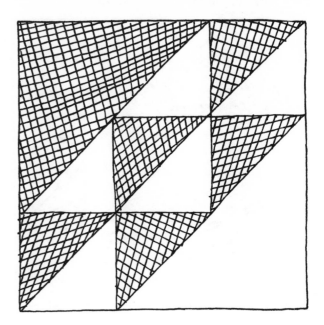

1.

2.

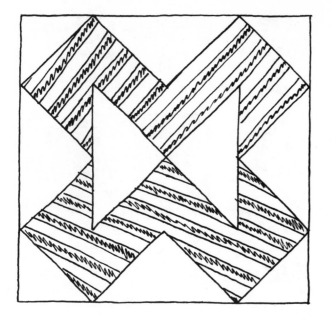

BROWN GOOSE

This old familiar pattern is also called the GREY GOOSE, DEVIL'S CLAWS and DOUBLE 'Z'. It dates back to the eighteenth century and is a New England pattern. It was probably made in the drab colors of grey and brown originally but it looks well in any dark color or print and white and is a fine scrap pattern. This design is much easier to piece than it looks.

Make sixteen dark and light squares with the No. 2 triangle; or piece it with the No. 1 large triangle and fill in the four corners, after putting the strips together, with the small No. 2 triangles. This may be an all-over pattern, with lattice strips or plain blocks as desired. It may be made with or without a simple border. A twin bed-size quilt takes seven rows of nine blocks each.

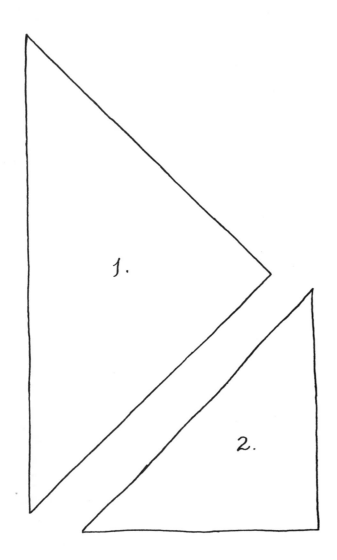

PUSS IN THE CORNER

This pattern is also known as PUSS IN BOOTS. It is another old pattern from the early nineteenth century. Its simplicity and ease of piecing will make it everyone's favorite quilt. It can be made into a scrap quilt with plain blocks between the pieced ones, an all-over pattern, or one with lattice strips. A border may or may not be used.

Piece four corner squares from one print No. 4 square and three white No. 4 squares. Piece four more squares from two print No. 1 diamonds, two small white No. 3 triangles and one white No. 2 triangle. The print diamonds should be formed into a chevron. For the two side rows, piece two rows of two corner squares on each side of a chevron square. Piece the center row of two chevron squares on each side of a print No. 5 square. The finished block should look like the one in the drawing. A twin-bed size quilt will take six rows of eight blocks each.

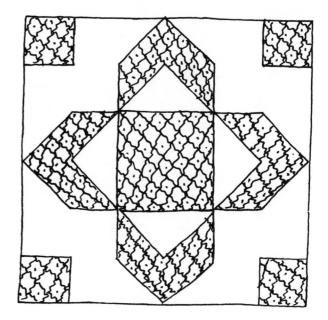

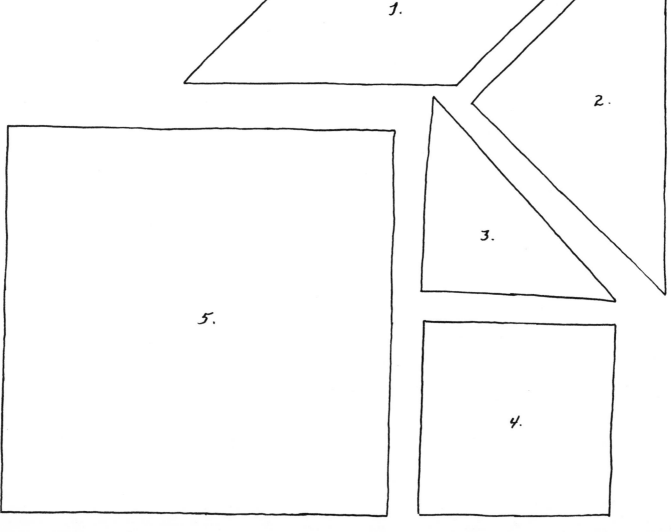

BOXED 'T'S

This looks like a design from the latter part of the nineteenth century although I cannot trace it back that far. Use any color with white or make a scrap quilt. It may be put together as an all-over pattern with lattice strips, or with plain blocks between the pieced ones. It may or may not have a border. To piece the block, sew one No. 4 triangle to the top of a No. 5 strip. Sew two of these strips and piece them to either side of a No. 6 strip to form the 'T'. Make four of these 'T' squares and sew a No. 3 triangle to the top of each. Make one strip of two No. 1 triangles on each side of a 'T' square. Then make a center strip of two 'T' squares on each side of a No. 2 square and repeat the first strip made. Sew these three strips together to form the finished square shown in the drawing. It will take six rows of eight blocks each to make a twin-bed size quilt.

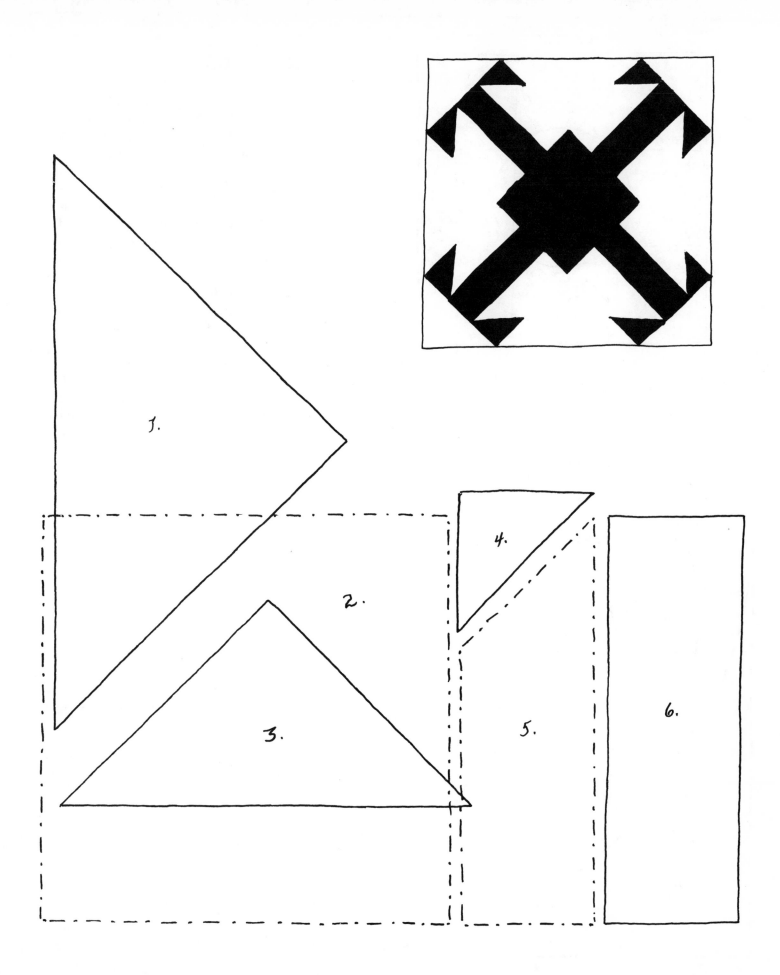

1.

2.

3.

4.

5.

6.

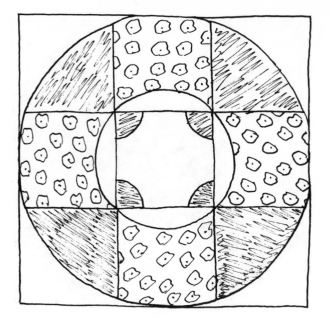

QUEEN'S CROWN

The simple design makes a pretty scrap quilt. It is a variation of some of the popular fan designs. Make each block with a pretty print and a matching color and white. Either lattice strips or plain blocks should be used between the pieced blocks. A border may or may not be used as preferred. To piece this design, cut one white square for the center and appliqué one of the No. 4 motifs in each corner. Piece the crescent No. 3 pieces to the No. 2 patterns. Sew two No. 5 pieces to each side of a No. 2 pattern. Make two rows of these. Make one row of two No. 2 squares on each side of the center block already appliquéd. Sew the two outside rows to each side of the center row. Piece the four corner No. 1 patterns to the block to finish the square. It will take eight rows of ten blocks each to make a twin-bed size quilt. The curved lines in this pattern are too difficult for a beginner.

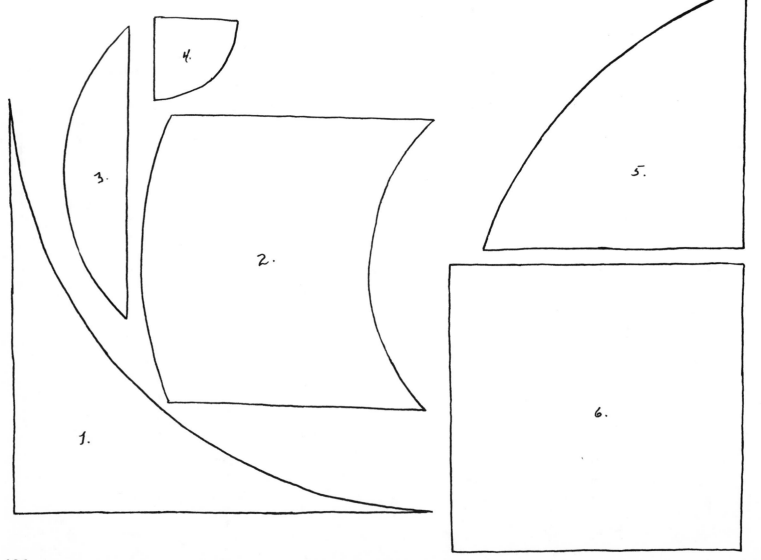

SINGLE WEDDING RING

This old pattern which dates from the middle of the nineteenth century was also called the WHEEL. It is made from one color or one print and white. It is much easier to piece than it looks. Piece four squares by piecing four No. 2 triangles to each side of a No. 3 square. Cut one white No. 1 square. Piece four squares from two No. 4 oblongs. Make two strips by placing a No. 3 square and No. 2 pieces on each side of a No. 4 pattern. Then piece the center row by placing a square of the No. 4 oblong on each side of the No. 1 square. Piece the three rows into the finished block. This can be made as an all-over pattern or it may be used with plain blocks between the pieced ones. Do not use a border with this quilt top. It will make an excellent scrap pattern. A twin-bed size quilt top will take five rows of six blocks each.

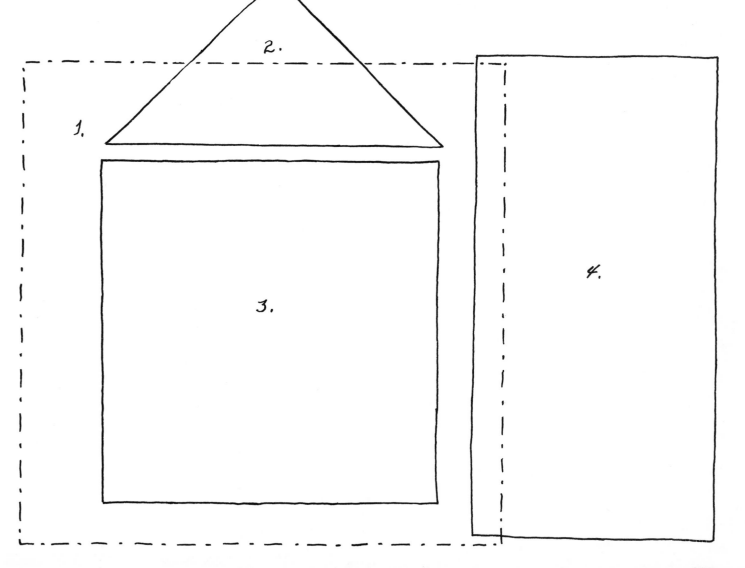

ORIOLE WINDOW

This pattern is also called CIRCULAR SAW and FOUR LITTLE FANS. During the 1870 decade no house was complete or fashionable without a window style prominent on its facade called an Oriole Window. The name of this pattern dates it effectively. Each block should be done in a print, a matching plain color and white. It will make a marvelous scrap quilt pattern with plain blocks between the pieced ones. If a border is used on this quilt top, make it a sawtooth pattern.

To piece the pattern, make four strips of sawteeth using the sections labeled 5–10 for half of each strip. The triangle marked 10 is folded in half on the dotted line. When each strip is finished, piece it to the top of piece No. 3 and finish a square with the No. 2 corner section. Piece two of these corner sawtooth squares to each side of a No. 1 section. Make two of these rows for the outside of the block. Make the center row of two No. 1 sections pieced to either side of the No. 4 pattern. Finish the block by piecing the outside rows to the top and the bottom of the center row. It will take six rows of eight blocks each to make a twin-bed size quilt. This is not an easy quilt to make and should not be attempted by beginners.

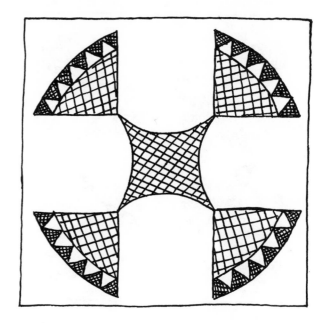

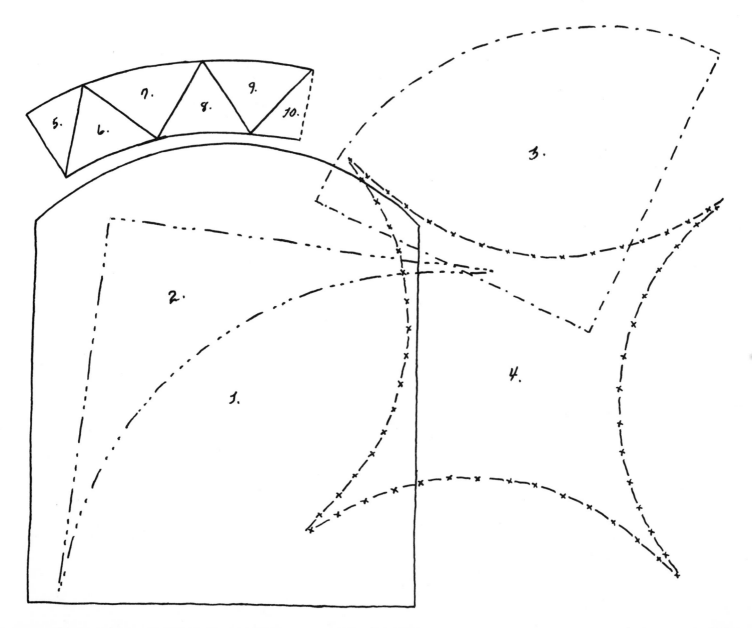

BLUE BLAZES

The slang term "Blue Blazes" dates from the last two decades of the nineteenth century, but the pattern may be earlier. Make this pattern alternate with a plain block and use a simple pieced border. Use one or two colors with white. There are eight white squares of the No. 1 pattern and one square is the pieced, simple nine patch. Put these squares together as shown with the nine patch in the center. Appliqué the No. 3 body and the No. 4 wings to the white blocks with the nine patch as the head of the insect. This is not a hard pattern to make if you are neat in piecing and appliqué. A twin-bed quilt will need six rows of eight blocks each.

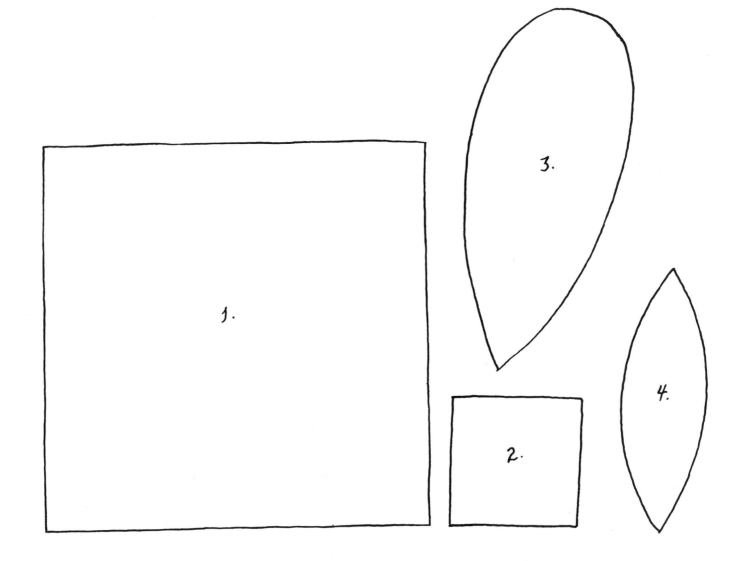

IMPROVED NINE PATCH

This is a pattern which was developed in the last half of the nineteenth century. It is one of the most outstanding of the nine patch patterns which is a joy to make and to own. Piece this pattern as a scrap quilt in an all-over design without a border. To make 122 nine patch blocks use four white No. 3, one dark No. 2 and four dark No. 4 pieces for each block. Then piece these together into ten rows of twelve blocks each with the No. 1 pattern between each two of the pieced blocks. Use half of the No. 1 pattern for the edges of the quilt by cutting the pattern on the dotted line. This is not a quilt for beginners. After you have mastered piecing a curve to lay flat, this will not be a hard quilt top to make.

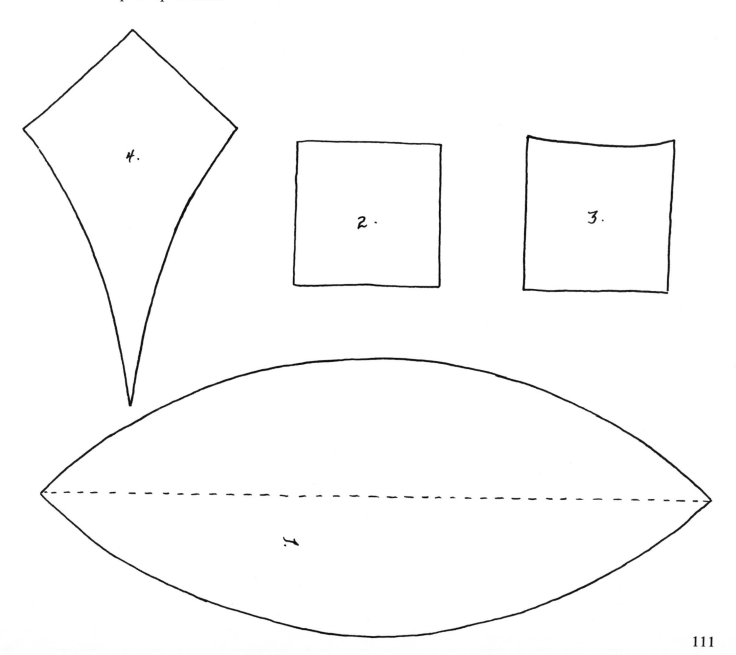

DUSTY MILLER

This design has the name of an old garden favorite. Because it has curved pieces it must date not earlier than the first decades of the nineteenth century. It may be made as a scrap pattern; however, it would look better with the more formal treatment of only two colors and white. Make this an all-over pattern or put it together with lattice strips or with plain blocks. A border may or may not be used. Piece the curved No. 1 and No. 2 sections and lay the four of them aside. Then piece strips of No. 11 and 12 sections, No. 9 and 10, etc. Put these together in four corner sections with the large No. 4 triangles as the actual corners. Piece one of the No. 2 sections to one of the pieced corner sections. Then piece all four of these to the center circular piece, one at a time. This design is not for beginners but it is not as hard as it looks. Be very careful and neat in piecing the sections. It will need six rows of eight blocks each for a twin-bed size quilt.

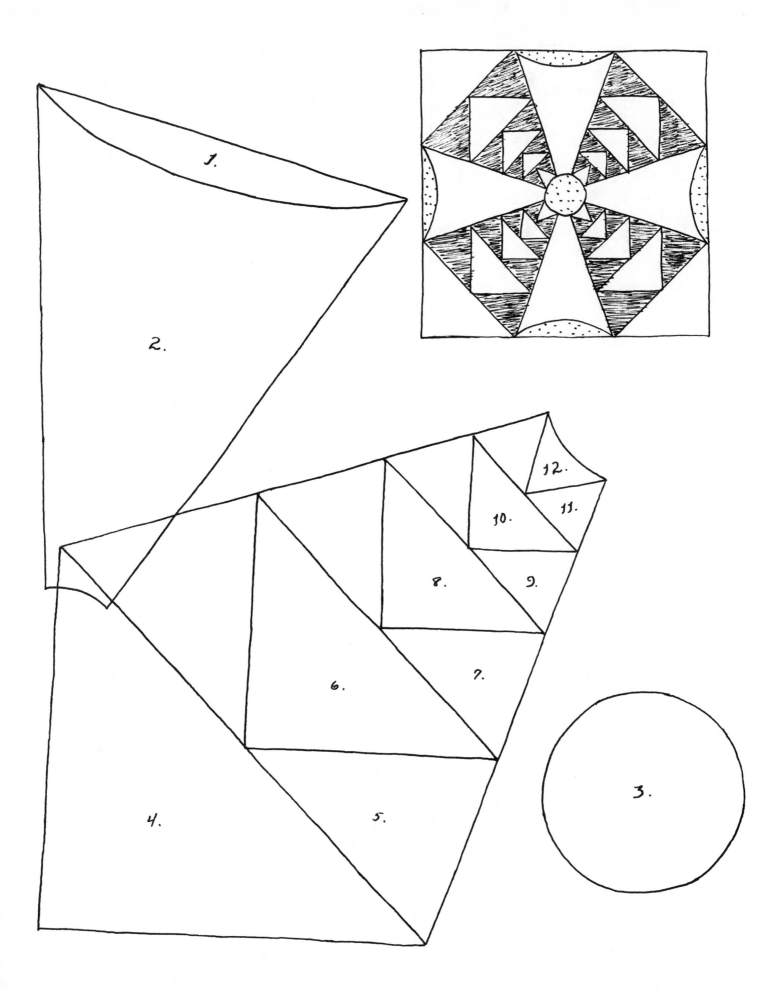

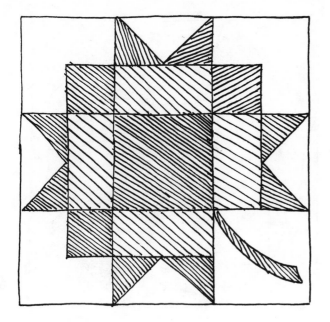

MAPLE LEAF

This is one of the neatest of the many leaf patterns I have found. It is from the early nineteenth century and should be made in two shades of green, or a green print and matching plain green on white. Cut two No. 1 squares, one white and one dark green. Piece three squares of three white, small No. 4 squares and one dark green No. 4 square. Then piece four strips of two small squares each. These squares should be pieced of a white and a dark green No. 3 triangle. The white triangles should be sewn into the strip, back to back (see drawing). Sew these strips to a light green No. 2 strip. Make three rows of squares, the first a strip of two corner blocks made of the No. 4 squares. The second strip should be made of the No. 2 strips and three on each side of the dark green No. 1 square (see drawing). The last strip is one of the squares made from No. 4 squares, one of the No. 2 and 3 strips and the white No. 1 square. Piece the three strips together and appliqué the No. 5 stem to the white No. 1 square. This is easy enough for a beginning quilter. It may be made either with lattice strips or plain blocks. Make this quilt with or without a border as desired. The top will need six rows of eight blocks each for a twin-bed size quilt.

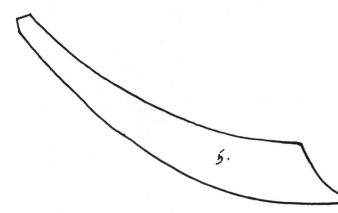

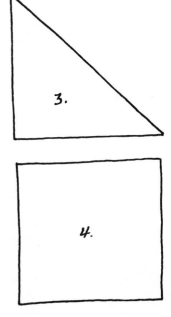

ROBBING PETER TO PAY PAUL

This pattern is a very old one which may date back to the middle of the eighteenth century. It was quite popular in the early nineteenth century for it was used quite often in the Friendship quilts of that era. It would look well as a scrap quilt in an all-over pattern, with lattice strips or with plain blocks. It does not need a border.

This block has several strips. The first strip consists of four squares (with each square made from two No. 3 triangles) and two corner blocks (made from No. 4 squares). Piece two more strips without the corner blocks. Two other strips are made by piecing four more squares (made from two No. 3 triangles) with two No. 2 oblongs between two of these squares. Another strip calls for piecing two No. 2 oblongs with a dark No. 1 square between them. Sew all of these strips together to form the block shown in the drawing. The cutting pattern is exactly like the Maple Leaf on the previous page. This is an easy pattern for a beginner; it is made with six rows of eight blocks each for a twin-bed quilt.

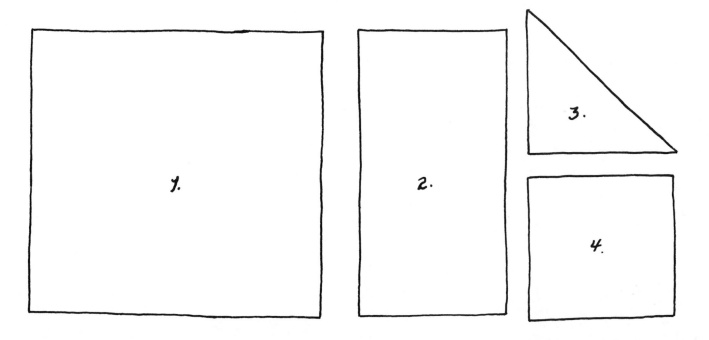

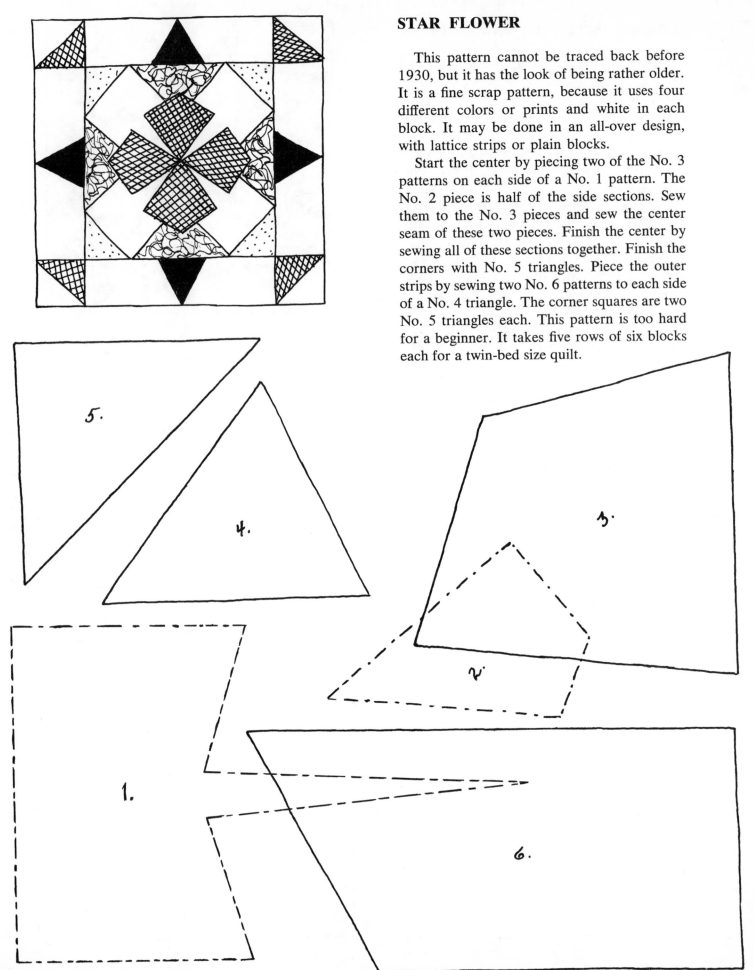

STAR FLOWER

This pattern cannot be traced back before 1930, but it has the look of being rather older. It is a fine scrap pattern, because it uses four different colors or prints and white in each block. It may be done in an all-over design, with lattice strips or plain blocks.

Start the center by piecing two of the No. 3 patterns on each side of a No. 1 pattern. The No. 2 piece is half of the side sections. Sew them to the No. 3 pieces and sew the center seam of these two pieces. Finish the center by sewing all of these sections together. Finish the corners with No. 5 triangles. Piece the outer strips by sewing two No. 6 patterns to each side of a No. 4 triangle. The corner squares are two No. 5 triangles each. This pattern is too hard for a beginner. It takes five rows of six blocks each for a twin-bed size quilt.

JOSEPH'S NECKTIE

To make the name meaningful we must make Joseph's necktie as colorful as his coat was. This is, then, an all-over scrap pattern which may or may not have a border. Piece the four No. 2 patterns around the No. 3 square to make the pieced squares. Add the larger plain squares between the No. 1 pattern. For a twin-bed size quilt there should be five rows of six blocks of the finished square (as shown in the drawing). Even a child might be able to do this very easy pattern.

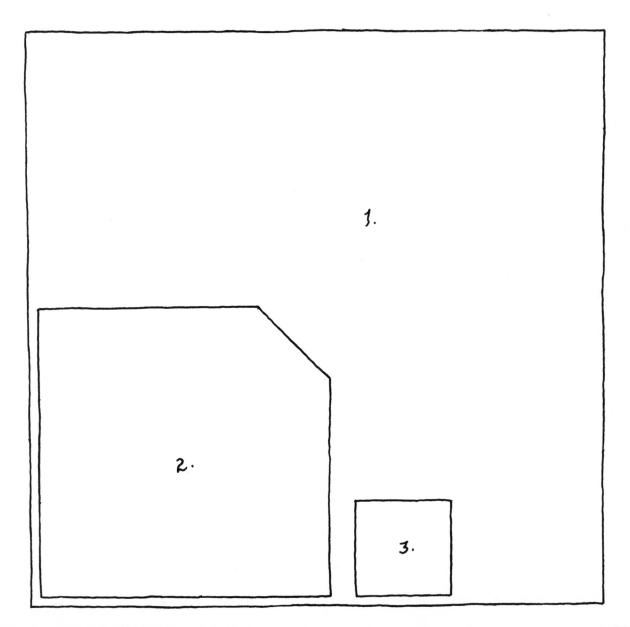

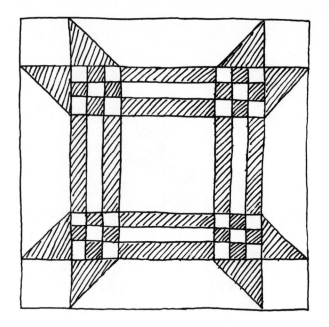

MISSOURI PUZZLE

This classic nine patch dates from around the middle of the nineteenth century. In one color and white it is one of the neatest and the most pleasant of the patterns in this book. It is one of my favorites. It is easy enough for any beginner to make. It will look nice with an all-over design, lattice strips or plain blocks, yet it can also be a scrap quilt. It can have a border or not.

Make the four, nine patch squares from the No. 4 square. Then put together the pieced strips of three No. 3 oblongs. Piece these strips with a plain No. 2 oblong and the pieced squares with one plain No. 6 square in white. The two squares are pieced together for two No. 5 triangles. Piece the eight squares thus formed into three strips by adding one plain No. 1 square for the center. Piece the strips into a block as shown in the finished drawing. A twin-bed size quilt will need five rows of six blocks each.

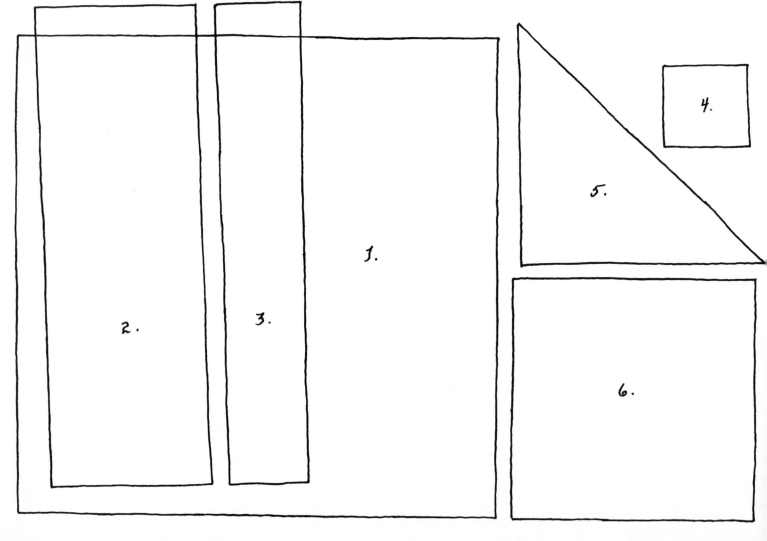

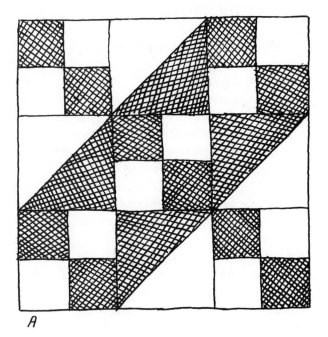

A

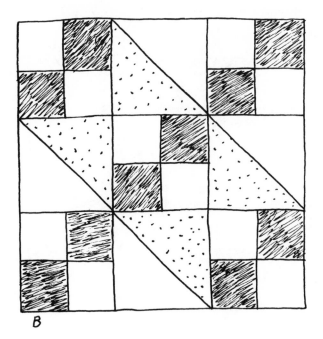

B

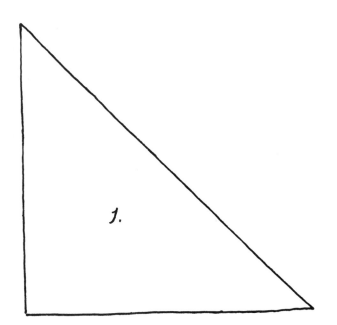

1.

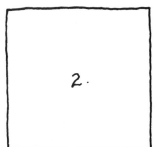

2.

JACOB'S LADDER

This is one of the oldest patterns in this book, dating as far back as the eighteenth century when pieced patterns could be found. This pattern has always been, and continues to be, a favorite of American quilters. It is considered an excellent pattern especially for a man or a boy's quilt. There are several favorite variations including the one in the second drawing where the ladder is reversed and the colors are multiplied. The traditional pattern is also called THE ROAD TO CALIFORNIA; the variation has several names, among which are: STEPPING STONES, THE TAIL OF BENJAMIN'S KITE, UNDERGROUND RAILROAD, THE TRAIL OF THE COVERED WAGONS, WAGON TRACKS, ROCKY ROAD TO CALIFORNIA and JACOB'S LADDER. This is quite an easy pattern to piece.

Make four squares of two triangles each and five squares of four No. 2 squares. Put these together in strips and then into the block shown in the drawing of the finished blocks. Use one color and white for the traditional pattern and two colors and white for the variation. This is not a scrap quilt and it needs to be put together into an all-over pattern without a border. It will take six rows of eight blocks each for a twin-bed size quilt.

54–40 OR FIGHT

It is seldom that a pattern keeps its name, shape and much of its popularity without change. The name refers to a popular slogan in the argument we had with the English over the boundary between the United States and Canada in the Northwest Territory. It almost became a fight but was stopped at the last minute when the present boundary line was agreed upon. The "Fight" slogan and the quilt pattern were all started in the year 1844.

Make four squares by piecing the No. 2 triangle and two No. 1 triangles together. Make five squares by piecing four small No. 3 squares together. Piece these squares into three strips. Then piece the strips into the square block as shown in the drawing. This is an easy pattern which can be a scrap quilt, but it should be put together with plain blocks between the pieced ones. It will take six rows of eight blocks each to make a twin-bed size quilt.

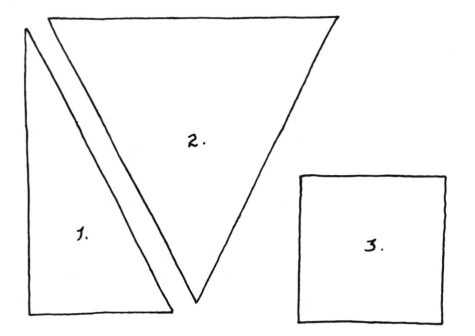

SHOO–FLY

This pattern is one of the old favorites which can be dated back as far as the eighteenth century. It has also been called by the names OHIO STAR, TIPPYCANOE AND TYLER, TOO, LONE STAR, TEXAS, LUCKY STAR, EASTERN STAR and EIGHT POINT STAR. This is such an old and popular pattern that my collection also has nine variations of it.

To make this pattern just make four squares pieced from four No. 2 triangles. Piece a strip of two plain No. 1 squares on each side of one of the pieced squares. Make two of these strips. Make the center strip by piecing the two remaining pieced squares on each side of a plain square. This is a marvelous scrap quilt which can be put together with plain squares or with lattice strips. It does not need a border. This is an easy quilt for anyone to piece. A twin-bed quilt from this pattern will need six rows of eight blocks each.

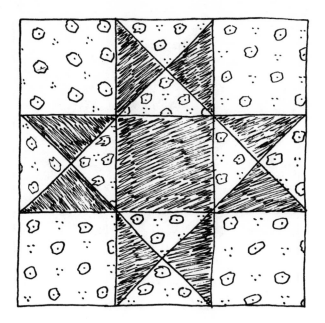

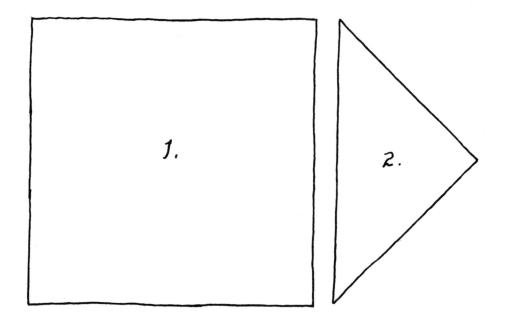

BLAZING STAR

This seems to be a fairly new pattern and a pretty one, too. It is done in one color and white. This might be pretty as a scrap quilt, but the top should be put together with plain blocks or with lattice strips. Use a border or not as you choose.

Piece together the following No. 3 diamonds: one dark, two light and another dark. Piece eight of these diamonds. Piece four light and one dark No. 4 triangles. Also piece four light No. 3 squares and one dark No. 2 corner triangle. Piece the eight diamonds into a star and add the triangles and the corner squares. This is not a hard pattern to make, although it should not be made as a first quilt. Five rows of six blocks each will make a twin-bed size quilt.

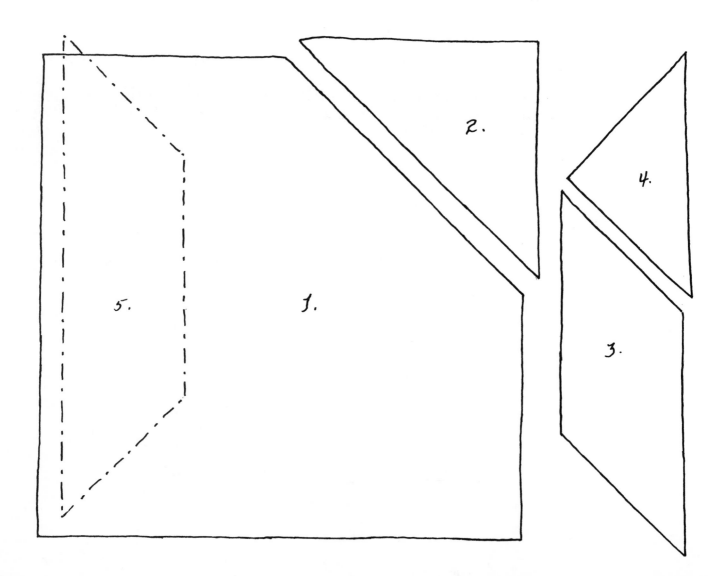

RADIANT STAR

This is one of the old Feathered Star patterns from the 1870's. It is one of the harder patterns in this section. It should be made in one color and white and should never be a scrap quilt. The top should be put together in an all-over pattern and should have a fairly complicated border. Start with the eight No. 1 diamonds for a center star. Add the No. 5 to No. 9 sawtooth strip with the No. 4 diamond and the No. 2 square to the upper point and lower corner. Put these strips around the No. 8 diamonds and add these to the center star. Fill in the corners of the block with the No. 11 square and the sides with the No. 10 triangle. This is too hard for any but a very good quilter to piece. Be very careful with all of the seams and points. It will take five rows of six blocks each to make a twin-bed size quilt.

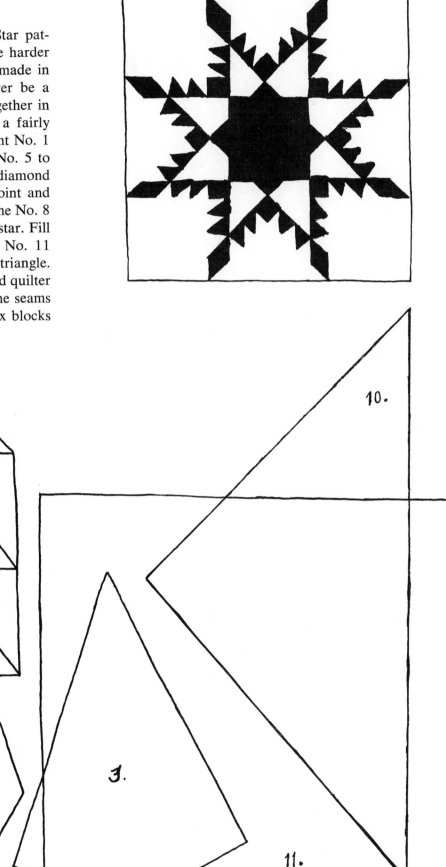

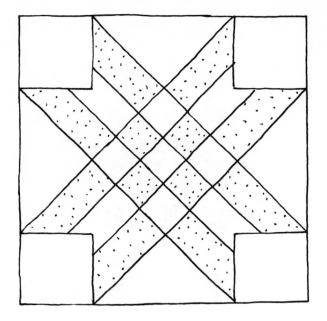

STAR AND CROSS

This is another simple pattern which dates from the nineteenth century but cannot be dated exactly. It is simple enough for any beginner and may be made with an all-over design, with lattice strips or plain blocks. It may also be made with or without a border as you wish. To make this patch, start in the center. First make the simple nine patch of the No. 3 square. Then piece the four corner star points by sewing three strips together: two No. 4 on each side of one No. 5 strip. Sew a large No. 2 square in the corner of the star points. Finish the square by sewing a No. 1 triangle on each side of one of the star points. Make two of these strips. For the center strip, sew one of the star point corners on each side of the center nine patch. Sew these three strips together to form the block shown in the finished drawing. A twin-bed size quilt top will need six rows of eight blocks each.

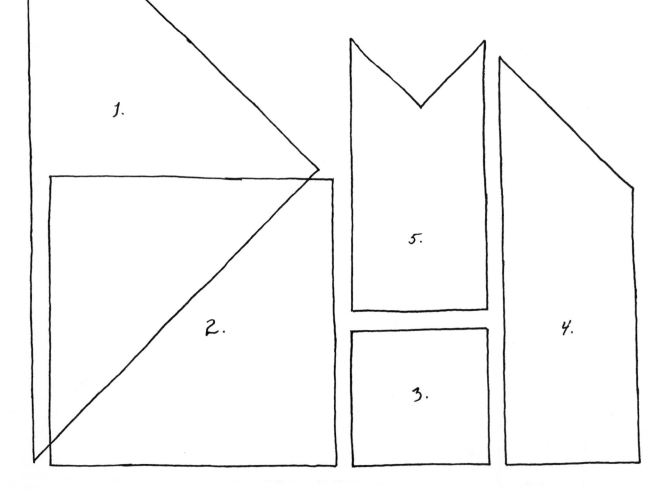

CHRISTMAS STAR

For your holidays I am including this pretty star pattern. It is easy enough for any beginner and may be made in an all-over pattern, with lattice strips or plain blocks. It may have a border or not as you wish. It would be easier to make this block in a series of nine squares.

The four corner squares are made by piecing together: two plain No. 4 squares and two squares made of four No. 3 triangles.

The four side squares are made of two white No. 3 triangles on each side of a No. 2 dark triangle. Piece two No. 6 triangles on each side of a No. 7 square. Put these last two strips together with two dark triangles for the bottom corners.

The center square is a plain No. 1 square. Sew all these squares together in three strips and sew the strips together to form the square shown in the finished drawing.

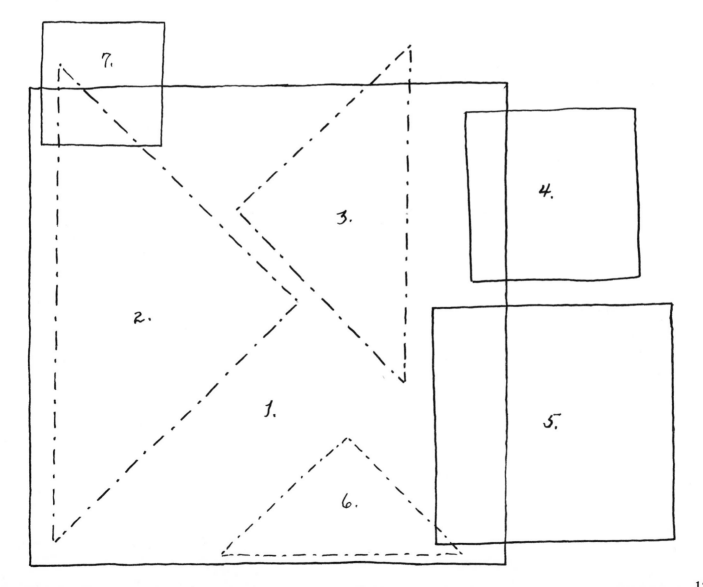

ROYAL STAR

I think this is a very pretty and dainty star. It cannot be traced back further than the 1930's. I believe that with care, even a beginning quilter could make a lovely quilt from this pattern. It takes four colors or shades of colors and should be done as an all-over pattern with a pretty border. Piece the four No. 1 rays and four No. 2 diamonds. Sew these together into a star and appliqué the star to a plain 12-inch block. It will take six rows of eight blocks each for a twin-bed size quilt.

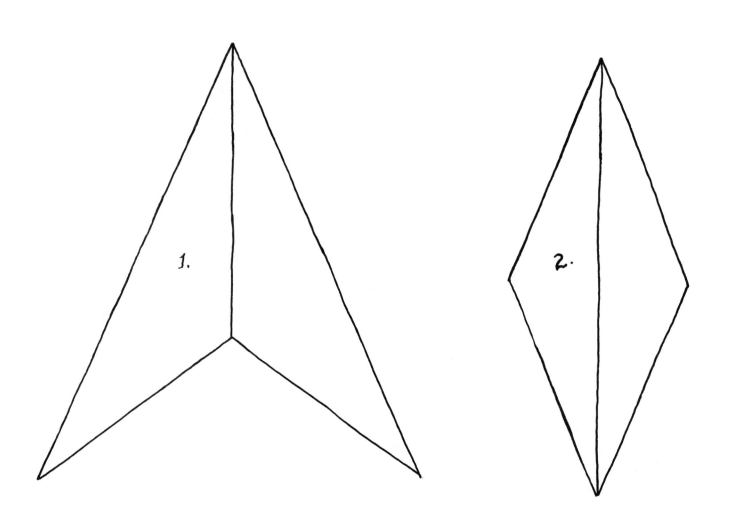

1.

2.

NINE PATCH

This pattern was taken from a mid-nineteenth century Friendship quilt. It is decorative and a very nice scrap pattern. It is easy to make and should be used as an all-over pattern without a border. Make the corner squares and side strips all of the same color over the entire quilt top, but make the inside dark squares different in each block. Piece the center of nine colored and four white squares, and twenty white No. 5 triangles. Use the No. 5 triangles for the four corners and eight No. 4 triangles for the sides. The squares are No. 3 pattern. Piece the lattice strips of No. 2 squares and No. 1 strips It will take six rows of eight blocks each to make a twin-bed size quilt.

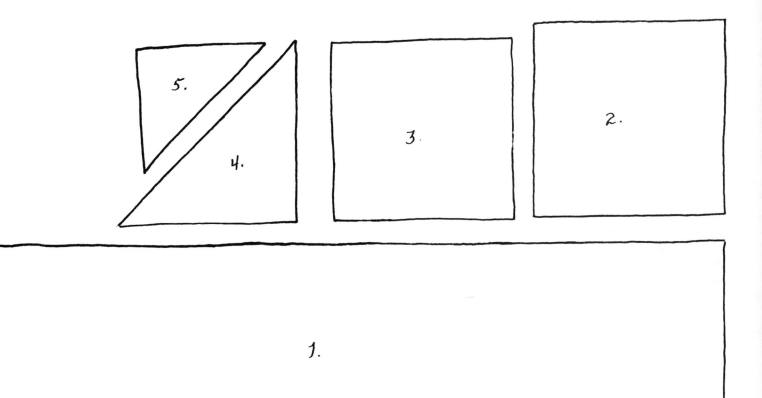

CACTUS BASKET

This pattern dates back to the middle of the nineteenth century. In its long popularity it has acquired several other names, such as BASKET OF SCRAPS, DESERT ROSE, TEXAS ROSE and TEXAS TREASURE. It should be put together with lattice strips or with plain blocks. The top may have a border or not as you choose.

To make this block, sew two No. 3 diamonds together with a No. 2 triangle between the points. Sew two of these sets. Then make a square by sewing two No. 4 triangles together. Add two white No. 1 squares to this last square to form a strip. Sew the two sets of diamond pieces together with a No. 1 white square between the points and a No. 4 triangle at the other corner to fill out the square. Also add two white No. 1 squares and the first strip to this section to make the finished block shown in the drawing. This is a very easy block to piece and makes an excellent scrap quilt. It takes six rows of eight blocks each for a twin-bed size quilt.

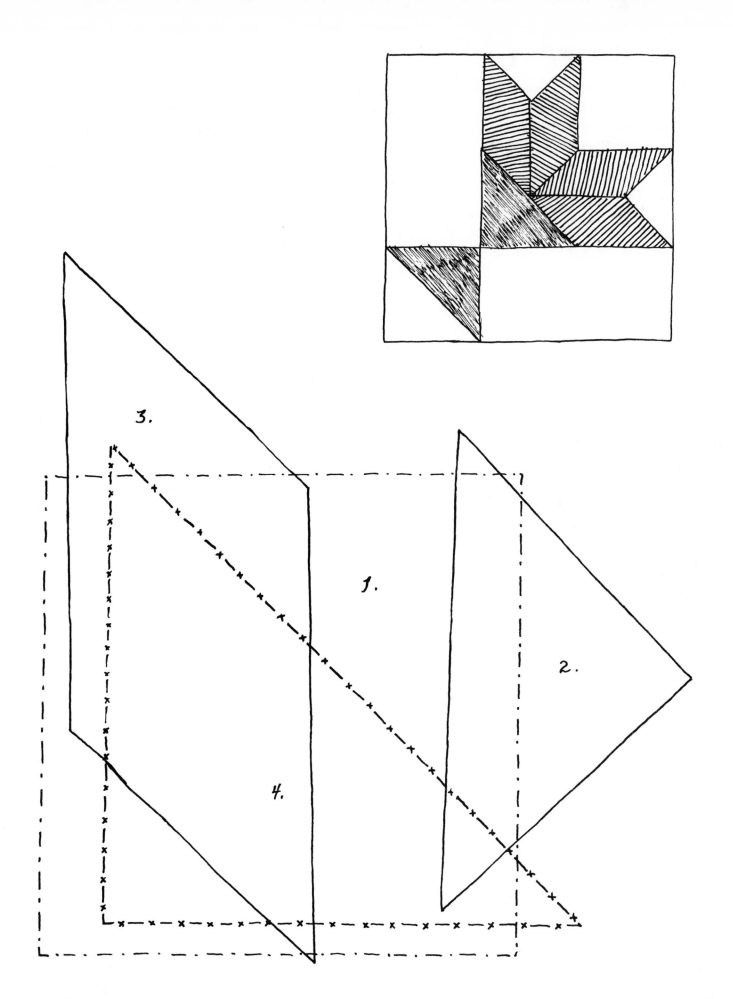

TULIP BASKET

This pattern dates back to the middle of the nineteenth century and is a very colorful scrap pattern. It may be put together with lattice strips or plain blocks and should have a simple border.

Piece four diamonds from the small diamond pattern No. 5. Make the bottom diamond in green, the next two in a lighter color or print and the top diamond in a dark color or print. Piece the brown No. 1 basket onto the large corner No. 3 triangle. Sew the four diamonds together with two white No. 6 triangles between the two side points and a No. 4 square between the center points. Sew the diamonds to the basket and add the No. 2 strip on both sides to fill in the remainder of the square. This is an easy pattern to make. It will take six rows of eight blocks to make a twin-bed size quilt.

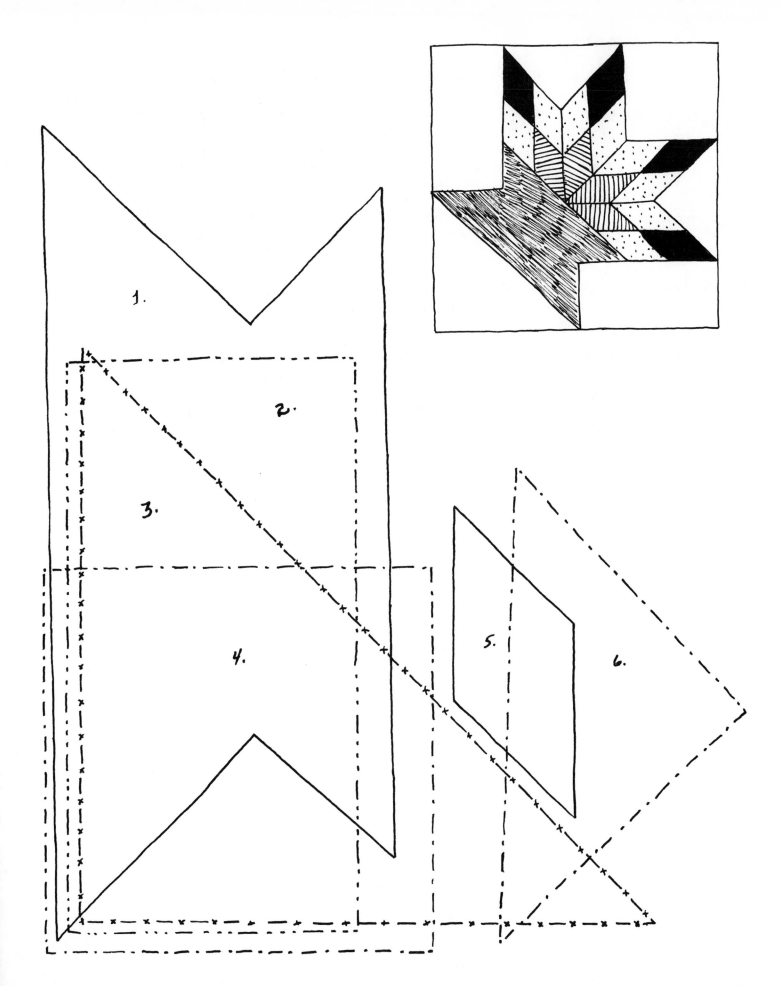

1.

2.

3.

4.

5.

6.

DOUBLE TULIP

This is a very old pattern which was popular with our grandmothers who left their eastern homes in the 1830, 1840 and 1850 decades to travel westward in covered wagons. It was popular then and remains popular now for its beauty as much as its historical importance. Other names for this pattern are: NORTH CAROLINA LILY, WOODS LILY, MEADOW LILY, TIGER LILY, MOUN—TAIN LILY, FIRE LILY, PRAIRIE LILY, MARIPOSA LILY, NOON DAY LILY and PENNSYLVANIA TULIP. This pattern can be placed straight on the square as shown or it may be placed diagonally with the point of the stem in the bottom corner.

If placed straight, part of the top tulip is appliquéd to the two corner blocks. Cut six white No. 8 squares. Sew two green No. 7 patterns to two red No. 5 diamonds with a white No. 4 triangle between the points. Sew these two sets together with a white No. 6 square between the remaining points. Make two other tulips with a triangle rather than a square on the top point. Make a strip with the two tulips and a white square between them and another strip of three white squares with the tulip appliquéd to the white center square. Put these together to form the finished block shown. Appliqué the stems to the center white squares of the block.

For the diagonal tulip, make three tulips with squares in the corners. Put the block together by making a strip with three white squares. Make one strip with one tulip and two white squares; the tulip is not in the center. The other strip has two tulips with a white square between. This strip is at the top, the three white squares come next, followed by the last square. The stems will have to be a little longer than the pattern given here.

Put this pattern together with plain white squares between the 12-inch blocks and a simple border. A quilt, in twin size, of straight blocks will take six rows of eight blocks each; a diagonal block will take seven rows of nine blocks each.

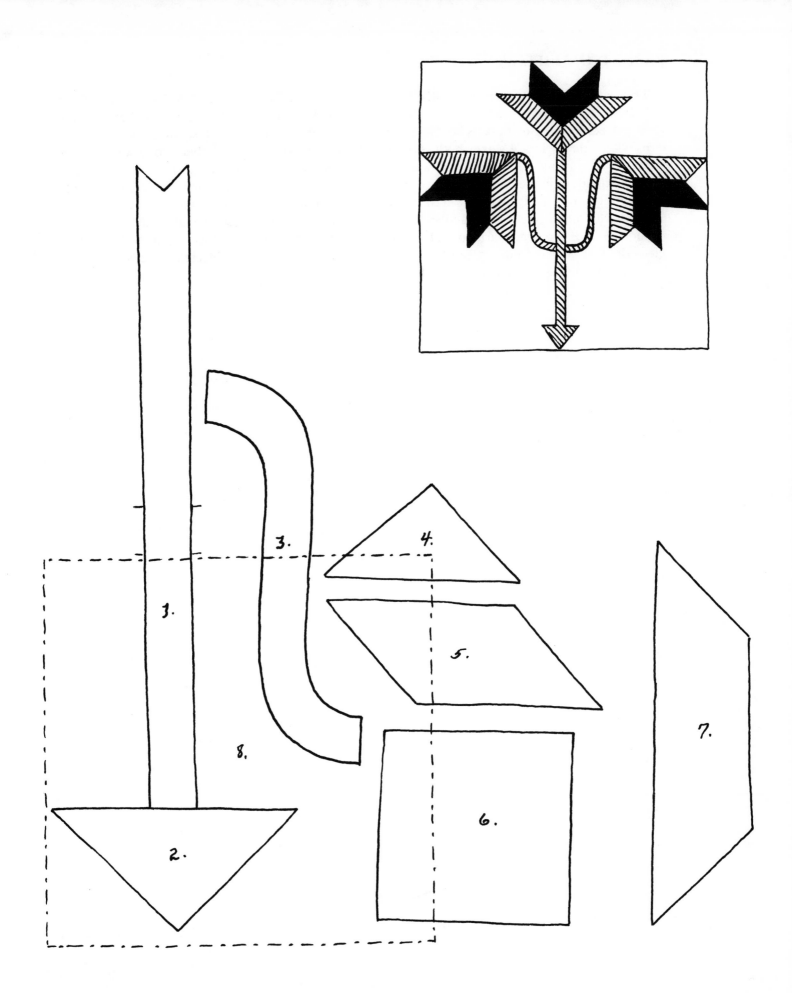

1.

2.

3.

3.

4.

5.

6.

7.

8.

BASKET OF LILLIES

This pattern is also known as BASKET OF TULIPS. By the 1870's and 1880's flowers were placed in vases or baskets so these patterns date themselves. Make both flowers pieced (see drawing A). Only the flowers for the second variation are of solid color, so they look appliquéd (see Fig. B). The baskets are triangles No. 5 and No. 7 with handles No. 11 appliquéd to the second variation (Fig. B). Piece the first flowers from a green No. 7 pattern and four red No. 2 diamonds. In the second variation, flowers are pieced from two No. 3 patterns and two No. 2 diamonds. Piece the background, all but the basket and top flower, in white No. 1 squares and No. 6 triangles. Appliqué the other two flowers and the three stems to this background. These two patterns are a little too hard for beginning quilters, but they are not as hard as they look. They should be put together with plain squares between the pieced blocks and with borders. There are six rows of eight blocks in a twin-bed size quilt.

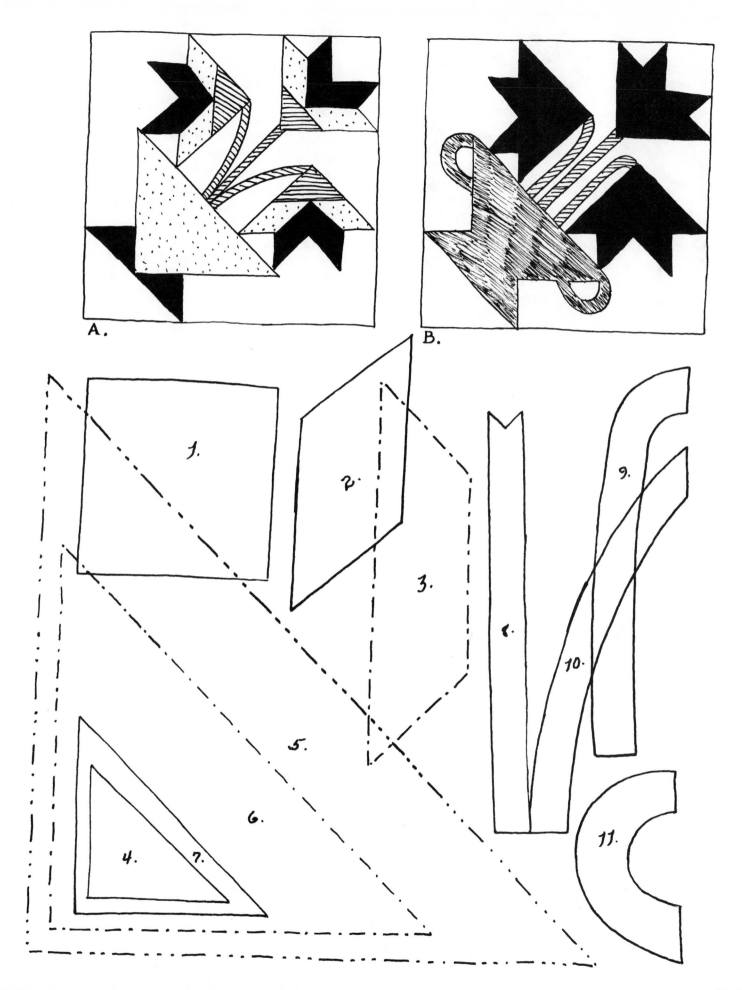

A.

B.

1.

2.

3.

4.

5.

6.

7.

8.

9.

10.

11.

FRIENDSHIP SQUARE

This is another block taken from a Friendship quilt of a later century than the previous one. It is not a perfect square. This one takes perfect accuracy in piecing to make it pretty so it should not be attempted as a first quilt. This is also a scrap quilt but as you can see from the drawing it could be a plain quilt in two colors and white. Make the side No. 1 triangles all the same plain color over the entire quilt top but you may use as many different print scraps to make the pieced blocks as you can find. Put the pieced hexagon together with alternating prints and white No. 2 diamonds in strips and then into the hexagon. Add the No. 1 triangles to fill in the corners. It will take six rows of 12 blocks each to make a twin-bed size quilt.

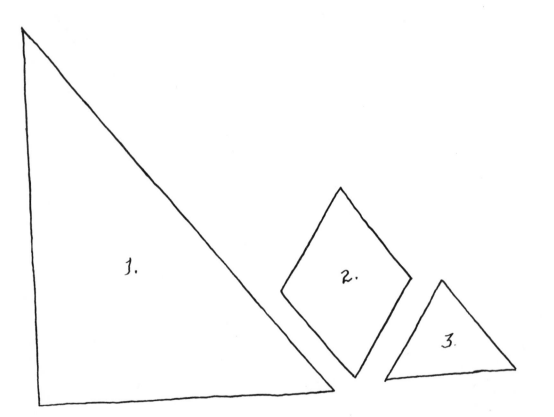

BEAR TRACKS

This is another pattern which has been traced back to the eighteenth century and has always been popular. Other names for this pattern are: BEAR'S PAW, DUCK'S FOOT IN THE MUD, LILY DESIGN, HAND OF FRIENDSHIP, CROSS AND CROWN, GOOSE TRACKS and BEAR'S FOOT. It is almost always done in red and white with yellow and white the next most popular color combination. Make a strip of two squares made from two No. 2 triangles and one No. 5 square. Make a second strip of the two squares of No. 2 triangles. Place these on two sides of a No. 4 square. This forms the bear's track. Make four of these squares. Then make two strips with two of the track squares on each side of one No. 1 oblong. Make a center strip of two of the No. 1 oblongs on each side of a No. 3 square. Sew these three strips together to form the finished block as shown in the drawing. A twin-bed size quilt will need eight rows of ten blocks each. This is an easy pattern. Put it together with plain blocks between the squares and do not use a border on this quilt.

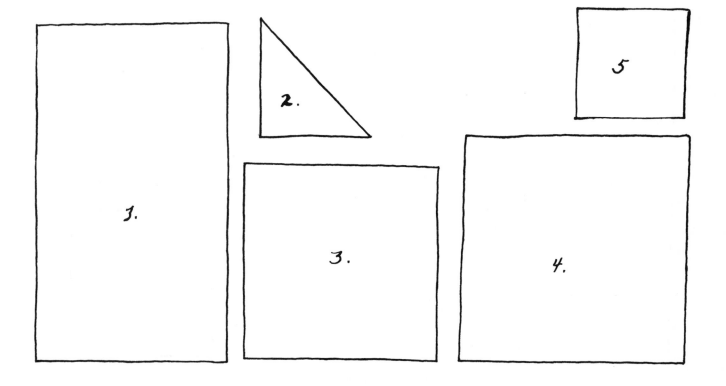

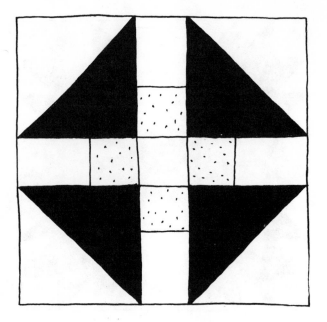

CHURN DASH

This pattern dates back to the early decades of the nineteenth century. Some of its other names are: LOVER'S KNOT and MONKEY WRENCH. It makes a fine scrap pattern and should be put together with either lattice strips or plain blocks between the pieced blocks. It is easy enough for any beginner. Piece the four corner squares of two No. 1 triangles. Make three strips of two of these squares with a No. 2 and a No. 3 strip between them for each of the two sides. The center strip will take two No. 2 and three No. 3 squares. Sew these together to form the finished pattern shown in the drawing. It will take eight rows of ten blocks each for a twin-bed size quilt.

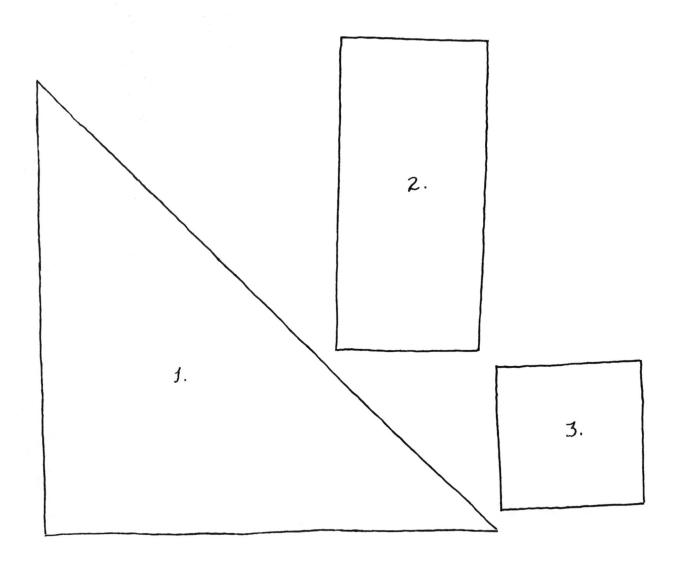

CORN AND BEANS

This pattern dates back to the eighteenth century. It has had several names, among which are: DUCKS AND DUCKLINGS, HEN AND CHICKENS and WILD GOOSE CHASE. It was most often done in red and white or yellow and white. This is a very easy pattern to piece. It may be done in an all-over pattern, with lattice strips or with plain blocks between the pieced squares. You may have a border or not as you please. Piece four triangles of four No. 3 triangles each. Sew these to a No. 2 triangle to form a square. Make two strips with two of these pieced squares on each side of a No. 1 strip. Make the center strip of two No. 1 strips on each side of a No. 4 square. Put these three strips together to form the finished square shown in the drawing. It will take eight rows of ten blocks each to make a twin-bed size quilt.

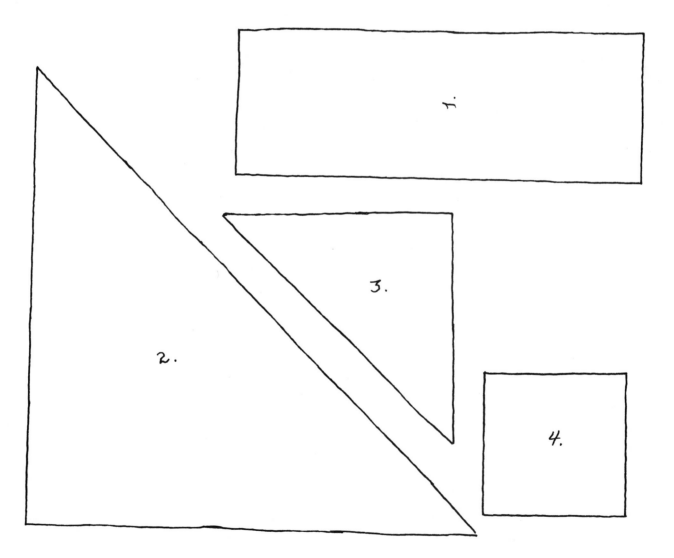

GOOSE TRACKS

The next four patterns are, in order, MEX-ICAN STAR, then comes the GOOSE TRACKS, DUCK PADDLE OR CROSS AND CROWN. Next is a pattern called FAN-NIES' FAN and last is another FANNIES' FAN. As you can see there are just slight differences between these designs. Using the directions of one pattern, I believe you can figure out the directions for all of them. Make the four corner squares first for the Mexican Star which is also the quilt pattern chosen for the quilt top drawing in this section.

The directions are: piece the No. 5 triangles to the bottom of the No. 6 shape. Sew two triangles each of two No. 4 triangles. Place these on two sides of a No. 2 square to form a large triangle. Sew these two triangles together. Sew two of these corner squares on each side of a No. 1 strip. Make two of these strips. Then for the center strip sew a No. 1 strip on each side of a No. 3 square. Sew all three strips together to form the finished square as shown in the drawing. The finished quilt top drawing shows this pattern used with a nine patch border and plain blocks between the pieced blocks. You may make it without a border and with lattice strips or in an all-over pattern as well.

For the two drawings on the next page use patterns No. 1 through No. 7 for the first drawing and patterns No. 1, 2, 3, 6, 7, 8 and 9 which is appliquéd to No. 7. All of these blocks will need six rows of eight blocks each for a twin-bed size quilt. Mexican Star is from the 1840's and the other patterns are from around that date also.

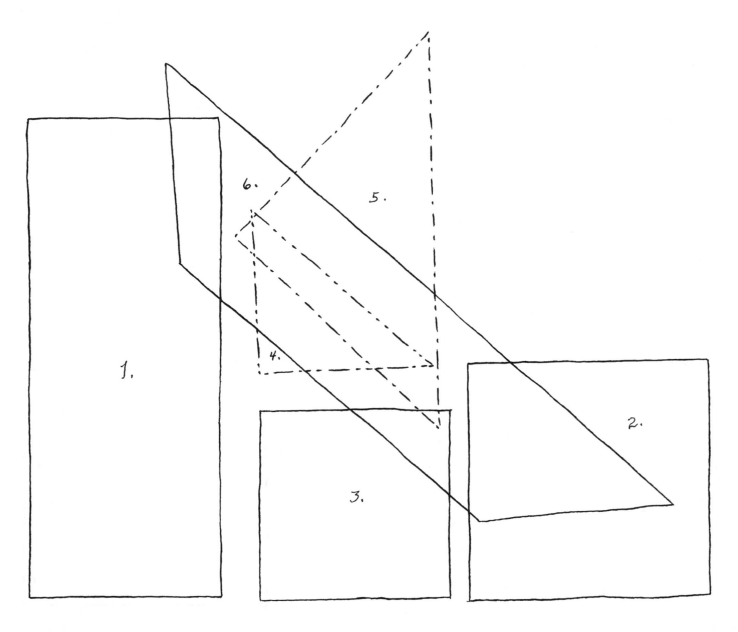

1.

2.

3.

4.

5.

6.

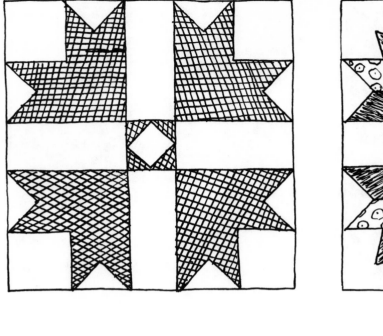

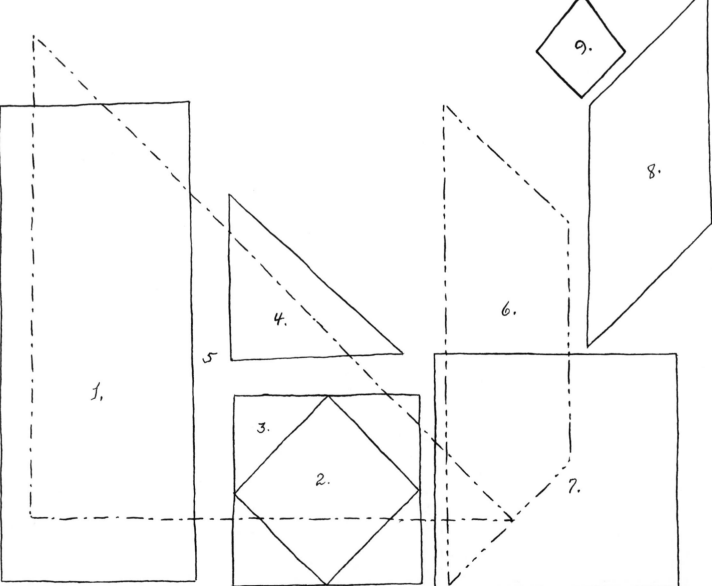

PUSS IN THE CORNER

This pattern is a pure uneven nine patch from the early nineteenth century. They are so easy to make and are a good pattern for a beginner to make as a first quilt. This pattern will make a prettier quilt top even as a scrap quilt than you can imagine by just looking at the patch.

Sew two strips of a No. 3 strip between two No. 4 squares. The center strip has two No. 3 strips on each side of a No. 2 square. Sew the three strips together. Make five of these squares and then sew them into the blocks shown using the plain No. 1 square between the pieced squares. Put this together into a top with either lattice strips or plain 15-inch squares between the large pieced squares shown in the drawing. A twin-bed size quilt will need five rows of six blocks each.

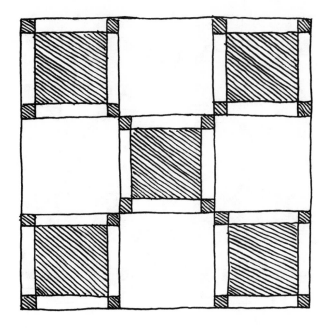

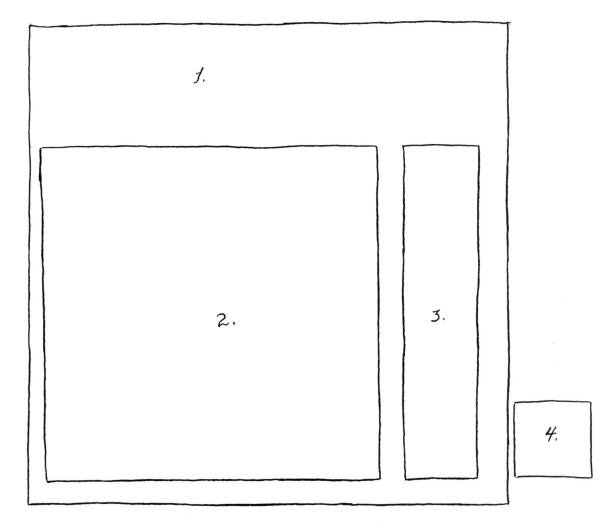

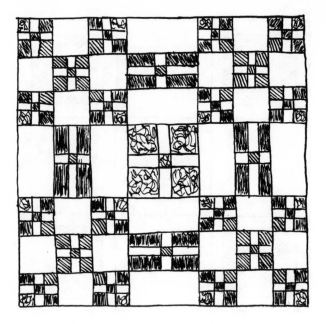

SAVE–ALL

The pattern certainly lives up to its name. This is a pattern which was taken from a weaving pattern and when put together in an all-over pattern will have the look of a woven blanket. It will need a border. Use the three-strip method of making all of the nine patches in this book. There are twenty small squares made from patterns No. 3, No. 4 and No. 5, four long, narrow squares made with patterns No. 9, No. 10 and No. 11, and one large square made with patterns No. 6, No. 7 and No. 8. To piece the four corners, piece five small squares and four plain No. 2 squares together. The four long, narrow squares should each be sewn between two No. 1 strips. The large square goes in the center. Piece these sections into strips and then into the finished square shown in the drawing. This is a tedious rather than a hard quilt, and unless you are tenacious you should not attempt this as a first quilt. There will be five rows of six blocks each in a twin-bed size quilt.

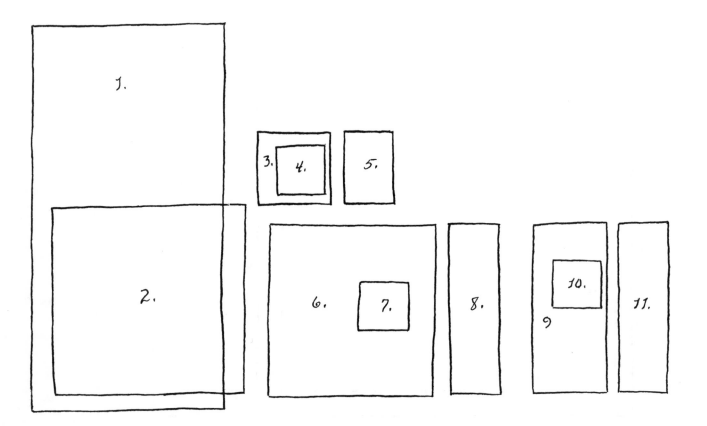

TILE PUZZLE

TILE PUZZLE or PUZZLE TILE—use this name any way you please; it stays the same. This is a pattern from the late nineteenth century. Make long strips of the square and triangle patterns given in one color and white. Try to follow each of the nine strips across the drawing and then piece the strips together in order. This pattern must be made in an all-over pattern and does not need a border. It makes an interesting quilt which will look very well with stark, modern furnitures and colors. It will take six rows of eight blocks each for a twin-bed size quilt. Be careful and be ready to rip out seams with this pattern, but be assured that the finished quilt will be beautiful enough to repay any efforts.

STRIPS AND SQUARES

This pattern is also called STRIP SQUARES. It is from about 1910 and is quite easy to piece. Put it together without borders and with plain blocks between the pieced ones. Make strips of the squares and strips No. 3 and No. 4. Wind these around the center of No. 1 squares and outside of No. 2 squares. Follow the drawing and you cannot go wrong. Use any two colors and white for your quilt. I do not think this should be a scrap quilt. It would be a very good, neat quilt top for a boy's room. A twin-bed size quilt will need six rows of eight blocks.

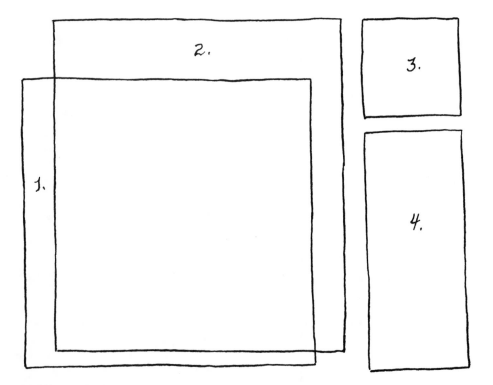

GORDIAN KNOT

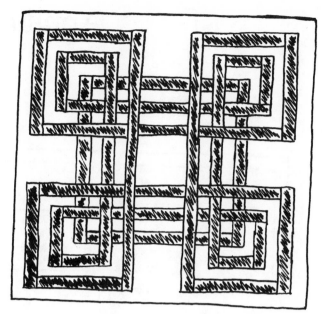

In the 1870's this type of complicated pattern was pieced in narrow strips and you may wish to use this traditional method of making it. The strips are ½ inch across. However, if you wish it would be much easier to cut twelve inch squares for the background and appliqué ½ inch wide bias tape strips in the twisted pattern. Remember to make the strips ½ inch apart. The strips are:

two strips 11 inches long
four strips 4½ inches long
four strips 3 inches long
sixteen strips 2 inches long
four strips 1½ inches long
four strips 1 inch long
twelve strips ½ inch long.

Follow the drawing as to placement of the various lengths of tape. The traditional color is brown on white. Place a plain square between each patterned one. A twin-bed size quilt will take six rows of eight blocks each. This would be quick, easy and modern if you appliqué the strips on your sewing machine. Note—Be sure to add the ¼ inch seam allowance to the 12-inch block making the actual size 12½ inches square.

Appliqué Patterns

Triple Tulips

APPLIQUÉ

To use these appliqué patterns, trace the designs on to tissue paper and then trace the design from these on to the material you use for a cutting pattern. This could be heavy, stiff plastic, cardboard or sandpaper. Trace a cutting pattern for each little section of the pattern which must be a different color. These sections are each labeled with a different number on the pattern. You may use the suggested colors when they are given or you may choose any pretty color combination.

Cut the background squares to the size given in the directions plus ¼ inch seam allowance on each of the four sides. Cut the sections of the pattern with a ¼ inch seam allowance on each side also. Draw the pattern on the RIGHT side of the material so you can use the pencil line as a sewing guide. Slit the seam allowance from the edge almost to the pencil line on all curved edges. Cut these slits closer together on tight curves and further apart on shallow curves. Pin or baste all the sections of the pattern to the background square before you begin to appliqué. This allows you to be sure your design is in the correct place and the colors look well together.

The appliqué stitch is the same stitch you use on a dress hem when you do not wish the stitches to show. (See the diagram in the foreword of this book.) Make your stitches as tiny and as close together as you can manage. Some people work appliqué by folding the seam allowance of each piece under, all the way around. Others use their sewing needle to push a small section of the seam allowance under as they sew. Use the way which seems less awkward to you, for either way is correct. Finish the quilt exactly as the directions in the foreword state.

TRIPLE TULIP

This design is from a 1930's Kit Quilt. That quilt was taken from an eighteenth century quilt design type which used only four large squares for a quilt top. However, I believe this tulip was designed in the 1930's to look like the older type of pattern. The original quilt was done in shades of pink, rose and green. The four large background squares are each 24 inches square, finished size. Patterns No. 1 and No. 2 are the stem and the leaf of the center tulip. Pattern No. 3 is the oval stem divided into three sections to get it into this book. Put the dotted lines together. Make a second stem by using the pattern reversed for the other side of the oval. The large tulip is the center one and the small tulip should be used for the two side flowers.

1.

2.

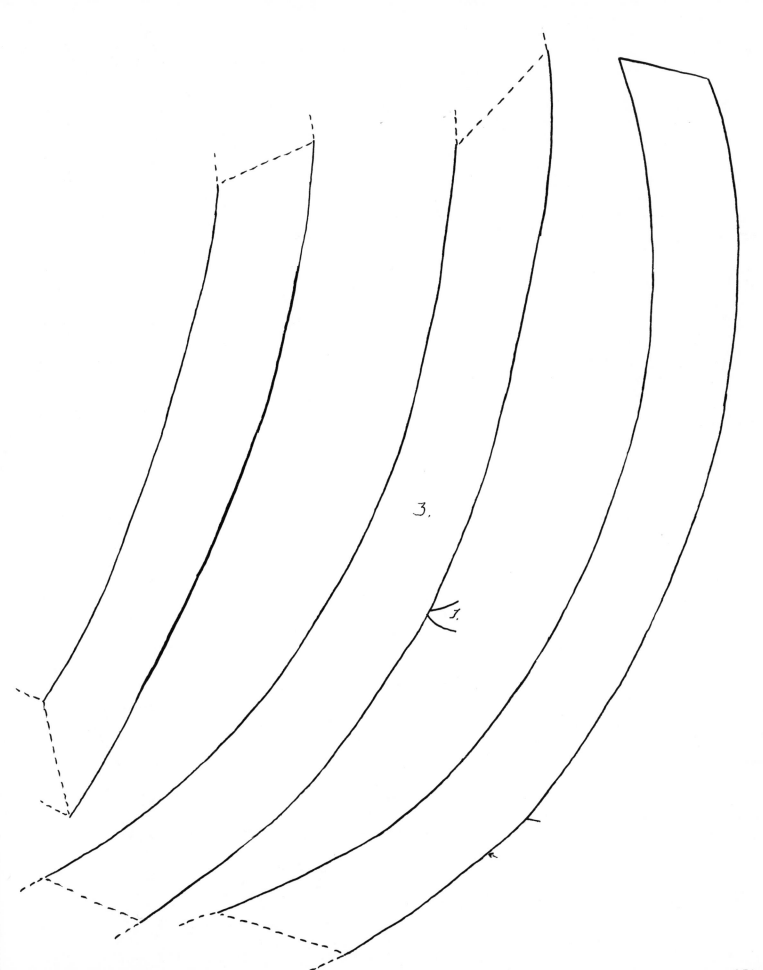

4.

5.

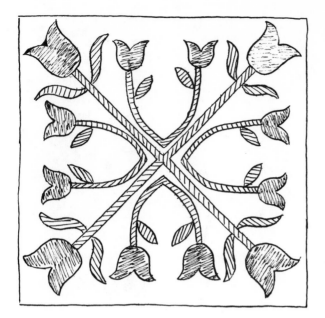

CONVENTIONAL TULIPS

The design for this block was taken from a picture in the Marie D. Webster book. This is the daintiest pattern in my collection. The original was pink and green on white. Mrs. Webster says of it: "Made from a pattern used 130 years ago"—(written in 1948)—"Colors: pink and green." Do try this pretty pattern because it will make a lovely quilt. The background squares should be 16 inches on one side when finished.

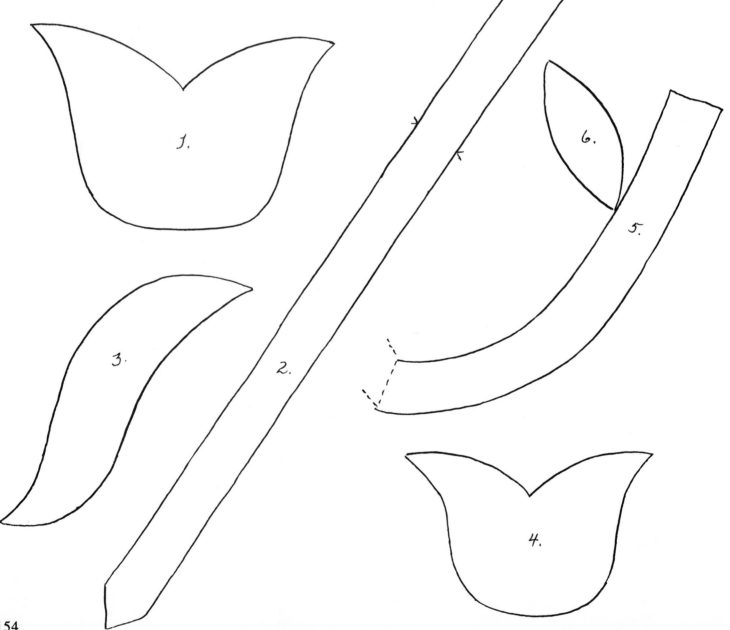

RARE OLD TULIP

This design was taken from an old quilt pattern book of the 1930's. The book said it was copied from a quilt over 100 years old then. The colors were red, yellow and orange with green. The background squares are 18 inches on a side. I have given two leaf shapes in one pattern. The two bottom leaves are oval and should have the point cut off on the dotted line marked 'a.' The stems are ¾ inch wide but they are too long to give as patterns. Pin or baste your other pieces to the background square and then cut the stems to fit the spaces.

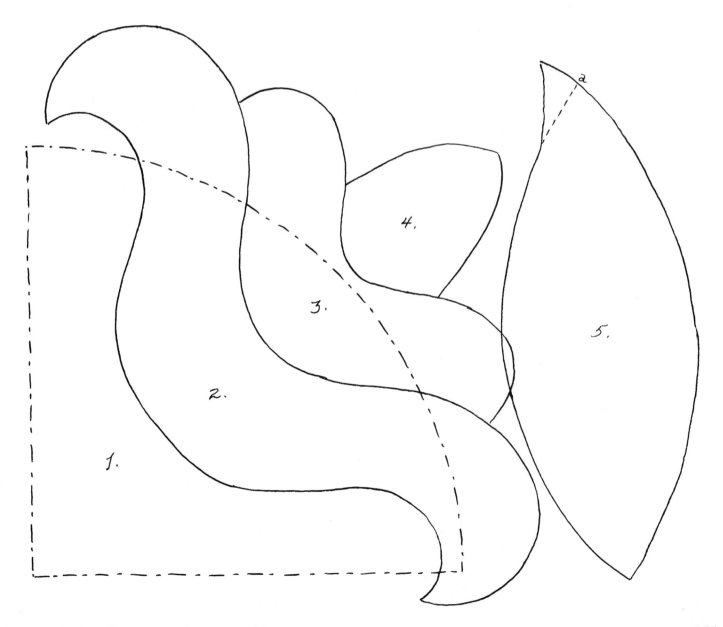

TULIP QUILT

This pattern is taken from a newspaper clipping from the 1932 Baltimore Sun. The background square is only 9 inches on a side so it would make a good design for making pot holders as well as for a quilt. The colors are green for the leaves and the stems and a solid color with matching print bud. It is a scrap quilt.

3.

2

4.

B

A

1.

B

A

A

B

5.

GRANDMA'S TULIP

This old pattern is also called BULL'S EYE. It is from the midwest and was designed during the middle of the nineteenth century. The original quilt was done in orange, yellow and green on a 12-inch background square. This makes a much prettier quilt than it looks from just seeing one block.

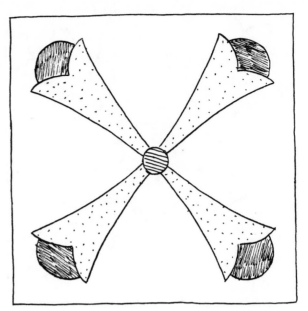

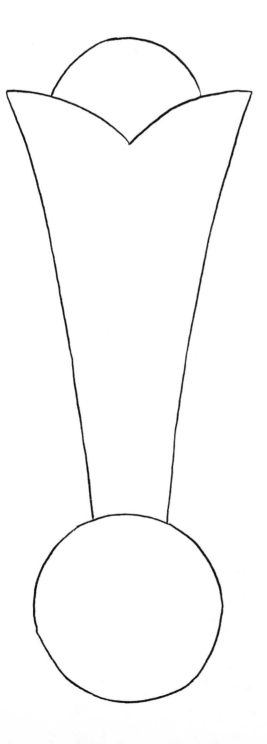

TULIP TIME

This is a design from a newspaper clipping of the 1940's. The original colors are yellow tulips, red-orange center and orange smaller circles with green stems and leaves. To make the center, cut out the No. 5 circle and surround it with eight of the smaller No. 4 circles. This pattern makes a charming quilt. The background square should be 20 inches on a side plus seam allowance.

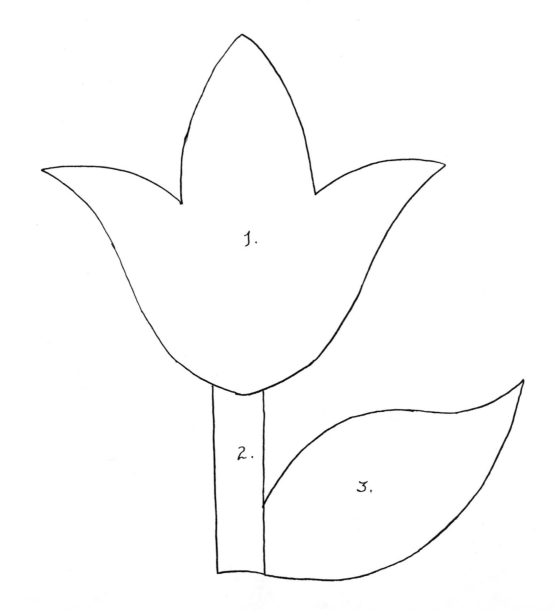

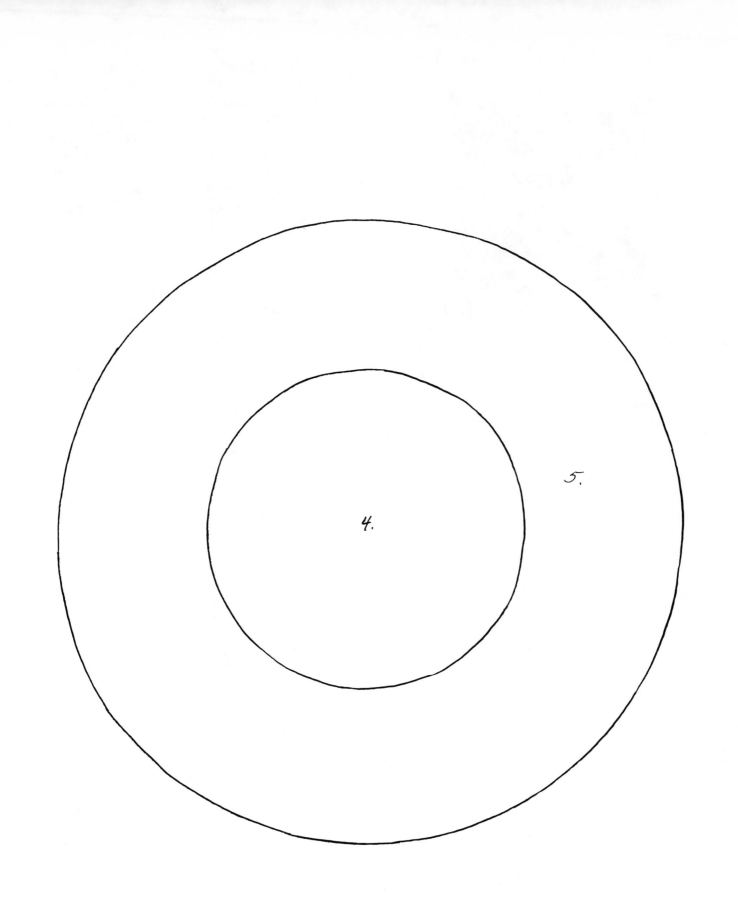

4.

5.

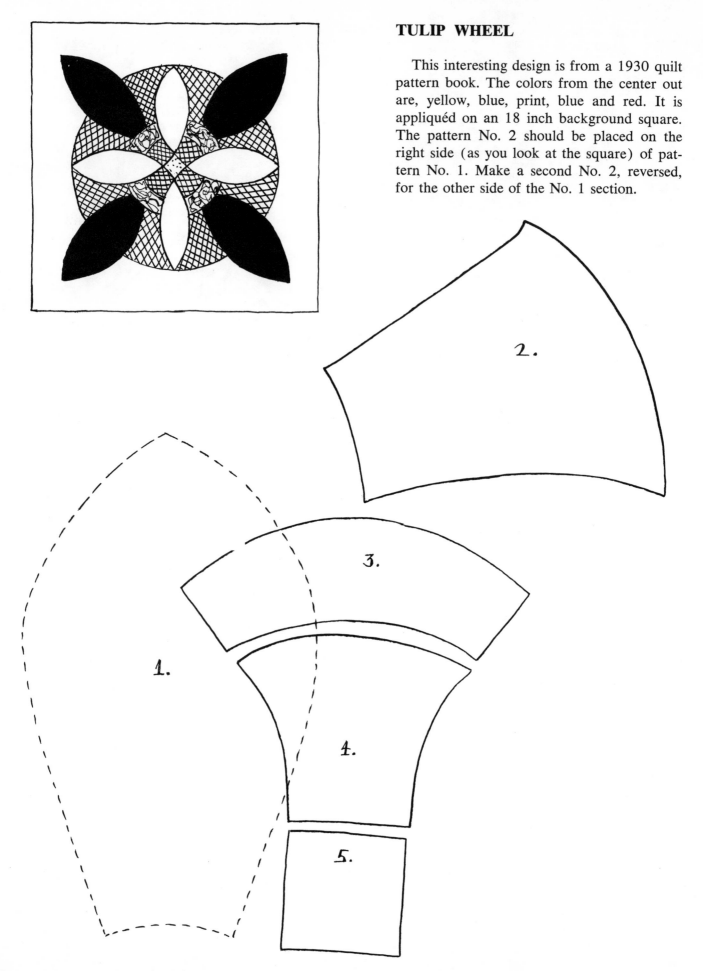

TULIP WHEEL

This interesting design is from a 1930 quilt pattern book. The colors from the center out are, yellow, blue, print, blue and red. It is appliquéd on an 18 inch background square. The pattern No. 2 should be placed on the right side (as you look at the square) of pattern No. 1. Make a second No. 2, reversed, for the other side of the No. 1 section.

2.

3.

1.

4.

5.

IRIS

The iris is one of my favorite flowers but there are not many iris quilt patterns because the shape of the flower is hard to catch and the stiff stems make awkward designs. This Iris pattern, however, makes a lovely quilt. The original quilt was shown in color in the Marie D. Webster book. It was light lavender and green in color and is dainty beyond belief. The background squares are 18 inches on a side. Patterns No. 1 through No. 4 are the larger corner iris, and patterns No. 5 through No. 8 are the smaller side iris. This pattern is an all-over design.

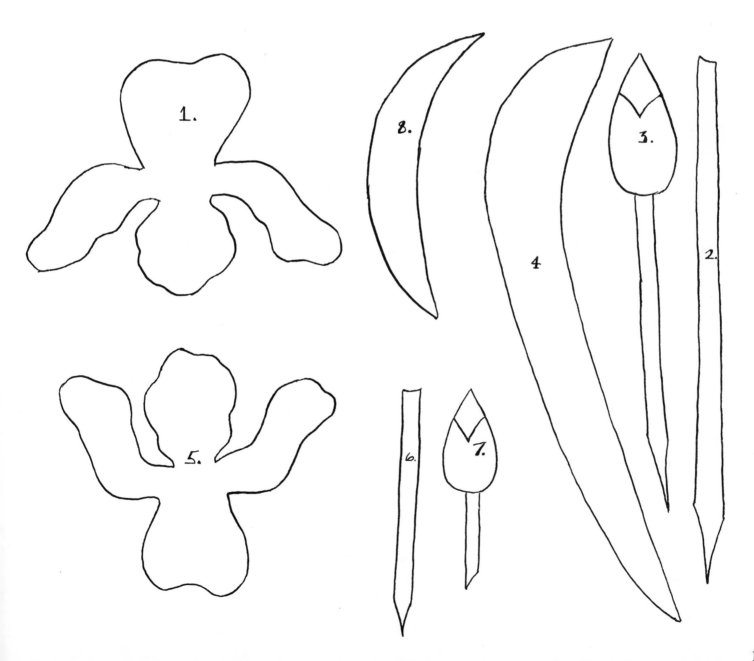

BEARDED IRIS

I took the inspiration for this design from my own garden several years ago. Each flower in each square may be a different color of a dark shade and a print or lighter shade of the same color. The background squares are 12 inches on a side. The beards are pale yellow and the leaves and stems are green. This makes quite a colorful scrap quilt and it is easy to make. It should be put together in an all-over design with a fancy border.

ROSE OF SHARON

There are literally hundreds of patterns called Rose of Sharon and it was hard to choose a representative. This block appeared in the Marie D. Webster book; it is one of the prettiest of the odd Rose of Sharon patterns. It was done on every other block with a white square in between the 14-inch appliquéd squares. The colors were pink, rose, green and a touch of yellow on white. The tiny dotted lines to the dots at the top of the buds are embroidered and the tiny dots may be embroidered in satin stitch also. This makes a lovely old-fashioned looking quilt.

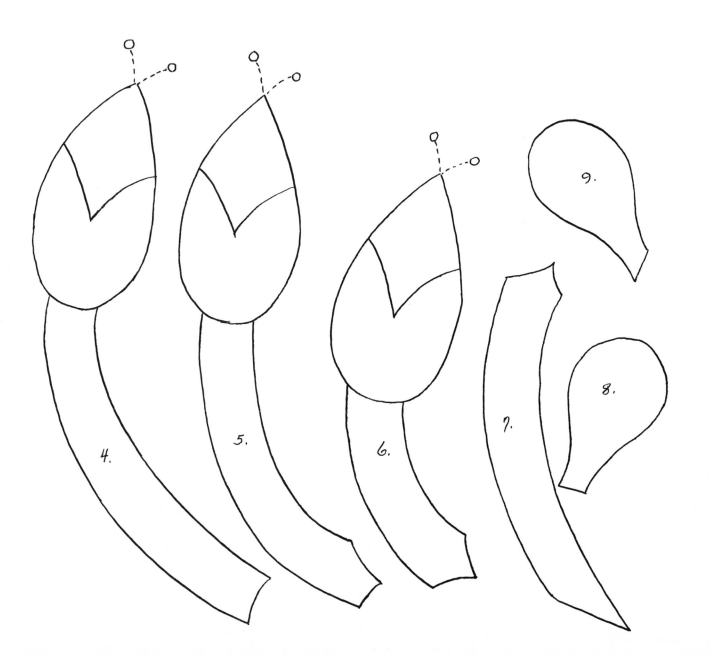

163

DEMOCRAT ROSE

This is another old pattern from the early nineteenth century. It is probably from around 1840 when the Democratic party was founded. The colors are pink, rose and dark rose with green. The white background square is 12 inches on a side. I wish I knew more about this pattern but there is nothing more to tell.

WHIG ROSE

The original quilt which this pattern was taken from was found in the attic of a Pennsylvania farmhouse. With it was a diary which said the quilt was completed in 1814. This quilt is now in a museum collection and this is the first time this pattern has been published. The background squares are 14 inches on a side and the colors are red, pink and blue-green. The dotted stem lines should be embroidered in green crewel yarns.

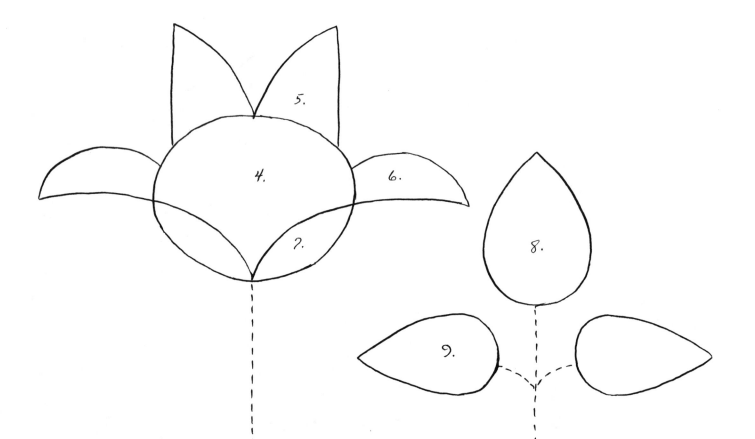

HARRISON ROSE

This is a political pattern as the other names given this pattern show. It was also called WHIG ROSE, DEMOCRATIC and RADICAL ROSE as well as having been named after President William Henry Harrison. The original colors were yellow, red, maroon, blue and green. The background square is white and 18 inches on a side.

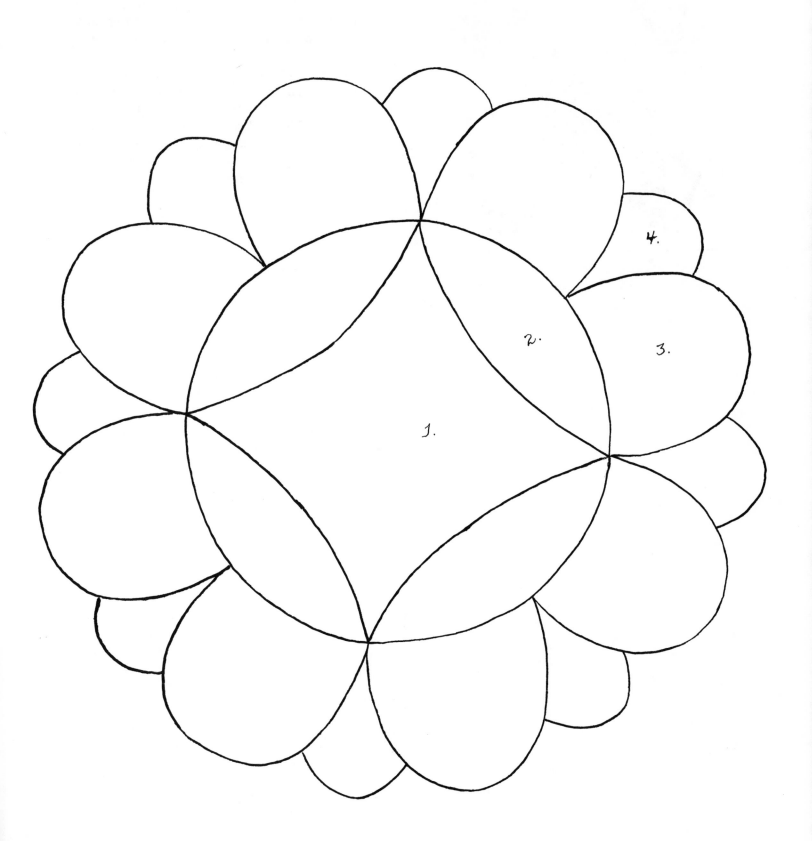

MEXICAN ROSE

This is a design which was popular during the Mexican War. During the 1840's and 1850's there was much trouble with our Mexican neighbors and quilters had several Rose and Star patterns which commemorated those troubles. This pattern in vivid red and green is one of the most Mexican looking of the Rose patterns. The background square is 12 inches on a side. This makes a different looking quilt which will go with the most modern of furnishings or the most traditional.

AMERICAN BEAUTY ROSE

This pattern was designed during the 1940's. It is a delicate design and was originally made in the purplish-rose color of the flower which was named the American Beauty Rose. The other colors are soft yellow and green. The stems are embroidered. This is a pattern from World War II. The background square is 14 inches on a side.

5.

4.

2.

3.

1.

SETH THOMAS ROSE

This interesting rose pattern was originally copied from a design painted on the glass panel of an antique Seth Thomas clock. Seth Thomas was a Yankee peddler who made wooden clocks and peddled them over the countryside in the early nineteenth century. The rose is made in three shades of rose and yellow. The tulips are rose and yellow and the vase is blue. The background squares are 14 inches on a side. I do not know who first made this pattern into a quilt, but it looks quite Victorian.

WILD ROSE

This is an odd pattern considered a modern style in either the 1930's or the 1940's. The colors are two shades of rose, green and yellow. The background square should be 12 inches on a side. This will make quite an interesting quilt.

WILD ROSE WREATH

This pattern was also called GARDEN WREATH. I do not know the original date of this design, but it is one of the prettiest and daintiest of the flower wreaths in my pattern collection. The flowers and buds are pale or shell pink and the leaves and vines are green. Work the design on a 12-inch square background block. Use the dot-dash line 'B' as a stem for the bud on the inside of the wreath, and dotted-line 'A' for the outside of the wreath. These stems are to be embroidered.

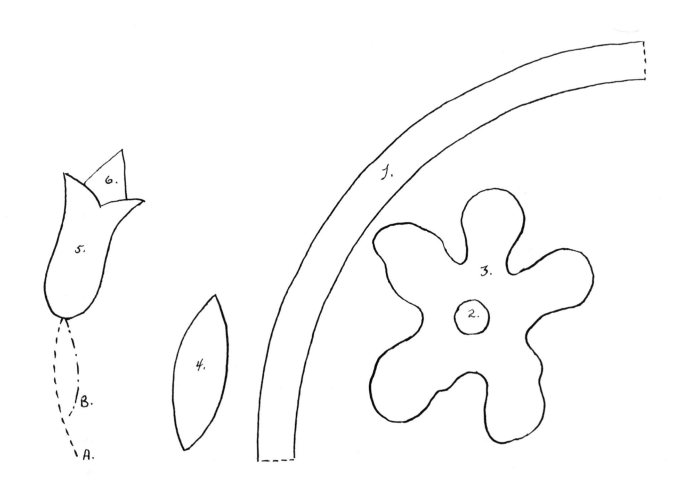

THE PRESIDENT'S WREATH

This wreath dates back to the early nine-teenth century when it was widely used, in many variations, in Friendship quilts. During the Civil War quilters named this type of wreath the President's Wreath and used it to represent President Lincoln. It has retained the association ever since. The colors are red and green and this pattern is to be worked on a 16-inch square background block.

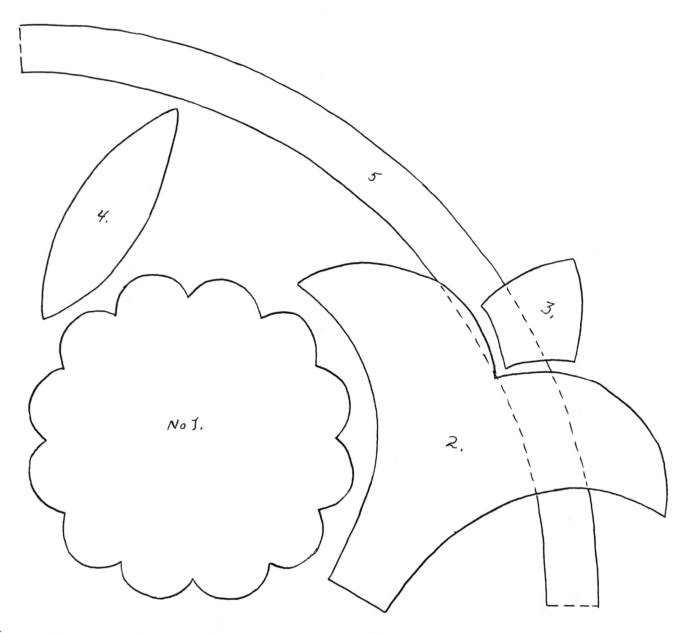

PANSY WREATH

This Pancy Wreath is from the 1920 to 1940 era. The flowers are two shades of any single color; blue, rose, yellow, etc. The leaves are a good medium green. This wreath is worked on a 14-inch square background block.

CURRANTS AND COXCOMBS

These red on white designs with their tiny berries were very popular in the mid-nineteenth century. This one dates back to about the 1870's. If you do not mind painstaking work this makes a striking quilt. It is worked on 20-inch square blocks.

1.

5.

6.

2.

4.

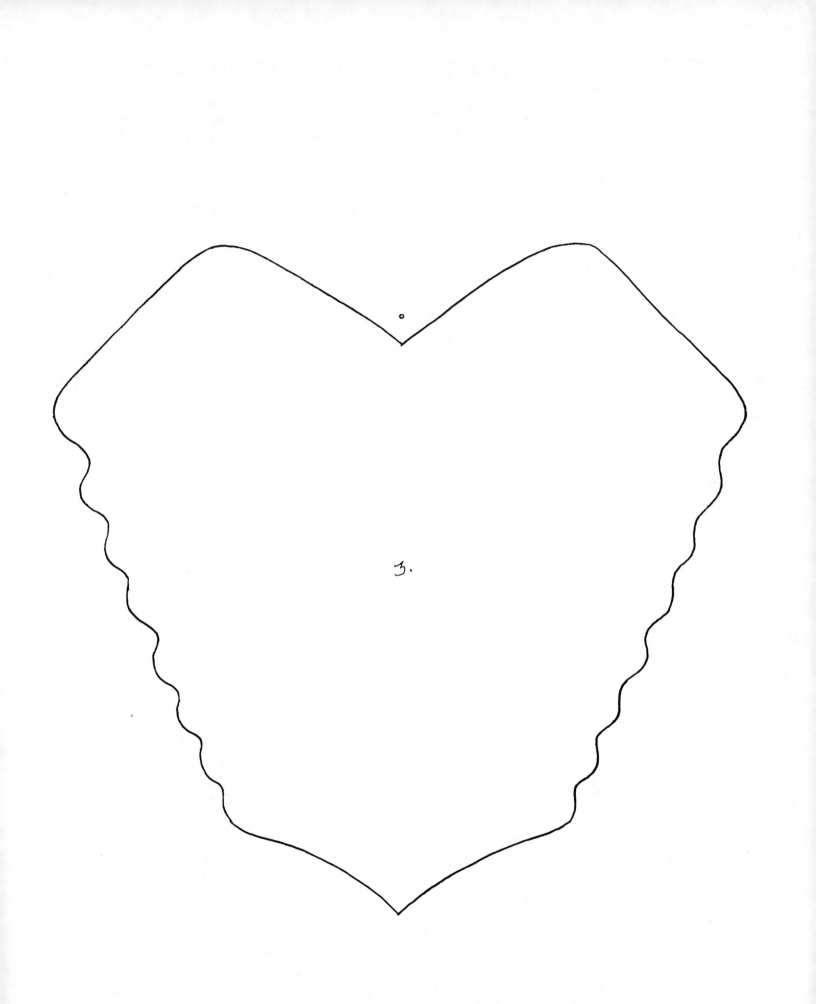

J.

YELLOW HEMSTITCH

This design is one of eight in a 1930 quilt pattern book which all have lines of embroidery and were named 'Hemstitch' patterns. This one is yellow and blue. Do not make this quilt a scrap pattern. The corner daisies will form complete flowers when the blocks are put together. It is worked on a 12-inch square background block.

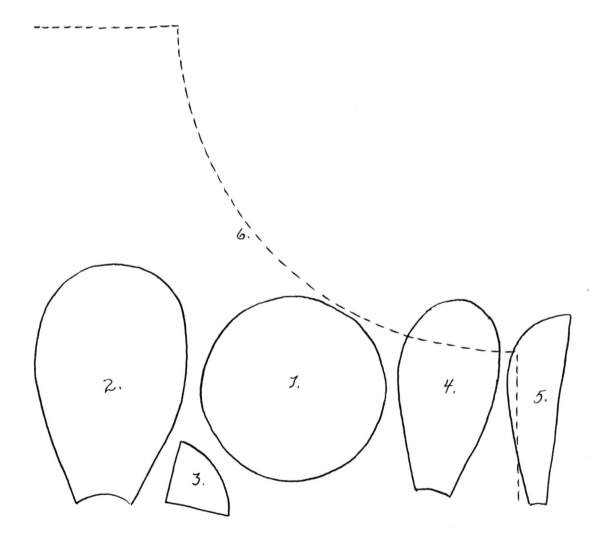

LOTUS FLOWER

I have seen many similar designs which are variations of the Lotus. They were very popular in the early part of the nineteenth century for Friendship quilt blocks. This one is light and dark rose with a light green stem and darker green leaves. It should be worked on a 14-inch square background block.

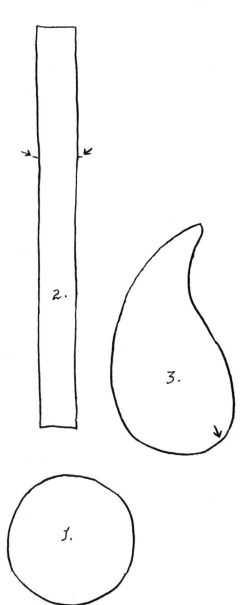

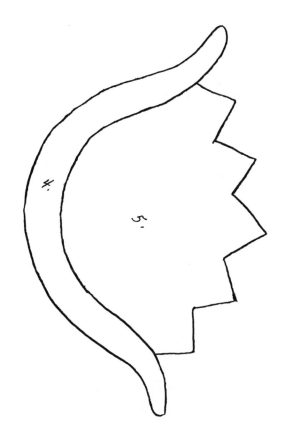

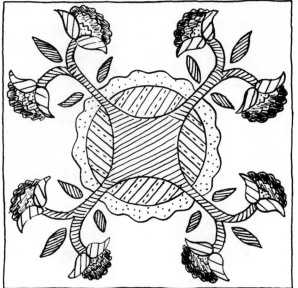

RAGGED ROBIN

This is a pattern from the late nineteenth century. It has several colors in the design, hence care must be used in blending them. This quilt looks better if all of the blocks have the same color combination, and the border matches the entire design. The leaves and stems (No. 5 and No. 4) should be medium green and of small print. The No. 2 oval sections around the center are a print and the rippled piece; the outside of these (No. 3)

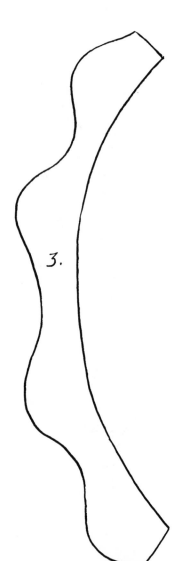

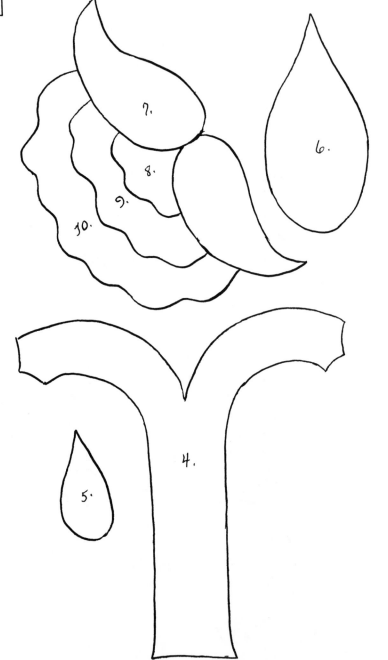

should be dark yellow. The same yellow should be used as piece No. 8 in the outer flowers. No. 9 should be a medium pink and No. 10 a maroon. The print in the center of the block may be a combination of the above colors. Use the colors in the print to be sure the other colors will blend with one another. The finished block should be 16 inches square. The twin-bed size quilt will use four rows of six blocks each with a six-inch border on all four sides.

POINSETTIA (see the next page)

This design must date from the middle of the nineteenth century and it is the only poinsettia design that I would call dainty. It is a red and green design on an 18-inch square block. This could be done as an all over design or with every other block white. The border should be quite fancy. For the center section use patterns No. 6, 7, and 8. For the corner motifs, use patterns No. 1, 2, 3, 4 and 5. For the motifs between the corner flowers use patterns No. 7 and 9.

1.

2.

THE THISTLE

This pattern is from sometime in the middle of the nineteenth century and should appeal especially to those with a good bit of Scot in their family tree. The colors are two shades of green and a thistle pink or rose. This pattern is not a scrap quilt so all of the blocks and the border should match in color. Use a very fancy quilting medallion between the appliqué motifs. The pattern should be done on a 16-inch block, finished size.

6.

7.

2.

3.

4.

5.

1.

WOODLAND FLOWER

This pattern was designed in the 1930's or 1940's. It used green bias tape for the stems, which you may also use if you choose to. The flowers in each block should be of a light and dark shade of one color in plain and print. Use either prints or plain colors in any of the blocks. Use at least two separate colors in this quilt. It would be pretty if all of the blocks are of different color. The finished size blocks are 12 inches square. There should be six rows of eight blocks each in a twin-bed size quilt.

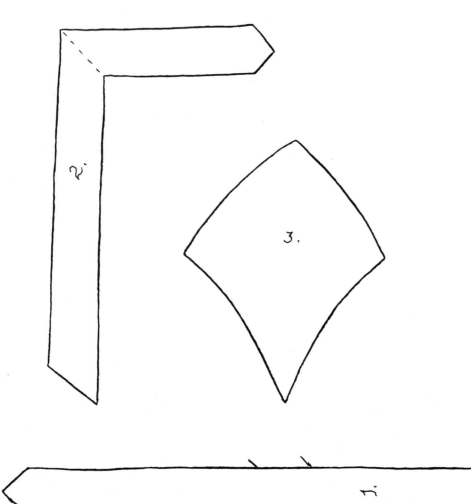

ZINNIA

This is an early twentieth century quilt and should be done in shades of yellow, orange and green with a touch of red in the center of each flower. The stems form a trellis pattern over the quilt top. It might be pretty to make half of the flowers in light tones of the above colors and the other half in dark tones of those colors. This quilt does not need a border if you do not wish to give it one. The finished size blocks are 14 inches square. A twin-bed size quilt will take five rows of seven blocks each.

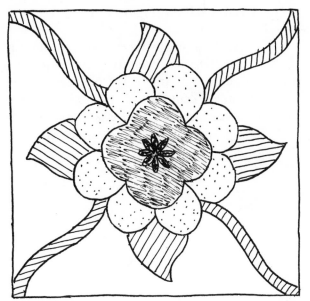

CHARMING NOSEGAY

This pattern is taken from an old quilt kit; the pattern has been long discontinued by the original company. It is from the middle of the twentieth century and is as dainty a pattern as I have ever seen. The basket (see the dot-dash line) must be cut from white, cotton, eyelet edging, four inches broad. The other flowers and leaves should be in light pastel tones. The finished size block is 12 inches square and a twin-bed size quilt will take six rows of eight blocks each. A baby quilt in this pattern will take two rows of four blocks each.

FLOWER TREE

This is a 1930 pattern from an old pattern book. It is a true scrap pattern using seven different prints and plain colors in each block. Use one color for the borders on all of the blocks. The finished size block will be 10 inches square without the border for each block. The twin-bed size quilt will need six rows of eight blocks each.

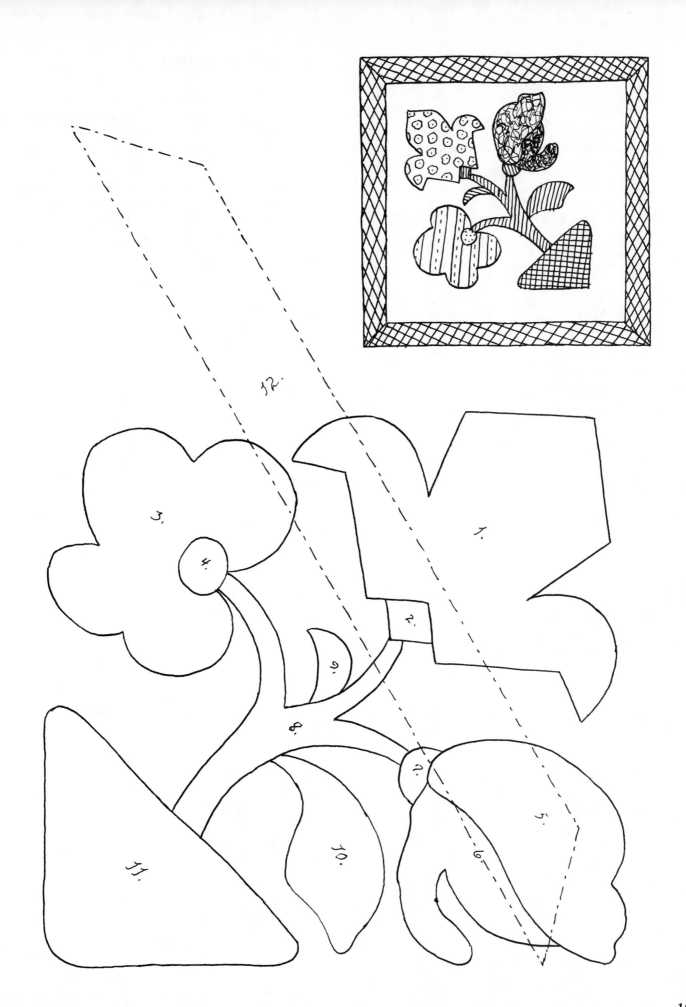

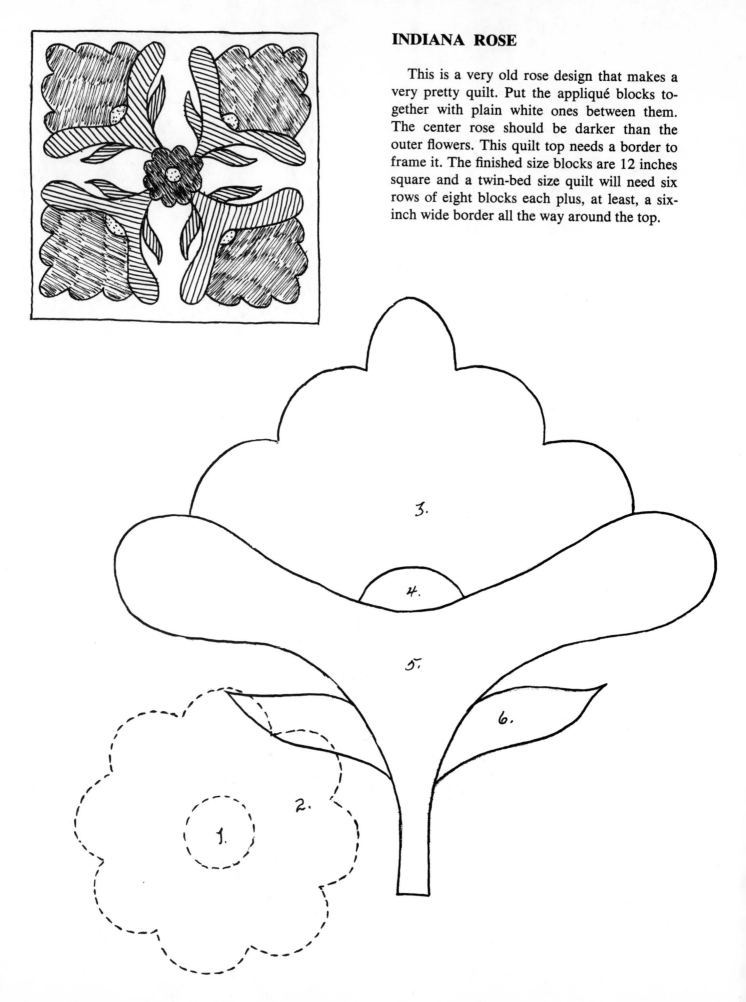

INDIANA ROSE

This is a very old rose design that makes a very pretty quilt. Put the appliqué blocks together with plain white ones between them. The center rose should be darker than the outer flowers. This quilt top needs a border to frame it. The finished size blocks are 12 inches square and a twin-bed size quilt will need six rows of eight blocks each plus, at least, a six-inch wide border all the way around the top.

3.

4.

5.

6.

2.

1.

192

ROSE TREE

This is a very early nineteenth century design. It is quite large; each block is a twenty-four-inch square when finished. The usual manner of putting this top together is to place two squares right side up at the bottom and two more upside down at the top. This quilt must have a very large, fancy border about eighteen inches wide.

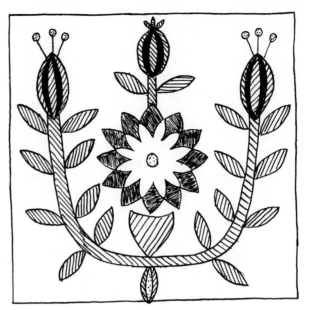

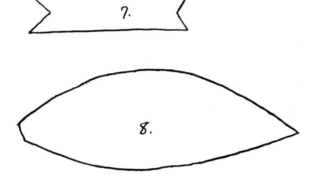

7.

8.

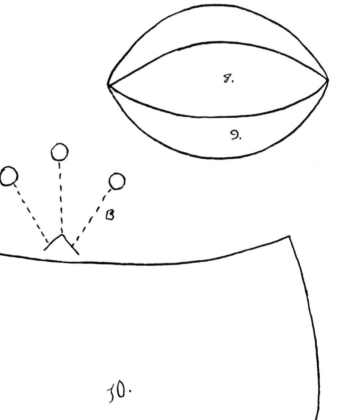

8.

9.

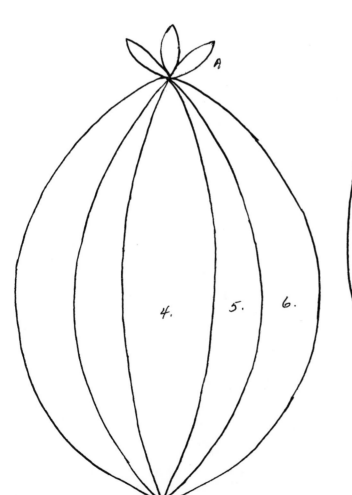

A

4.   5.   6.

B

10.

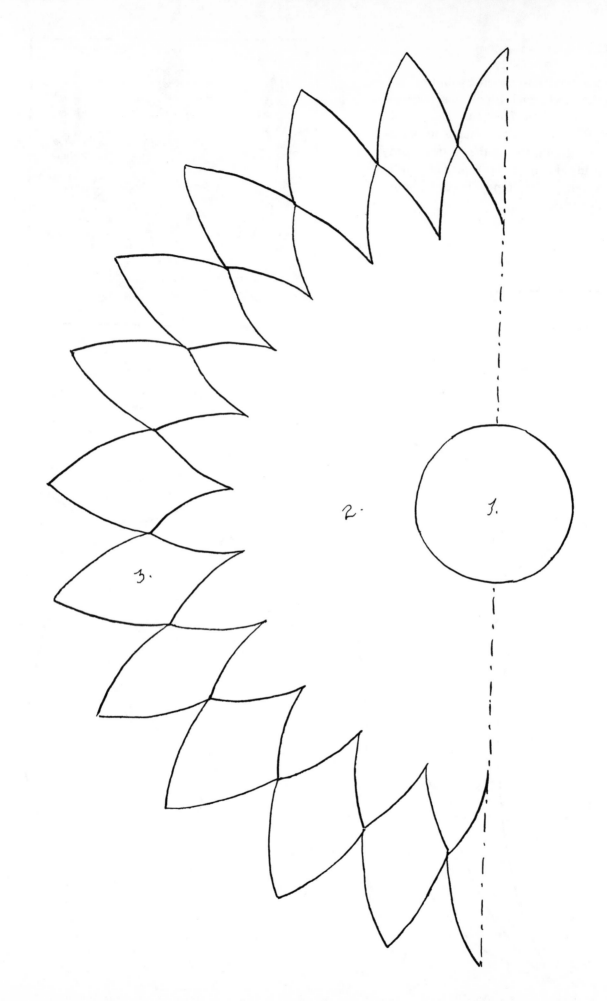

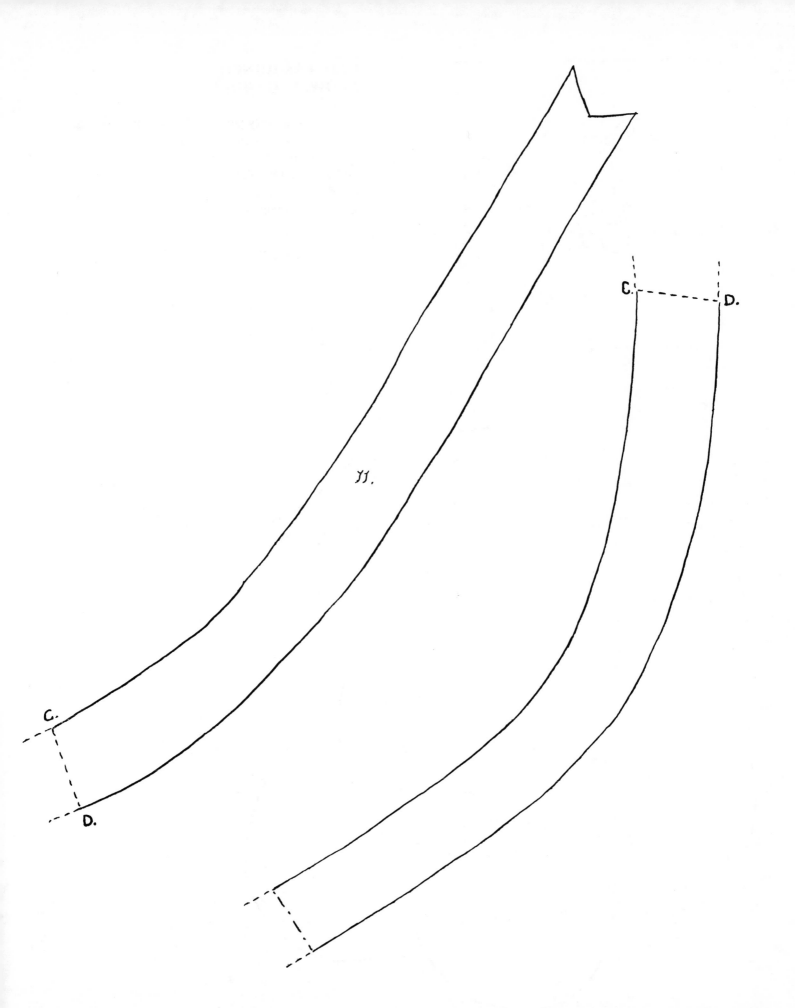

C.

D.

II.

C.

D.

OLD FASHIONED FLOWER GARDEN

This is a very simple 1930 quilt pattern good for beginners in appliqué. The flowers are of print or plain yellow with green stems and leaves. The block is 12 inches square (finished size) and a twin-bed size quilt will need six rows of eight blocks each.

OHIO ROSE

This is a delightful old design from about 1840. It is a red and green pattern typical of that era but this design is sparked with a touch of rose (pattern No. 2). If you cut four layers of flower design for the center rose, the resulting flower will be quite hard to quilt. To appliqué the design, cut out the center flower and the eight petals for each of the other layers. Pin each of these in place and baste the pieces before appliquéing them permanently. A plain block between each of the appliquéd ones, is pretty when the plain block is quilted in an elaborate medallion. This quilt also needs a border. The finished blocks are 14 inches square and a twin-bed size quilt will need five rows of seven blocks each. You may also turn this pattern diagonally for a pretty top design.

199

WREATH OF GRAPES

The pattern is also called FRUITFUL VINE. It is an early nineteenth century design which was popular for Friendship quilt blocks. The copy here has a blue ring for the wreath, green leaves and stems and redish-maroon grapes. Every other block in this quilt should be plain white with a quilting pattern exactly the same as the appliquéd pattern. This top will look best with a border. The blocks in this quilt are 16 inches square, finished size. A twin-bed size quilt will take four rows of six blocks each.

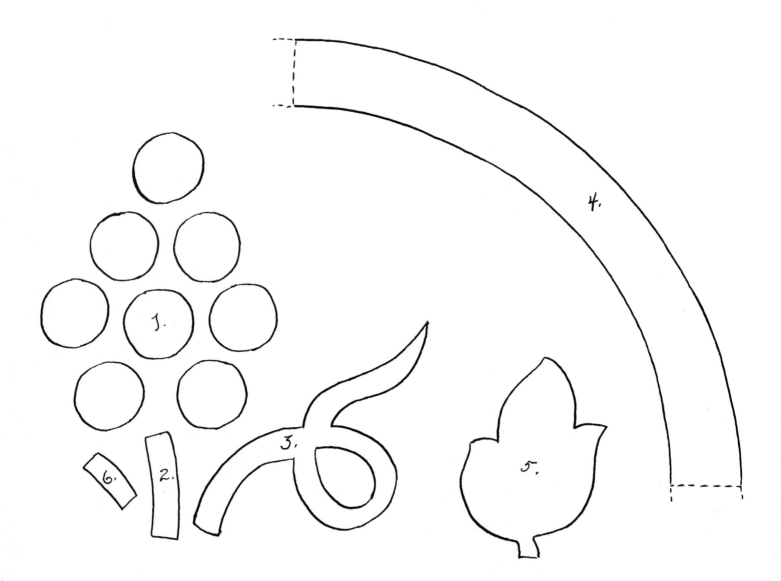

OAK LEAF AND CHERRIES

This design is a very early red and green pattern probably from the 1820's. It may be made with or without plain blocks between the appliquéd ones. The finished block size is 14 inches square and a twin-bed size quilt will need five rows of seven blocks each. This quilt should have a border. This pattern was very popular for use in early Friendship quilts.

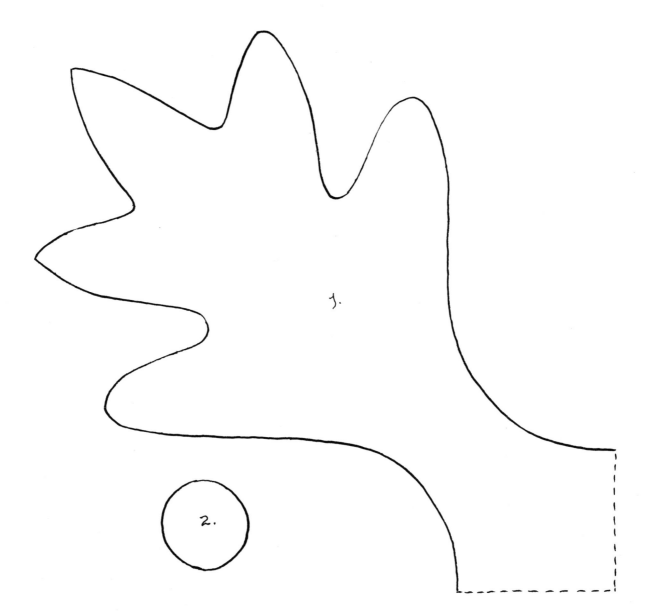

THE LOVE APPLE

This design is from the middle of the nineteenth century and is primarily a red and green quilt sparked with some yellow. The old Love Apple was the name for the tomato when it was used as a garden plant in the flower beds and believed to be poisonous. The design shows the ripe tomato cut in half with the seed sections represented by the yellow sections.

The appliqué blocks can be arranged diagonally with plain blocks between them or with the blocks arranged to point to the center of the quilt from both sides. This quilt does not need a border but you may use one. The finished block size is 12 inches square and a twin-bed size quilt will need six rows of eight blocks each.

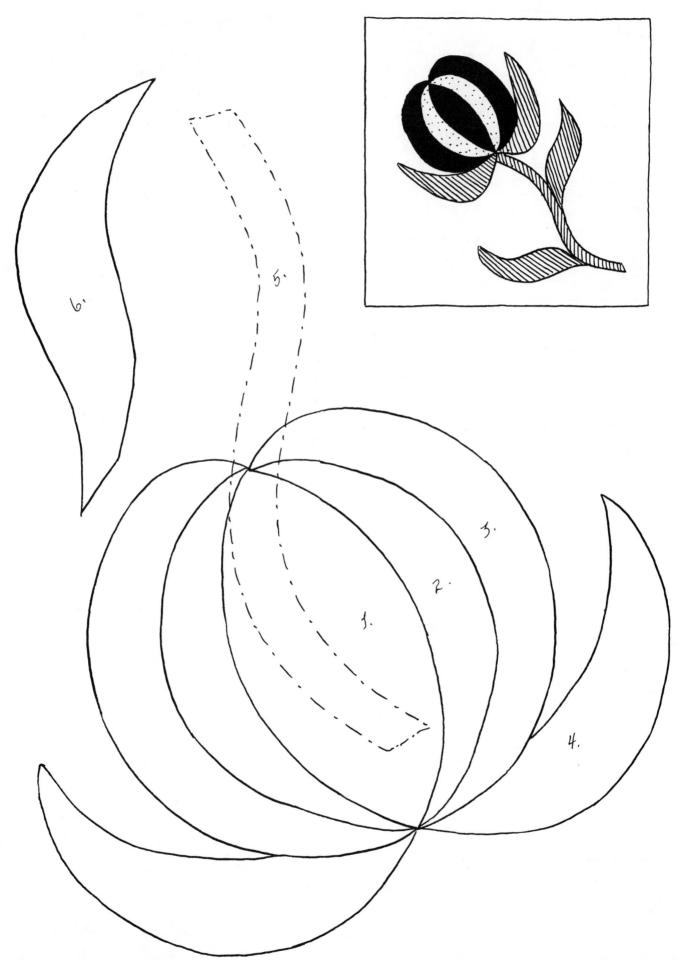

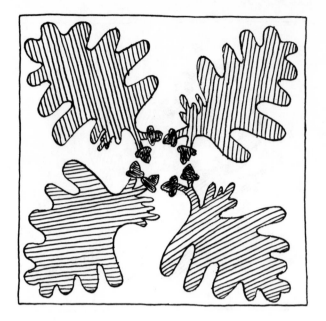

CHARTER OAK

The early nineteenth century, called the Federal Period, had many favorite patriotic motifs. One of them was called the Charter Oak. It represented the oak tree which hid the colonial charter of Connecticut when the English government threatened to revoke it. This all happened in 1687. Many representations of the Oak Tree were designed by American needlewomen. This is one of my favorite motifs. The leaves are green and the acorns are brown. Another name for this pattern is OAK LEAF WREATH. The finished size blocks are 18 inches square and a twin-bed size quilt will need four rows of six blocks each plus, at least, a six inch border all the way around.

1.

2.

3.

PRINCESS FEATHER

From the beginning of quilting in America, a favorite motif was any of the variations of the old English PRINCE'S FEATHER. Americans have changed the name and used it both for appliqué or for quilting designs. The present pattern is from an early red and green quilt. The design can be made either mostly red or mostly green by making the center star either of those colors. Make every other block in this quilt a plain one and use an appropriate border. The quilting should be quite elaborate. The blocks are 24 inches square, finished size. A twin-bed size quilt will need three rows of four blocks each.

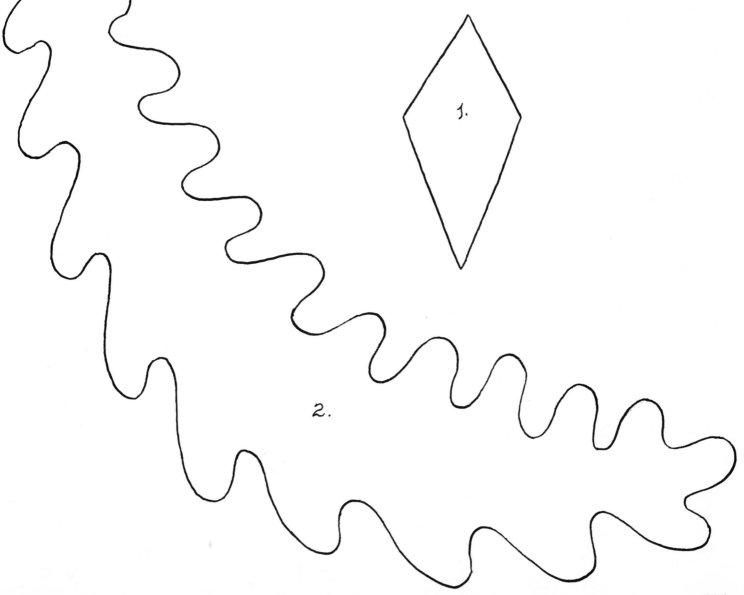

QUEEN BUTTERFLY

It seems that all quilters love butterfly patterns. This is a particularly pretty one. The wings of each butterfly should be a combination of a print and a plain color. The body is brown in each block plus brown embroidered antennae. This pattern should be done on 12-inch square blocks. A twin-bed size quilt will take six rows of eight blocks each.

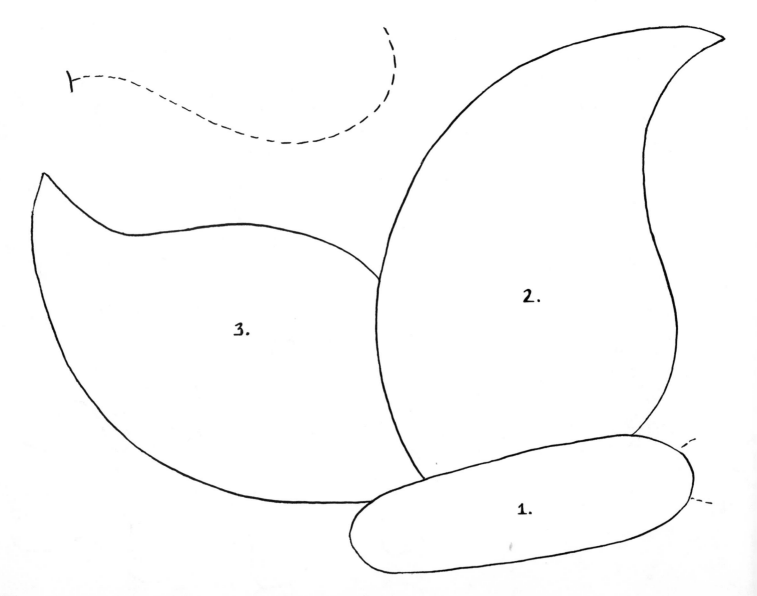

2.

3.

1.

RECOLLECT and REMEMBER

These cute patterns are from the turn of the twentieth century and are used for memory quilts. The hands, feet and faces should be done in flesh color and the hats are yellow to represent straw. The dress or overalls should be made from many different prints which should be saved from your sewing. A little girl's quilt may be made from scraps saved from her own clothing, or each figure could be made from the scraps of her friends' cloth-ing. The same kind of quilt can be made for a boy. A friendship quilt for an adult can be made of both figures dressed in scraps traded from friends. A friendship quilt block is always signed by the persons represented on the block in either indelible ink or embroidery. The finished size of the blocks is 12 inches square and a finished twin-bed size quilt top will take six rows of eight blocks each.

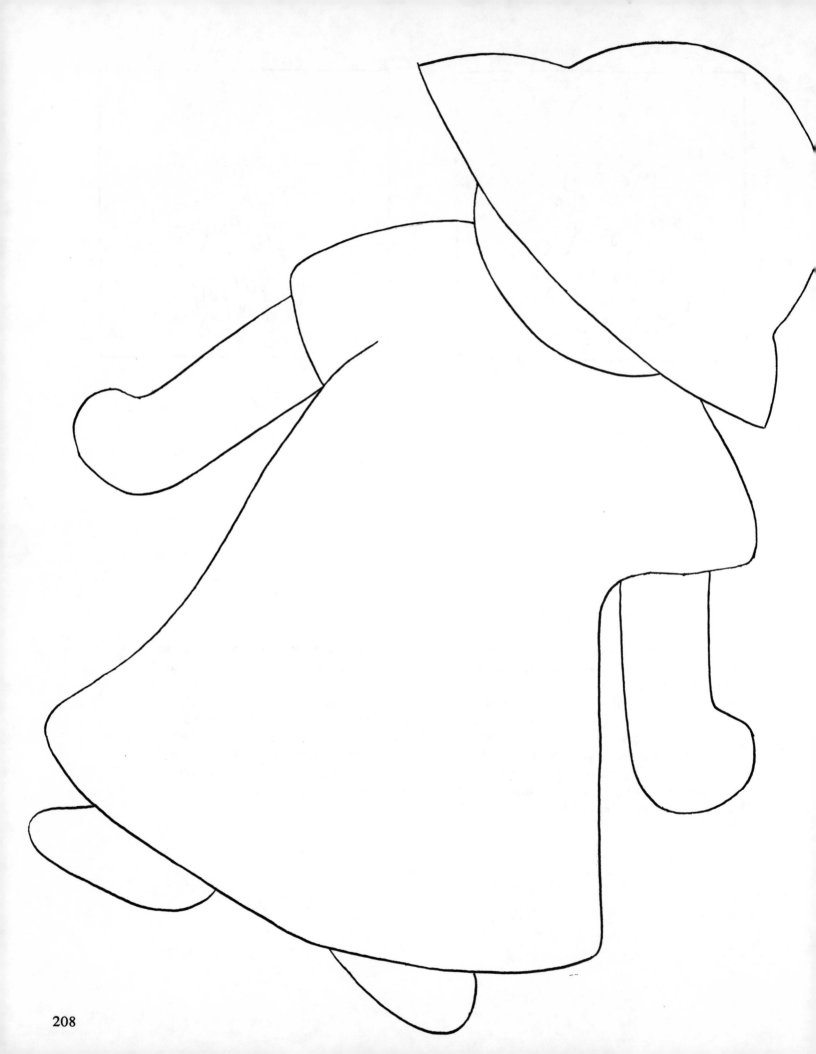

COLONIAL LADY

These quilts have been popular since the 1920's, but this design was taken from a 1930 pattern book. You may make a quilt from the six designs, each represented eight times. Or you may make a whole quilt from one or two of the designs. This quilt will look best with three-inch lattice strips between the blocks. It is a scrap quilt design. The dotted line pat-terns are meant to be embroidered on the squares while the solid line patterns must be cut out and appliquéd. Each dress should have a print and a matching solid-colored trim. Finished blocks should be 12 inches square and the twin-bed quilt size should be composed of six rows of eight blocks each.

A

B

C

D

E

F

211

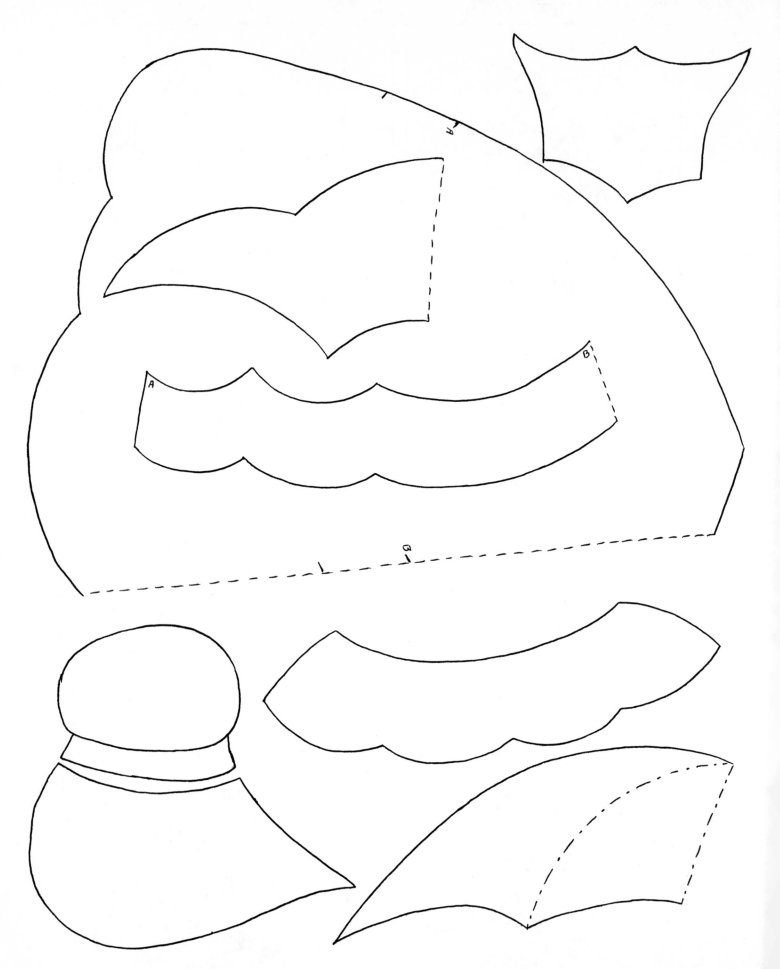

A.

D.

G.

C.

B.

E.

F.

213

Border Patterns

BORDERS AND INSERTIONS

Not all quilts, whether pieced or appliquéd, need a border. However, many of them look better and more finished if they do have a pretty border around them. Indeed, the old Medallion quilts are essentially a small center with several rows of borders in graduated size around this center. Any of the borders in this section may be used to make a Medallion quilt.

There are only three pages of appliquéd borders. These can be used to make many different borders which will match the quilt top they are used with. First is a SWAG AND TASSEL BORDER. In the original the colors were red and blue. There was a small quilters rose in the center. I have given the pattern for this also, but it may be left out. Something

which will match one of the quilt pattern motifs may be used in its place. This swag should be appliquéd to the center of a 12-inch wide strip of white cloth. The colors may match those used in your quilt. Instead of the tassels, use one of the small flower patterns from the appliqué section, at the top between two of the points of the swags. Pattern No. 5 of Iris; No. 2 and No. 6 of Conventional Tulips with the leaf No. 6 used in the place of the tassels; No. 4, No. 5, No. 6 and No. 7 of the Whig Rose; No. 7 and No. 8 of Harrison Rose; No. 4, No. 5 and No. 6 of Wild Rose; No. 2 and No. 3 of Wild Rose Wreath; No. 4 and No. 5 of Lotus Flower; and No. 7, No. 8, No. 9 and No. 10 of Ragged Robin may be used in this manner with the basic swag. In this way the swag border will be made quite suitable for these quilts.

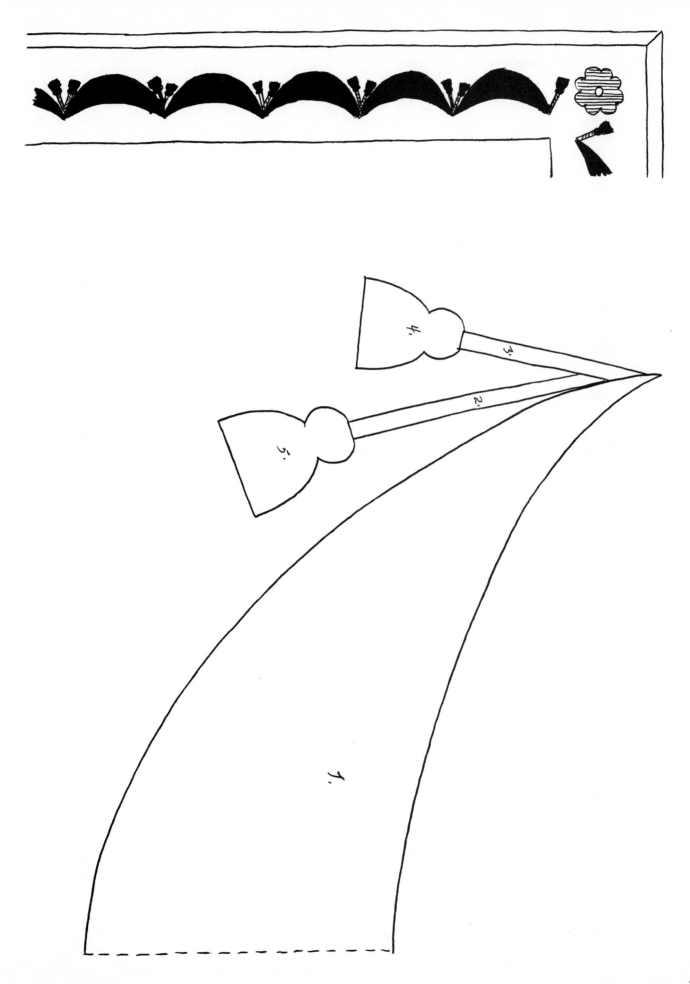

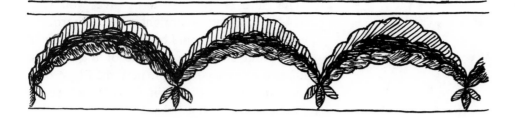

The second border, RIPPLED SWAG BORDER, is a fancy, dainty one suitable for use with any of the flower motif quilts. It should be appliquéd to a white strip nine inches wide or wider. The original colors were pink, rose, green, pink and green, in that order. Any range of complementary colors may be used which match the colors in your quilt top. Again the ornament at the top of the swags may be changed to one of the small flowers used in your quilt top to make this border match your quilt pattern.

4.

5.

3.

2.

1.

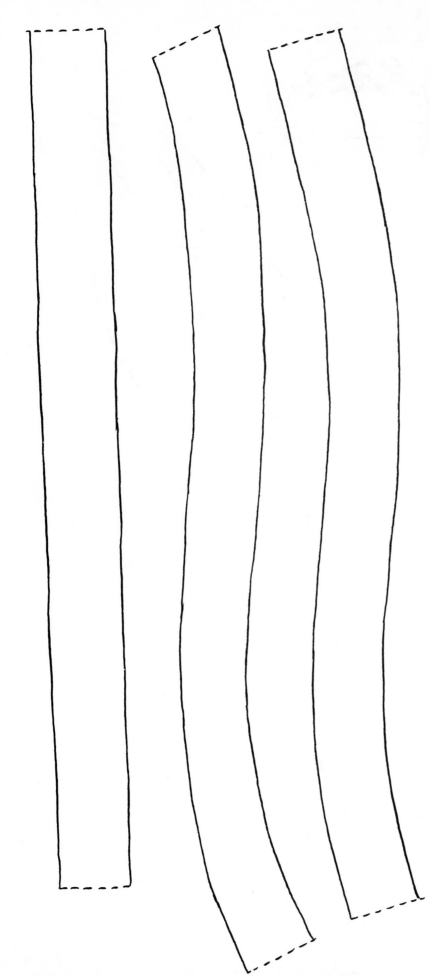

The third sheet of patterns gives you two MEANDERS and a straight vine for borders. The straight vine should be used with a six-inch wide border strip. Choose one of the flowers and leaves from your quilt pattern. Place one flower at each end of the vine and place several leaves along the vine. Continue this until the border entirely surrounds your quilt top. The shallow meander should be appliquéd to an eight-inch wide or wider border. The other meander needs at least a 12-inch wide border. You may use any of the flowers and leaves from your quilt top patterns. Scatter these flowers and leaves along the length of the swags formed by putting several of the meander sections together. Or place a flower on each of the seams where the sections join and scatter leaves and buds on either side of the meander until the border is complete around the entire quilt top. If you repeat the pattern of the placement of the motifs on your border, it is easier and neater than an entirely haphazard pattern.

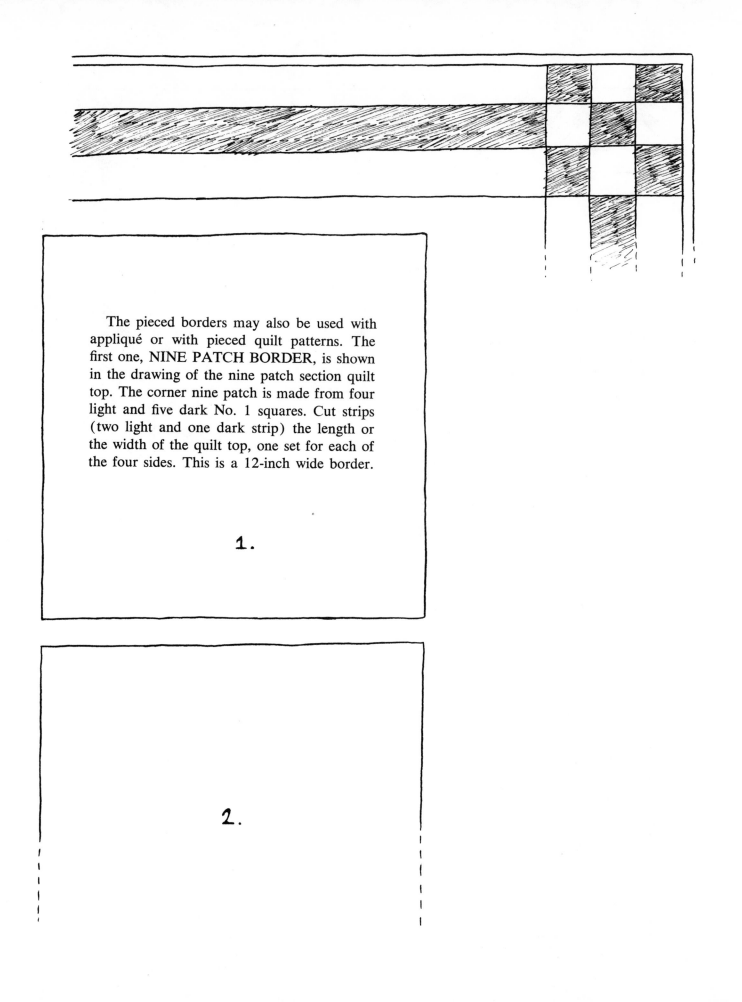

The pieced borders may also be used with appliqué or with pieced quilt patterns. The first one, NINE PATCH BORDER, is shown in the drawing of the nine patch section quilt top. The corner nine patch is made from four light and five dark No. 1 squares. Cut strips (two light and one dark strip) the length or the width of the quilt top, one set for each of the four sides. This is a 12-inch wide border.

1.

2.

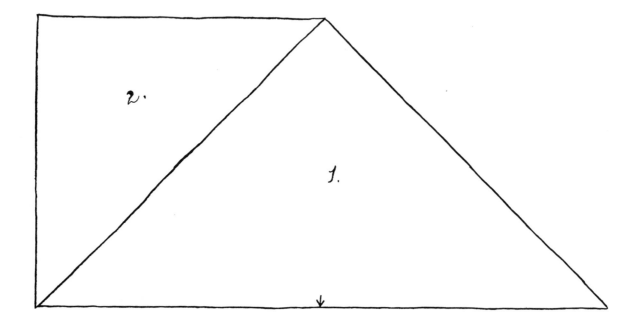

The next border is called STREAK O'-LIGHTNING. The corner is made of two triangles each, one twice the size of the No. 1 pattern. Make two strips the length or the width of the quilt, by sewing together No. 1 light and dark triangles. The No. 2 triangles finish off the bottom strip to complete the lightning. To make a 12-inch wide border like that in the drawing, the pieced strip should be made of the two sections six inches wide when finished. Add two 3-inch wide strips to each side of the pieced strips.

2.

1.

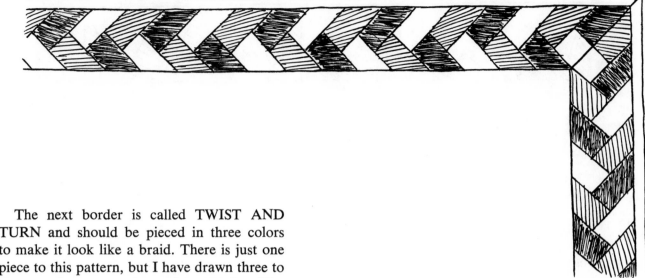

The next border is called TWIST AND TURN and should be pieced in three colors to make it look like a braid. There is just one piece to this pattern, but I have drawn three to show you how to put the sections together. The pieced border will be four inches wide.

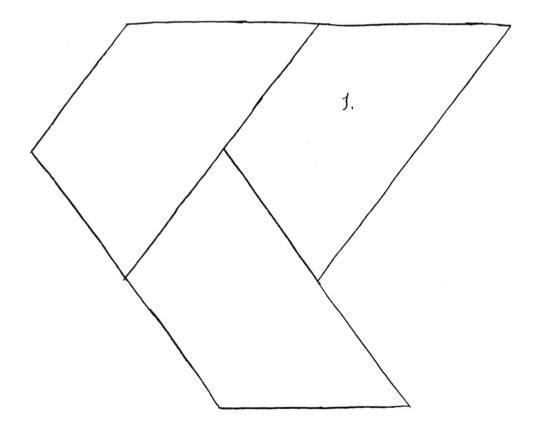

1.

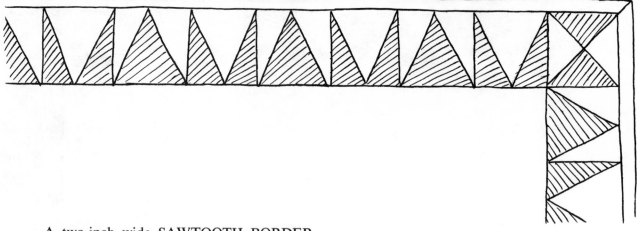

A two-inch wide SAWTOOTH BORDER called SHADE AND SHADOW is next. Piece together little squares from two No. 2 and one No. 1 patterns and make strips by sewing them together with every other square reversed. The corner is made from four of the No. 3 triangles. This pattern could be put together in two-pieced strip with a plain strip between them like the next DOUBLE SAWTOOTH BORDER.

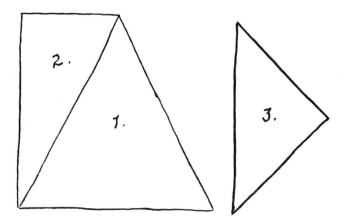

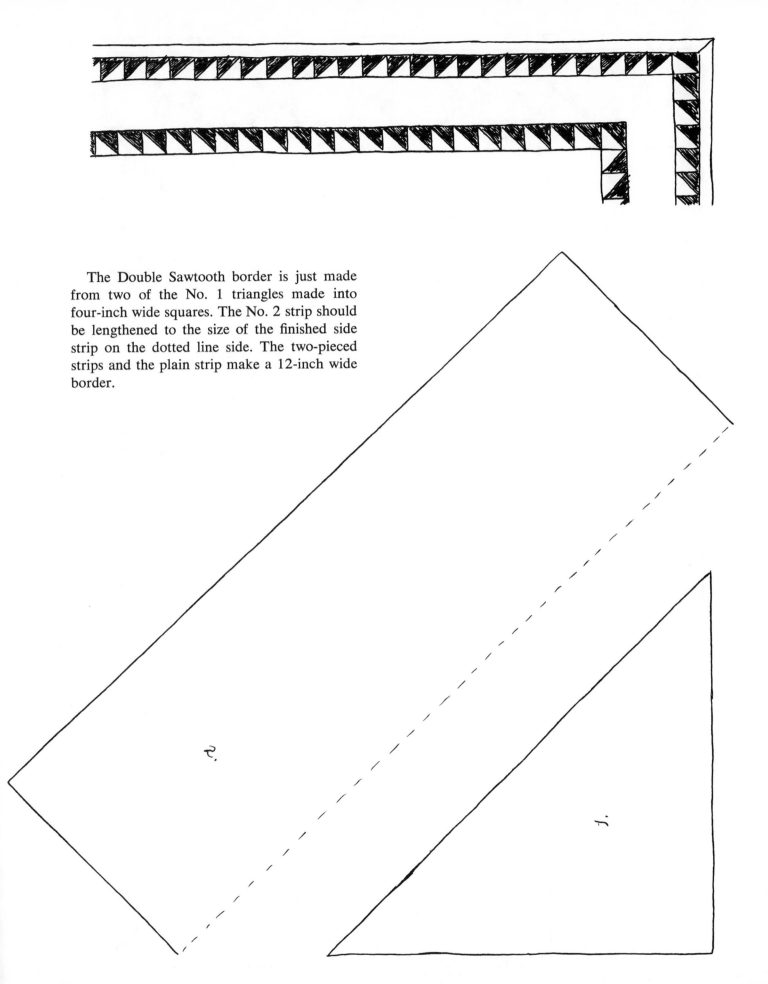

The Double Sawtooth border is just made from two of the No. 1 triangles made into four-inch wide squares. The No. 2 strip should be lengthened to the size of the finished side strip on the dotted line side. The two-pieced strips and the plain strip make a 12-inch wide border.

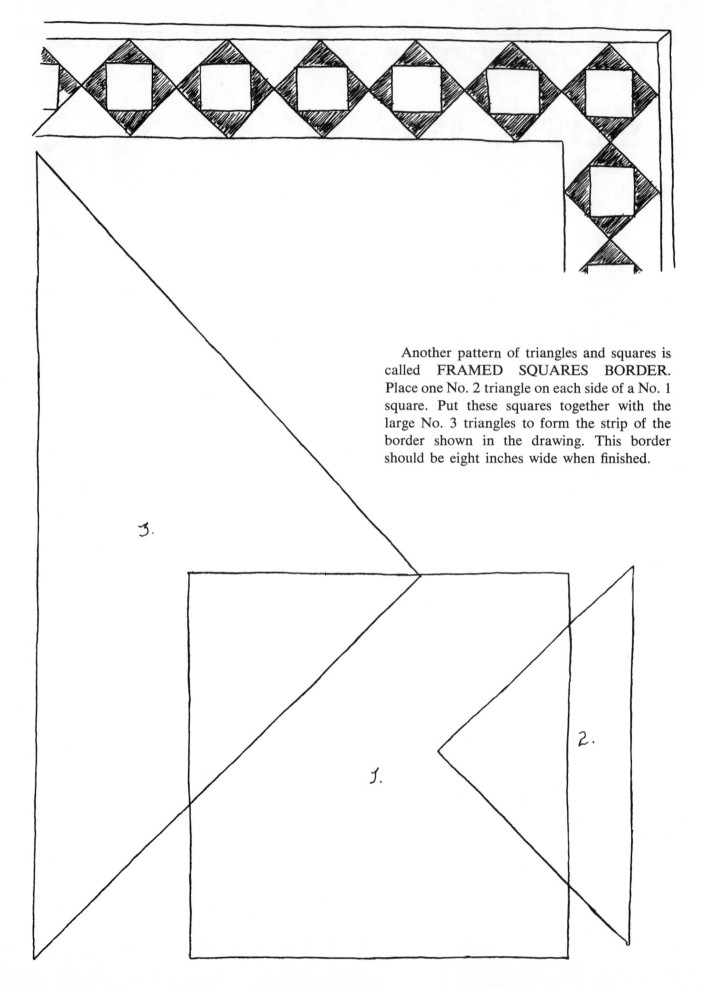

Another pattern of triangles and squares is called **FRAMED SQUARES BORDER**. Place one No. 2 triangle on each side of a No. 1 square. Put these squares together with the large No. 3 triangles to form the strip of the border shown in the drawing. This border should be eight inches wide when finished.

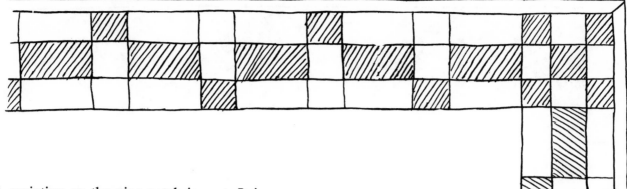

A variation on the nine patch is next. It is called **TWISTED TRAIL BORDER.** Just put the No. 1 square and the No. 2 oblongs together to make a six-inch wide strip.

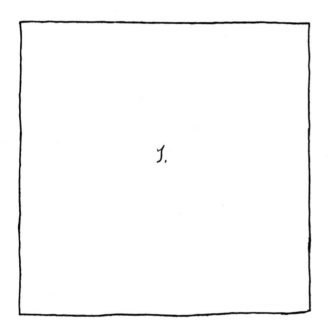

1.

2

The next border is called TWISTED RIB—
BON BORDER and it is eight inches wide. It
is shown in full on the quilt top illustrating the
Five Patch Section. Again make squares from
two No. 2 and one No. 1 patterns. Put them
together into strips.

1.

2.

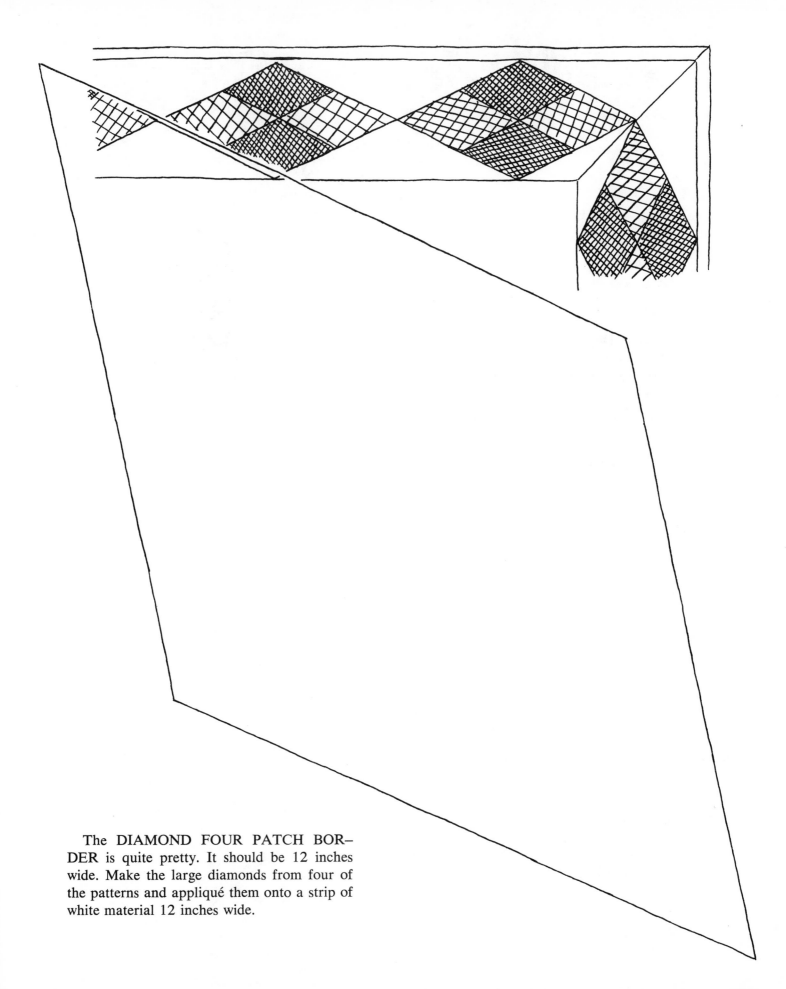

The DIAMOND FOUR PATCH BOR–DER is quite pretty. It should be 12 inches wide. Make the large diamonds from four of the patterns and appliqué them onto a strip of white material 12 inches wide.

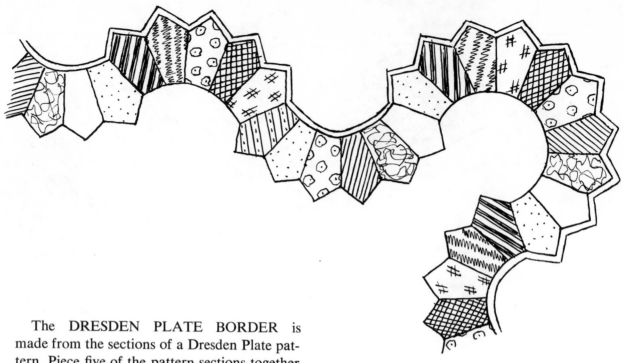

The DRESDEN PLATE BORDER is made from the sections of a Dresden Plate pattern. Piece five of the pattern sections together and then make the border by putting these sections together with every other section of five reversed. Appliqué the strip of sections onto a white strip eight inches wide to give a straight strip to sew onto the quilt top.

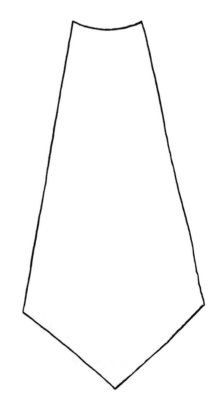

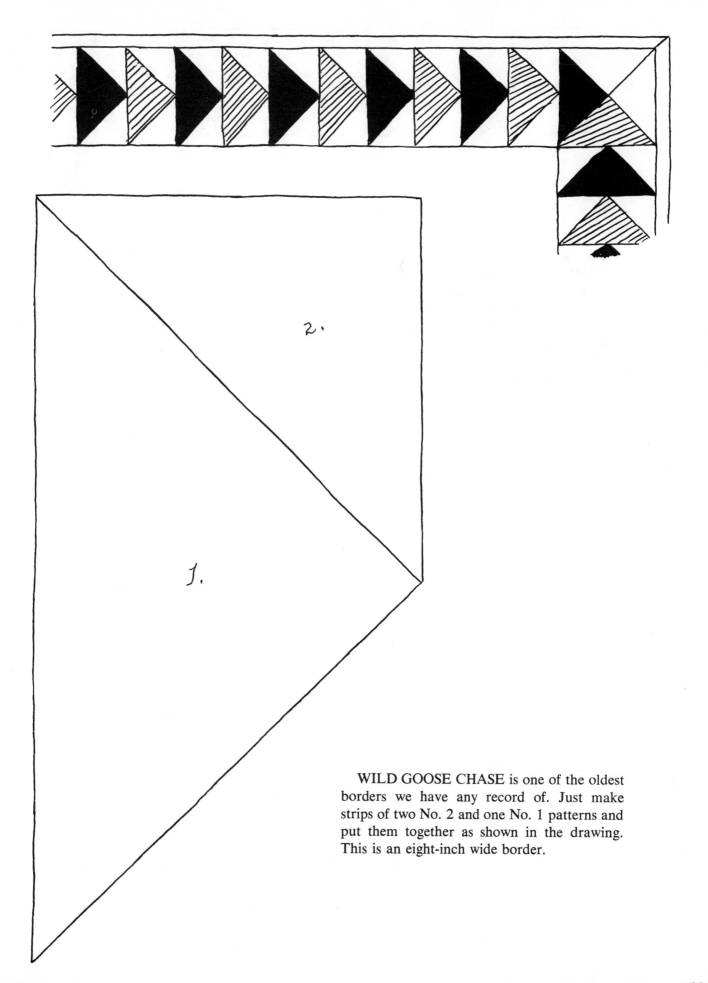

2.

1.

WILD GOOSE CHASE is one of the oldest borders we have any record of. Just make strips of two No. 2 and one No. 1 patterns and put them together as shown in the drawing. This is an eight-inch wide border.

The last pattern is called CHECKERED BOARD and it has a STAR CORNER. Put two rows of the squares together for the sides of the border and make four of the Star corners for the corners of the quilt. Try several of these borders with each of your quilts so you can choose the one which will make each of your quilts the prettiest when finished.

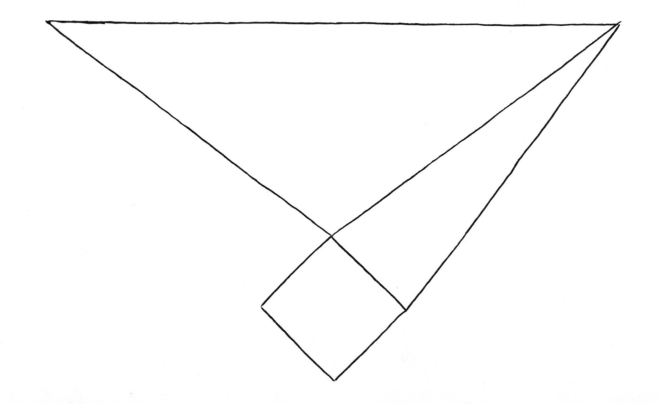

Quilting Patterns

THE QUILTING DESIGNS

Choosing a quilting design that will complement the pieced or the appliqué design of your quilt top and add the finishing touch to your quilt is very important. I have indicated a few quilting patterns in the drawings of quilt tops in this book, but choose most of the patterns yourself. There are 33 patterns in this section—medallions, insertions and borders. All are beautiful, old and little published versions which should become as popular as the more widely known patterns already in use.

There are several ways of transferring these designs to your quilt. The simplest way would be to trace the designs on tissue paper and transfer them to thin cardboard or plastic. Cut slits along the lines without severing the sections entirely. Use a pencil on the slits and finish joining all the lines after lifting the pattern.

Patterns No. 4, 5, 7, 9 and 30 are one fourth of their finished designs. Patterns No. 14, 15 and 29 are one half of their patterns and patterns No. 16, 17, 18, 19, 20, 21, 22, 23, 24, 25, 26, 27, 28 and 33 are all border patterns and must be extended. Pattern No. 17 has the corner as well as the straight side of the border.

1.

2.

3.

234

4.

6.

5.

7.

8.

9.

10.

11.

12.

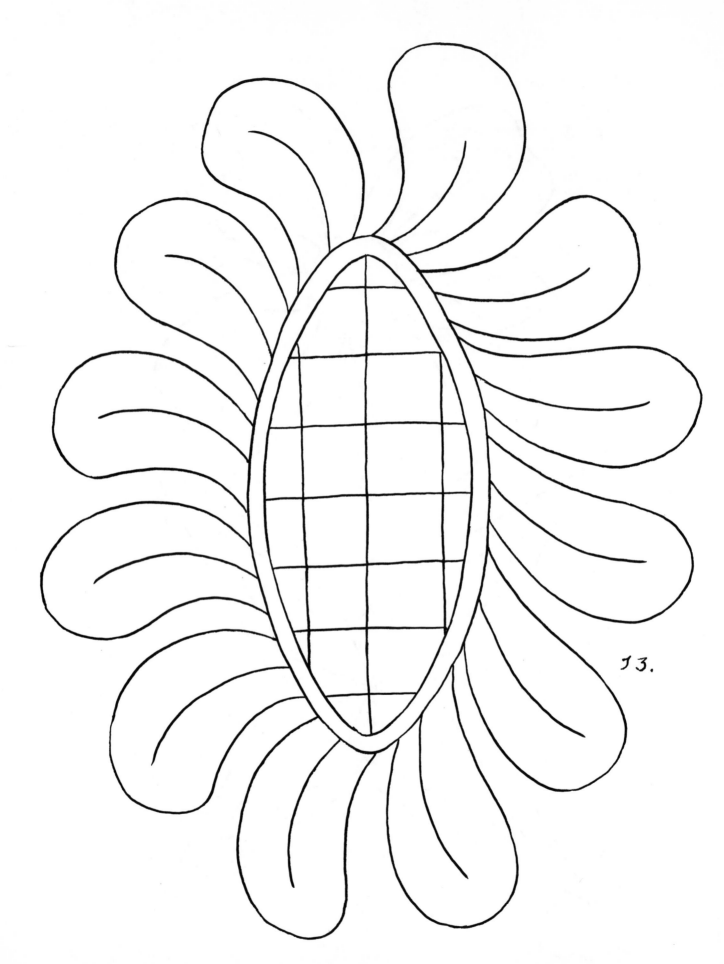

13.

14.

15.

244

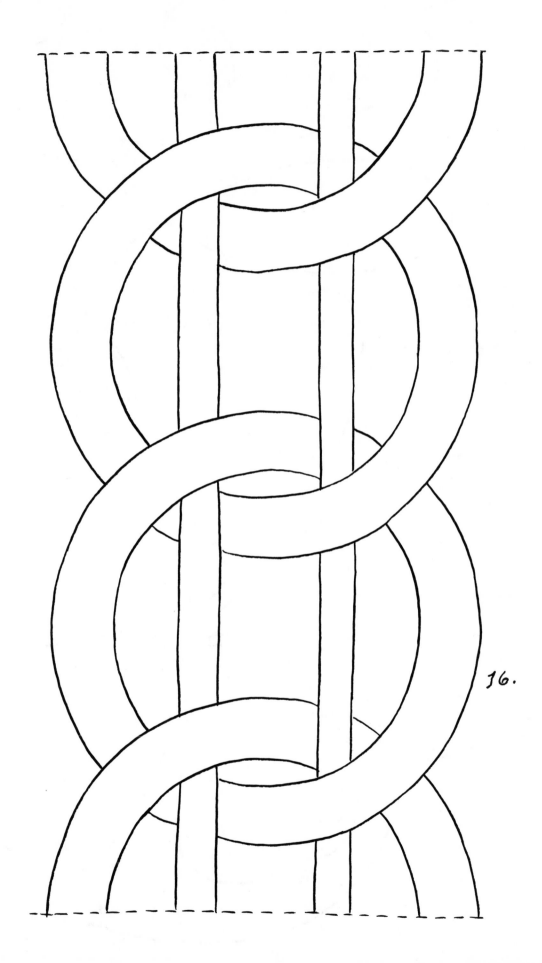

16.

17.

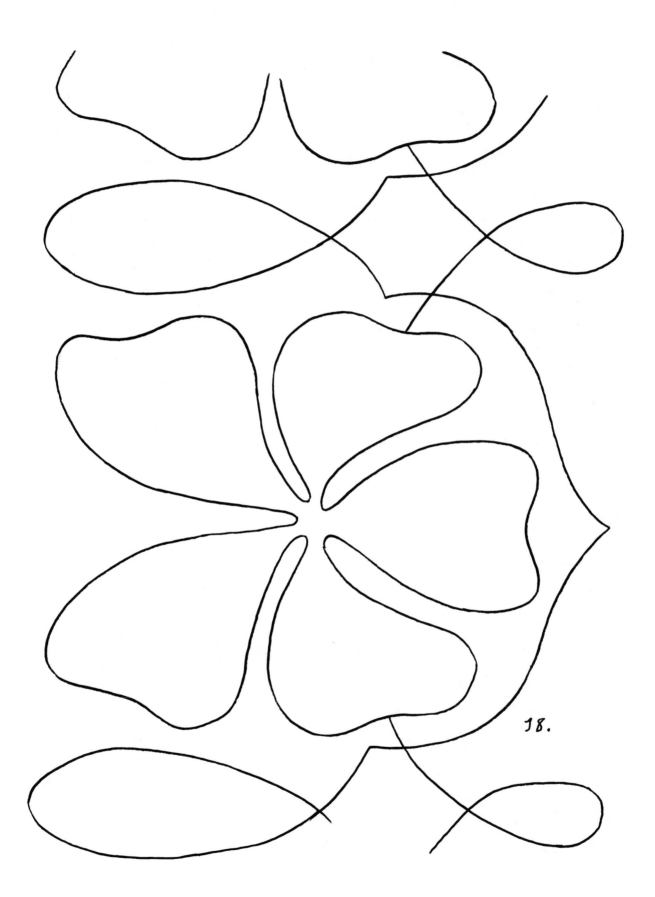

18.

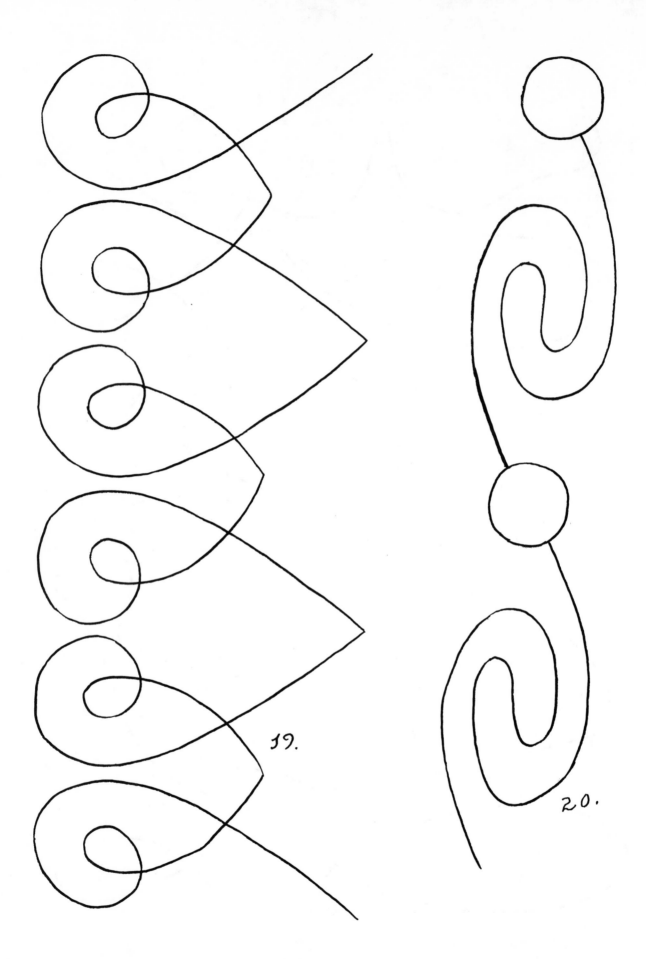

19.

20.

21.

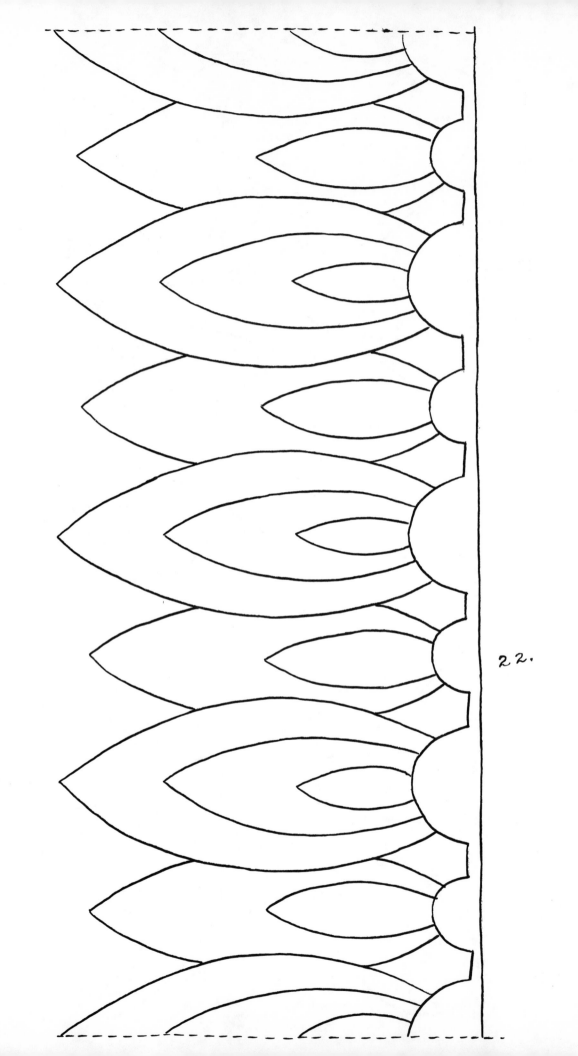

250

22.

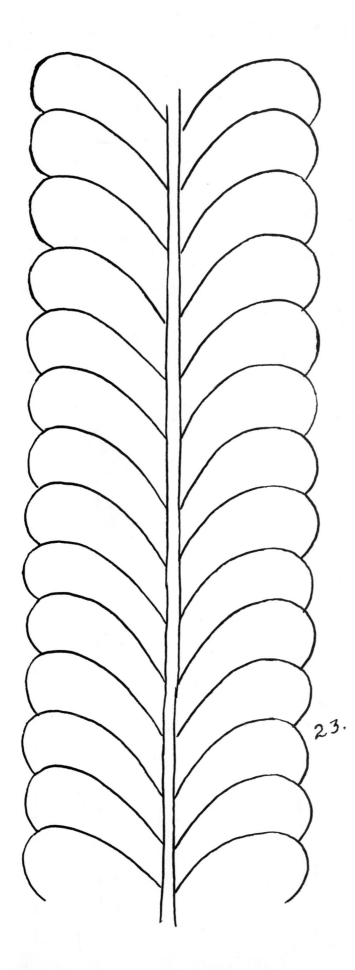

23.

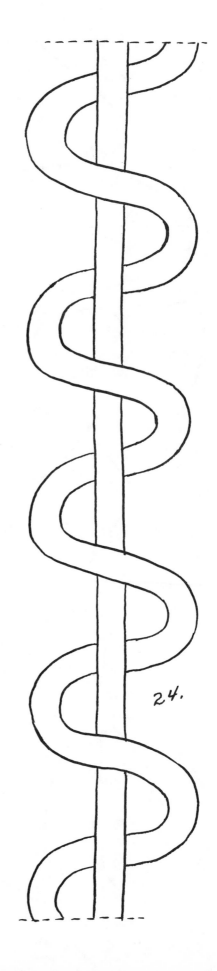

24.

25.

26.

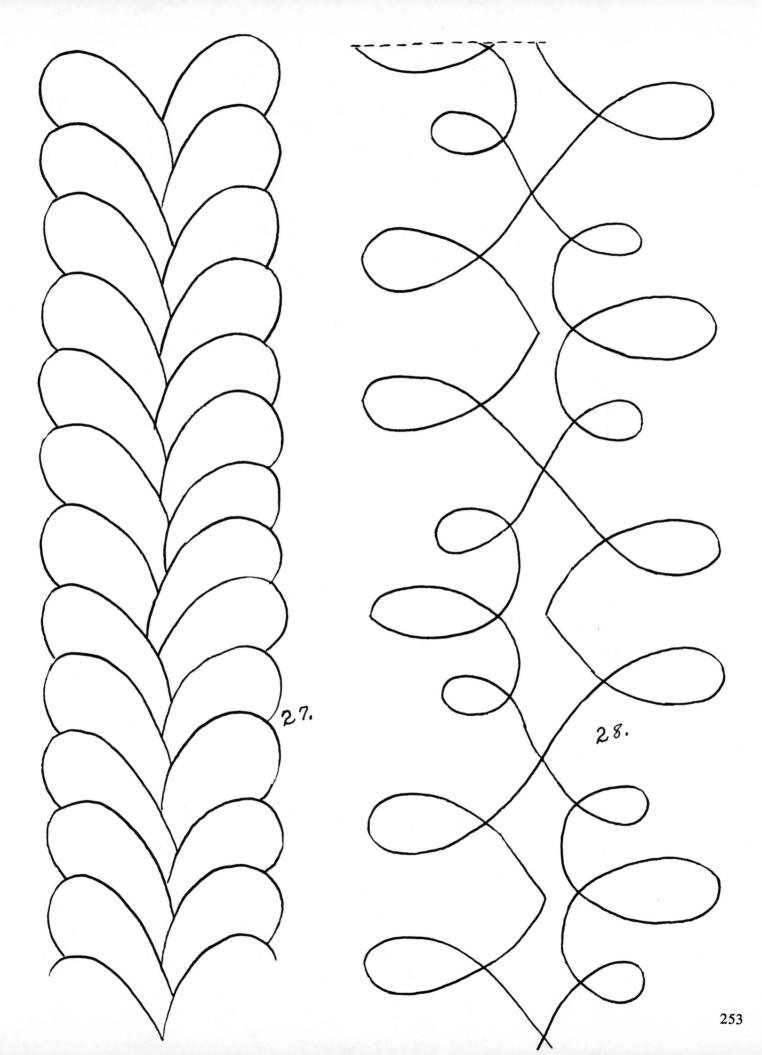

27.

28.

29.

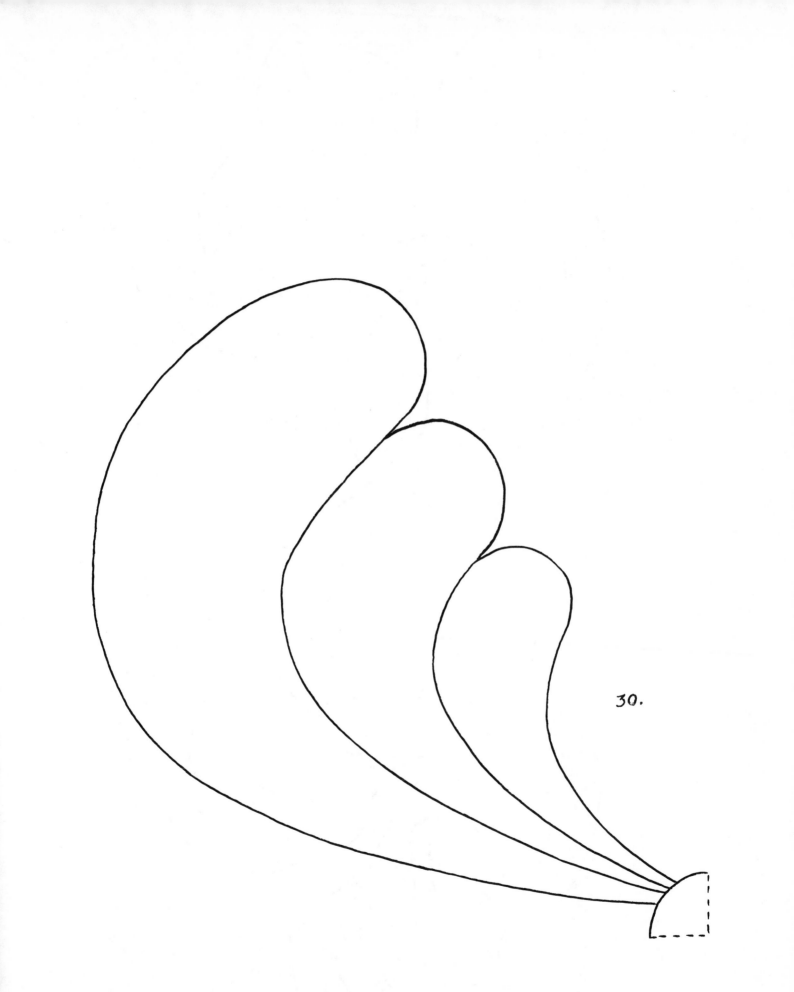

30.

31.

32.

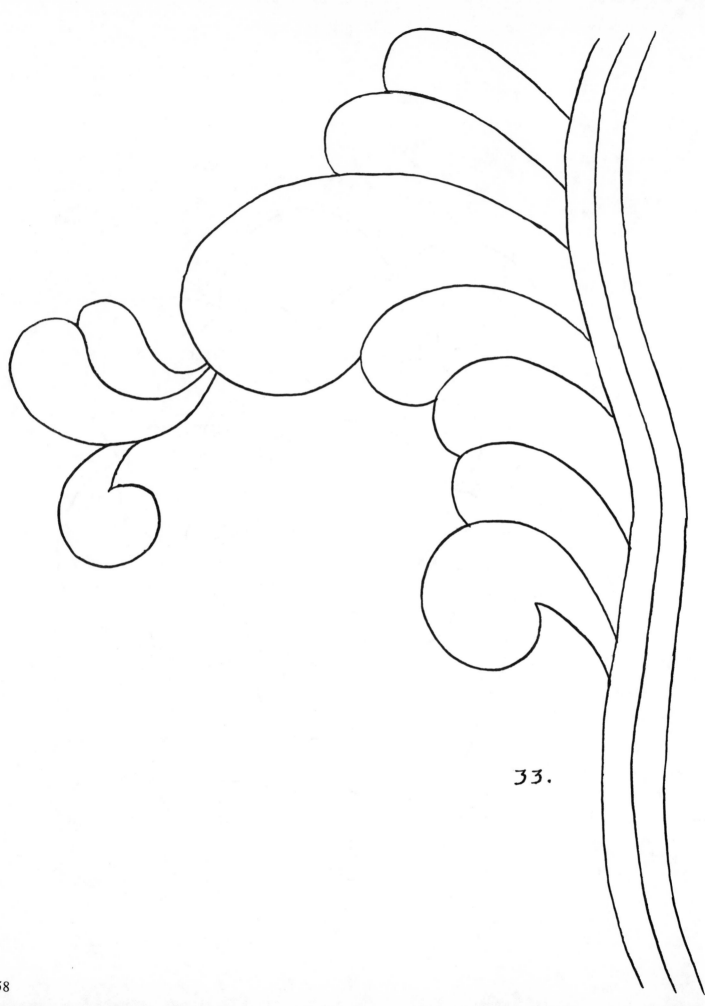

33.

Embroidery Patterns

Nursery Rhyme Baby Quilt

EMBROIDERED OR PAINTED QUILTS

There are four patterns represented in this chapter. The first is a child's or baby quilt three feet by four feet in size. Cut the diamond shaped blocks 16½ inches by 19½ inches across the points. Embroider four of these diamond shapes with the four nursery rhyme figures in any color combination that pleases you. Write the baby's name and vital statistics on the center block and then embroider those also.

The second set of patterns is a butterfly quilt dating from the 1930's. The patterns are to be done on 12-inch square blocks and the top should be made with every other block a print.

Next is a 1930 Flower Basket design which may be made on 12-inch square blocks or may be enlarged by the graph method to cover the whole top of a bed.

The last set of designs is for an Antique Car quilt designed by one of my readers, Mrs. Arthur Brown, of Washington, North Carolina. Work these designs on 12-inch square blocks also.

The car quilt should be put together with a print or plain color block between the embroidered blocks. The colors to be used for the different cars are:

Buick—1915	Brown with yellow trim
Studebaker	Red body, brown upholstery, grey top
Stanley Steamer	Blue body, yellow trim
Pierce Arrow	Brown with yellow trim
Stearns	Brown, red upholstery, red trim
Cadillac—1905	Green, yellow trim
Mercer	Yellow, red trim
Siegfried Marcus	Black, grey wheels
First Ford	Black, brown seat
Duryea	Red, grey top
Diamler	Grey, brown upholstery

Oldsmobile	Blue, red trim
Model T Ford—1909	Lavender, grey top, black and yellow trim, brown upholstery
Stutz Bearcat	Blue, red and yellow trim
Ford Model T—1913	Red, grey trim and top
Locomobile	Yellow, grey trim, black upholstery
Chevrolet	Green, grey trim and top, brown upholstery
Overland	Lavender, grey trim and top, brown upholstery
Packard	Blue, black top, grey trim
Crestmobile	Brown, green fenders and wheel spokes, brown upholstery
Cadillac—1906	Grey, red trim, black upholstery

All of the tires are black. The accessories are brass and chrome. The lights are white. The wheel spokes are either the same as the body color or the trim color. Use a darker shade of the car body color to fill in the areas that are marked with an X on the pattern. For the plain colored blocks, use a color or print which matches a car color and the color of the room the quilt will be used in.

To use these patterns, trace them onto tissue paper. Tape this tissue paper to the back of a white square of cloth ½ inch larger all the way around than the dimensions of the square given in the directions. This will allow for the seam. Tape the cloth and tissue paper to the glass of a window. The picture will show through and you may draw the picture on the cloth. These patterns are for embroidery, but you may also use fabric paints to color them if you wish.

To
Banberry
Cross

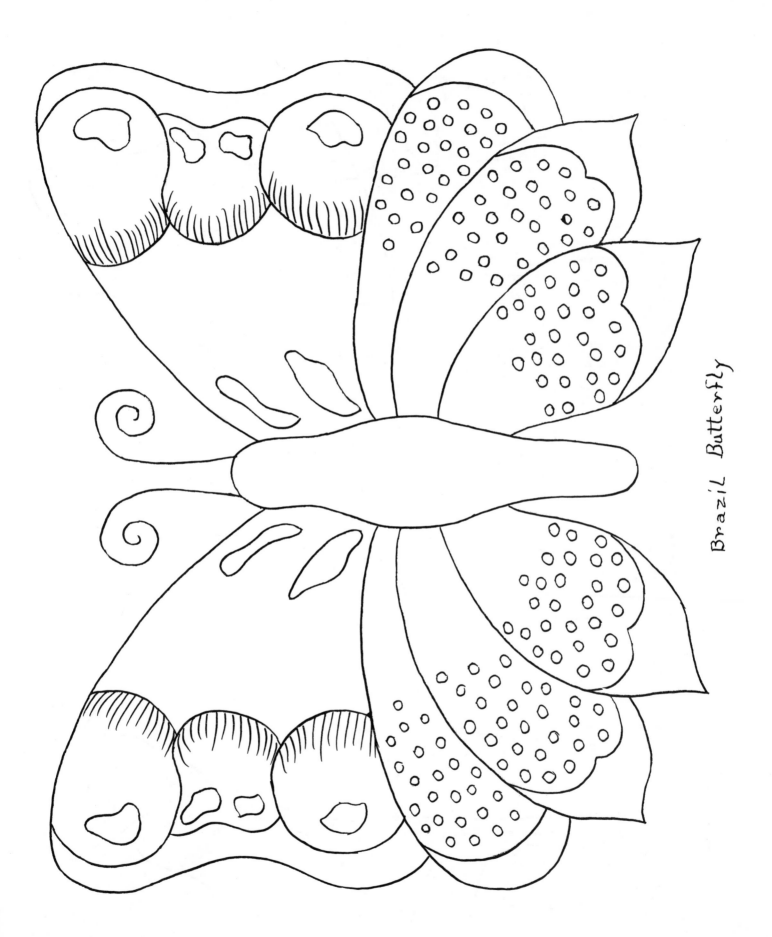

Brazil Butterfly

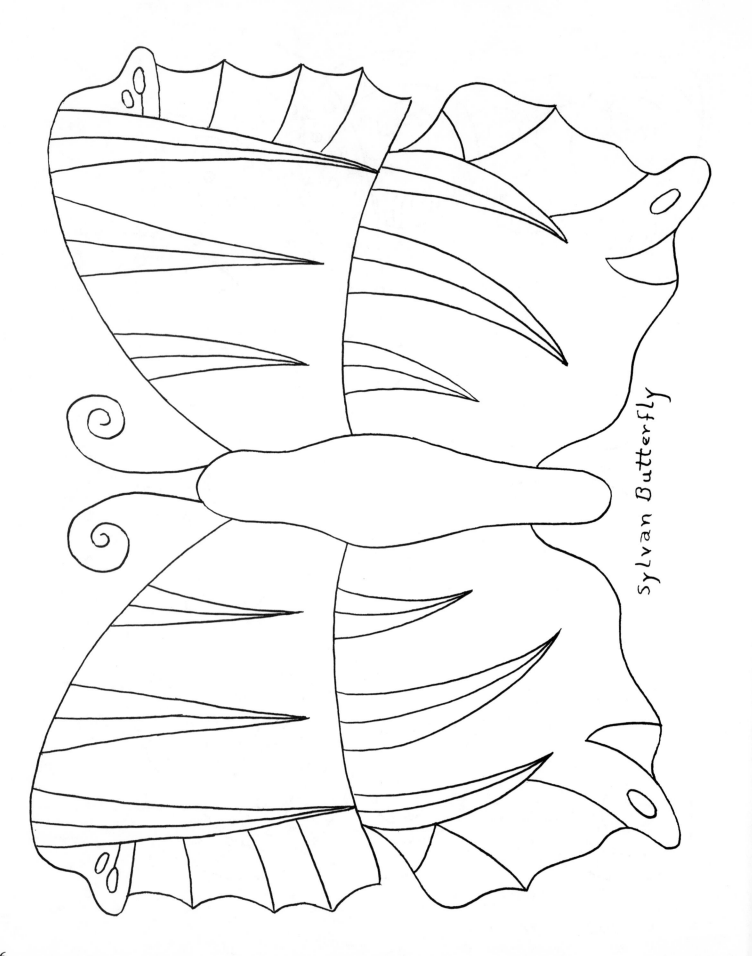

Sylvan Butterfly

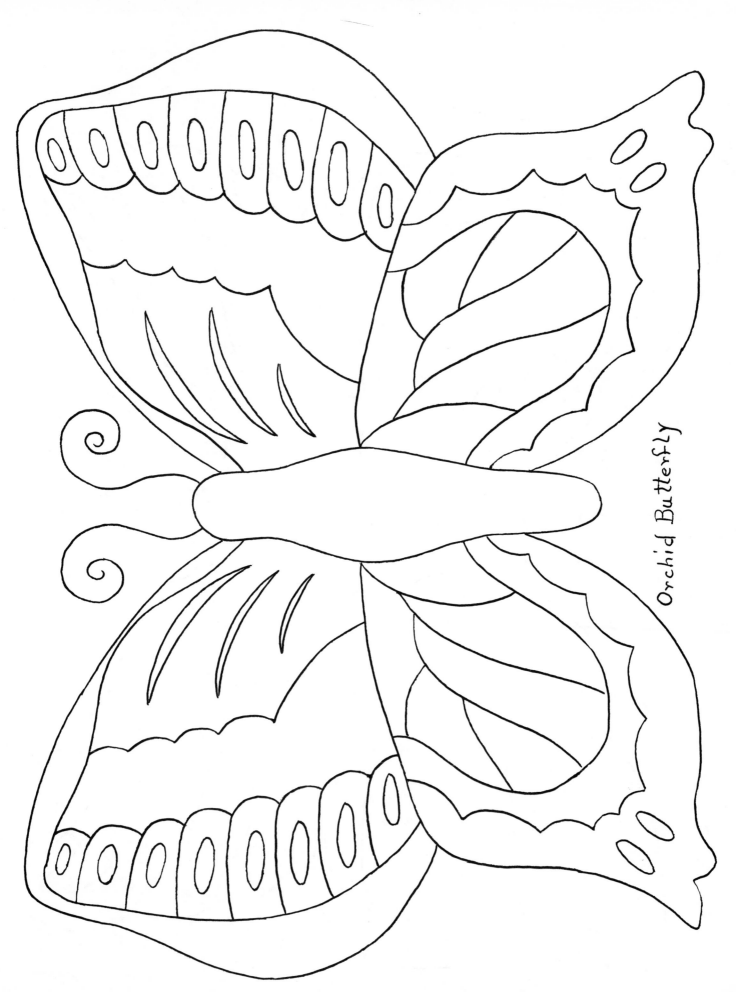

Orchid Butterfly

Queen Butterfly

269

BUICK 1915

DURYEA

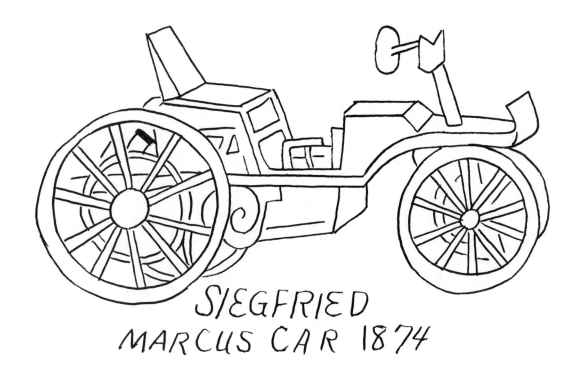

SIEGFRIED
MARCUS CAR 1874

MERCER
1914

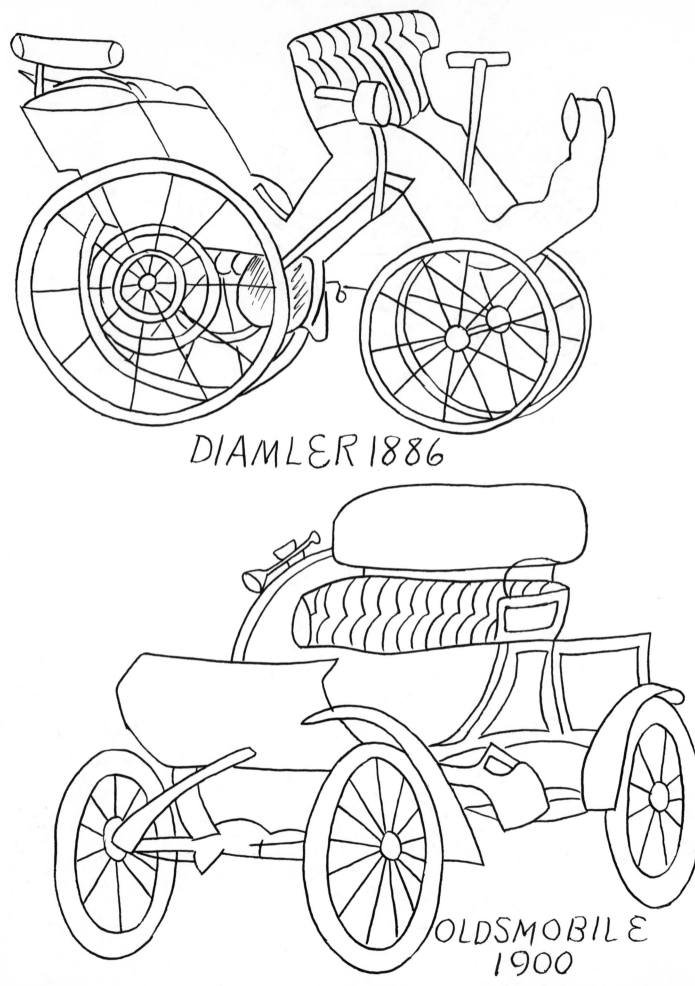

DIAMLER 1886

OLDSMOBILE
1900

FIRST
FORD

CADILLAC
1905

Studebaker
Electric
1902

The Stanley Steamer
1911

Packard 1910

Overland 1910

Cadillac 1906

Crestmobile 1904

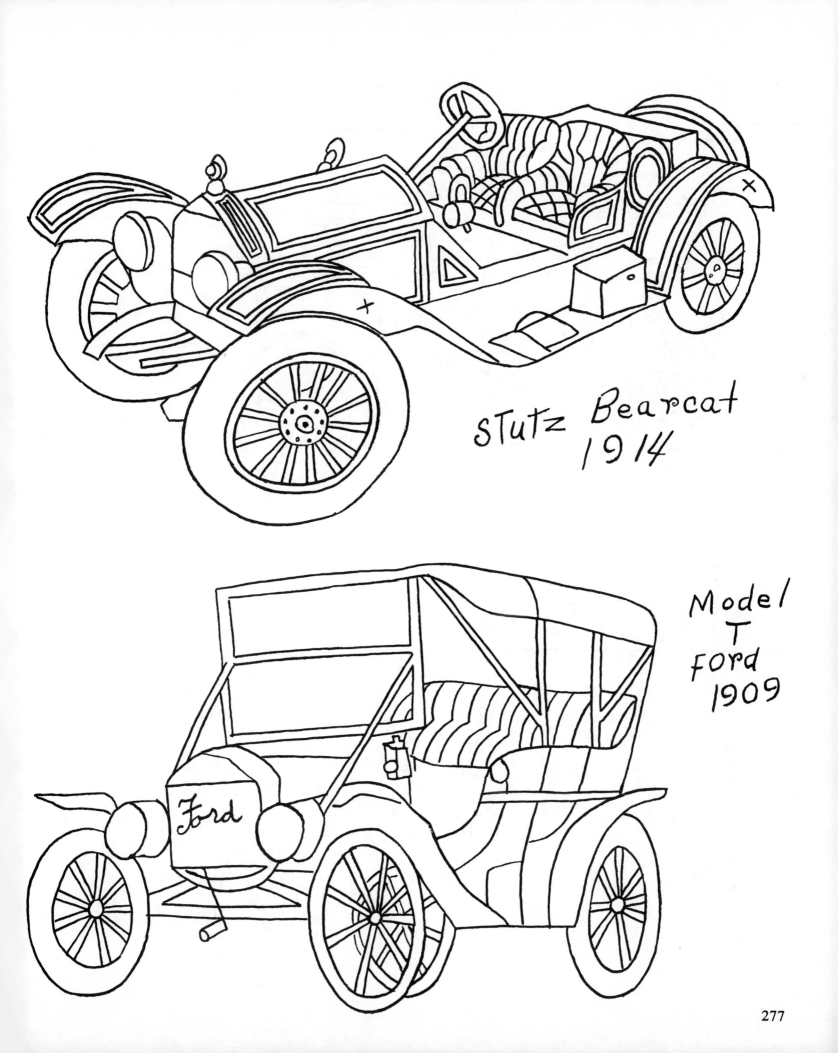

Stutz Bearcat
1914

Model
T
Ford
1909

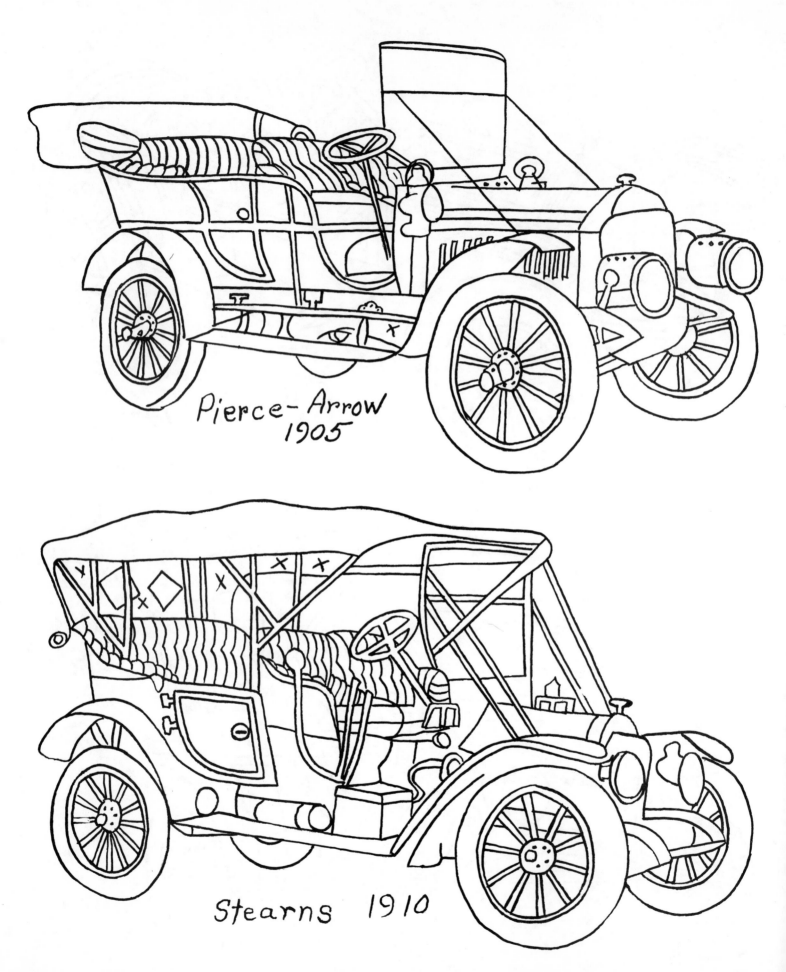

Pierce-Arrow 1905

Stearns 1910

Ford Model T 1913

The Locomobile 1907

Chevrolet 1915

Index